D1377381

BEST OF
Country Cooking

Mama's Blackberry Cobbler (p. 180)

Visit us at tasteofhome.com for other Taste of Home books and products.

International Standard Book Number: 978-1-62145-721-3
International Standard Series Number: 2166-0522
Component Number: 117000100H

Executive Editor: Mark Hagen
Senior Art Director: Raeann Thompson
Editor: Hazel Wheaton
Deputy Editor, Copy Desk: Dulcie Shoener
Copy Editor: Sara Strauss
Contributing Designer: Jennifer Ruetz

Front Cover
Photographer: Dan Roberts
Senior Set Stylist: Stacey Genaw
Food Stylist: Shannon Norris

Pictured on front cover:
Dutch-Oven Bread, p. 63

Pictured on title page:
Red, White & Blue Summer Salad, p. 47

Pictured on back cover:
Four-Cheese Stuffed Shells, p. 120;
Ham, Potato & Pepper Chowder, p. 54;
Cheesy Caramelized Onion Skillet Bread, p. 11

Printed in China
1 3 5 7 9 10 8 6 4 2

Come Home to Country Cooking!

MAKE YOUR KITCHEN THE HEART OF YOUR HOME!

With hearty, satisfying breakfasts to start the day off right and delicious, home-cooked meals to bring your family together in the evening, create dishes your loved ones will remember and memories they'll treasure. Tasty snacks and comforting stews, tempting appetizers and scrumptious side dishes, heartwarming casseroles and delectable desserts—the newest edition of ***Best of Country Cooking*** has all these and more!

Whether you're looking for excellent recipes to make in the slow cooker or Instant Pot™, meals for two or spreads for a potluck, home-baked bread or a stunning Sunday roast, we have you covered. Every recipe was shared by a home cook like you and has been approved by the experts in the *Taste of Home* Test Kitchen, so you know each one will work right the first time.

LOOK INSIDE FOR:

Contest Winner

Blue-Ribbon Recipes
A special blue ribbon badge identifies a dish chosen for honors by our tasting experts in one of our *Taste of Home* recipe contests. Each one is—literally—a winner!

Freeze It!
For recipes you can have ready at short notice, look for the special ❄ icon. With these dishes in the freezer, you'll always have something delicious to serve family and guests.

It doesn't get any better than sharing an amazing meal while creating memories with loved ones. ***Best of Country Cooking*** delivers the warmth and tradition of down-home cooking—heirloom recipes that are bound to become new favorites in your own home.

CONTENTS

Snacks & Beverages 4

Side Dishes & Condiments 22

Soups, Salads & Sandwiches 40

Breads, Rolls & More 58

Main Dishes 76

Meals in Minutes 100

Cooking for Two 118

Slow Cooker & Instant Pot™ 134

Cookies, Bars & Candies 152

Dazzling Desserts 170

The Cook's Quick Reference 188

Index 190

Snacks & Beverages

Looking for party appetizers, afternoon snacks or between-meal nibbles? The tasty bites and delicious drinks in this chapter have you covered! A special section puts the spotlight on scrumptious pocket-sized treats that work well as appetizers or light meals!

HEAVENLY DRINKING CHOCOLATE

The name says it all—sipping this beverage is like experiencing an out-of-this-world blend of dark and milk chocolate. The only thing that could make it better? A dollop of whipped cream on top.
—Taste of Home *Test Kitchen*

Takes: 20 min. • **Makes:** 5 cups

- **4 cups half-and-half cream**
- **2 bars (3½ oz. each) 70% cacao dark chocolate, chopped**
- **2 oz. milk chocolate, chopped**
- **1 tsp. vanilla extract**
- **¼ tsp. ground nutmeg**
- **Dash salt**
- **Optional: Sweetened whipped cream or marshmallows**

In a large saucepan, heat the cream over medium heat until bubbles form around sides of pan (do not boil). Remove from the heat; whisk in the chocolates, vanilla, nutmeg and salt until smooth. Return to the heat; cook and stir until heated through. Pour into mugs; top with whipped cream or marshmallows.

1 cup: 489 cal., 35g fat (23g sat. fat), 105mg chol., 130mg sod., 37g carb. (33g sugars, 4g fiber), 9g pro.

STICKY SESAME CAULIFLOWER

Sesame chicken is one of my favorite take-out dishes, but I'm doing what I can to cut unnecessary calories and fat. This recipe gives me an alternative that uses fresh vegetables and never compromises on flavor.
—Anthony Ashmore, Bohemia, NY

Prep: 40 min. • **Bake:** 25 min.
Makes: 12 servings

- **1 cup dry bread crumbs**
- **½ cup cornmeal**
- **2 Tbsp. all-purpose flour**
- **½ tsp. salt**
- **½ tsp. garlic powder**
- **½ tsp. pepper**

BATTER

- **1 cup all-purpose flour**
- **1 Tbsp. adobo seasoning**
- **1 tsp. garlic powder**
- **½ tsp. salt**
- **½ tsp. pepper**
- **1 bottle (12 oz.) beer**
- **1 large head cauliflower, broken into florets (about 8 cups)**
- **1 Tbsp. peanut oil**

SAUCE

- **¼ cup orange juice**
- **¼ cup sweet chili sauce**
- **¼ cup island teriyaki sauce**
- **2 Tbsp. sesame oil**
- **1 tsp. soy sauce**
- **½ tsp. rice vinegar**
- **½ tsp. Sriracha chili sauce**
- **Optional toppings: Thinly sliced green onions, grated orange zest and sesame seeds**

1. Preheat oven to 400°. In a shallow bowl, combine the first 6 ingredients. For batter, in a large bowl, mix flour, adobo seasoning, garlic powder, salt and pepper; whisk in beer until smooth.
2. Dip the cauliflower in the batter, then in the bread crumb mixture. Place on a greased baking sheet. Drizzle with peanut oil; gently toss to coat. Bake until golden brown and cauliflower is just tender, 25-30 minutes.
3. In a small saucepan, combine orange juice, chili sauce, teriyaki sauce, sesame oil, soy sauce, vinegar and Sriracha chili sauce. Cook and stir over low heat just until warmed, about 5 minutes.
4. Transfer the cauliflower to a large bowl. Drizzle with sauce; gently toss to coat. Serve with toppings of your choice.

⅔ cup: 140 cal., 4g fat (1g sat. fat), 0 chol., 714mg sod., 23g carb. (8g sugars, 2g fiber), 4g pro.

SOUTHWESTERN EGG ROLLS

At my church potluck, these crispy, spicy snacks went fast thanks to the triple kick from the Italian sausage, Mexicorn and chiles. Want to balance the hot with a little cool? Sour cream and guacamole are a tasty party trick.

—Jacqueline Bower, Washington, IA

Takes: 30 min. • **Makes:** 1½ dozen

- **1 lb. bulk hot Italian sausage**
- **1 can (15 oz.) black beans, rinsed and drained**
- **1 can (11 oz.) Mexicorn, drained**
- **1 can (10 oz.) diced tomatoes and green chiles, undrained**
- **1 pkg. (8.8 oz.) ready-to-serve Spanish rice**
- **18 egg roll wrappers**
- **Oil for frying**
- **Optional: Sour cream and guacamole**

1. In a large skillet, cook the sausage over medium heat for 6-8 minutes or until no longer pink, breaking it into crumbles; drain. Stir in beans, Mexicorn, tomatoes and rice; bring to a boil. Reduce heat; simmer, uncovered, 5 minutes, stirring occasionally.

2. With 1 corner of an egg roll wrapper facing you, place ⅓ cup filling just below center of wrapper. (Cover the remaining wrappers with a damp paper towel until ready to use.) Fold bottom corner over filling; moisten remaining wrapper edges with water. Fold the side corners toward center over filling. Roll up tightly, pressing at tip to seal. Repeat.

3. In an electric skillet, heat 1 in. of oil to 375°. Fry the egg rolls, 2 at a time, 1-2 minutes or until golden brown, turning occasionally. Drain on paper towels. If desired, serve with sour cream and guacamole.

1 egg roll: 333 cal., 19g fat (4g sat. fat), 21mg chol., 643mg sod., 31g carb. (2g sugars, 2g fiber), 10g pro.

LEMONY BACON-ARTICHOKE DIP

Move over, spinach artichoke dip—bacon adds much more flavor! You might want to double this fabulous recipe because there are never any leftovers.

—Heidi Jobe, Carrollton, GA

Prep: 20 min. • **Bake:** 25 min.
Makes: 12 servings (3 cups)

- **5 thick-sliced bacon strips, chopped**
- **1 can (14 oz.) water-packed quartered artichoke hearts, drained and chopped**
- **2 garlic cloves, minced**
- **2 pkg. (8 oz. each) reduced-fat cream cheese**
- **⅓ cup sour cream**
- **½ tsp. onion salt**
- **¼ tsp. salt**
- **⅛ tsp. pepper**
- **2 Tbsp. lemon juice**
- **½ cup grated Parmesan cheese**
- **Pita bread wedges, toasted**

1. Preheat oven to 400°. In a large skillet, cook the bacon over medium heat until crisp, stirring occasionally. Remove with a slotted spoon; drain on paper towels. Discard drippings, reserving 2 tsp. in pan. Add artichoke hearts and garlic to drippings; cook and stir 1 minute.

2. In a large bowl, beat the cream cheese, sour cream, onion salt, salt and pepper until smooth. Beat in the lemon juice. Fold in the artichoke mixture and half the bacon.

3. Transfer to a greased 2-qt. baking dish. Sprinkle with the remaining bacon; top with Parmesan cheese. Bake, uncovered, until golden brown, 25-30 minutes. Serve with pita wedges.

¼ cup: 141 cal., 11g fat (7g sat. fat), 35mg chol., 421mg sod., 4g carb. (2g sugars, 0 fiber), 6g pro.

TOMATO-ONION PHYLLO PIZZA

With a delicate crust and lots of lovely tomatoes on top, this dish is a special one to serve to guests. I make it often when fresh garden tomatoes are in season. It freezes well unbaked, so I also keep one on hand to pop in the oven for a quick dinner.
—Neta Cohen, Bedford, VA

Prep: 20 min. • **Bake:** 20 min.
Makes: 28 slices

- **5 Tbsp. butter, melted**
- **14 sheets phyllo dough (14x9 in.)**
- **7 Tbsp. grated Parmesan cheese, divided**
- **1 cup shredded part-skim mozzarella cheese**
- **1 cup thinly sliced onion**
- **1 lb. plum tomatoes, sliced**
- **1½ tsp. minced fresh oregano or ½ tsp. dried oregano**
- **1 tsp. minced fresh thyme or ¼ tsp. dried thyme**
- **Salt and pepper to taste**

1. Preheat the oven to 375°. Brush a 15x10x1-in. baking pan with some of the melted butter. Unroll the phyllo dough; cut stack into a 10½x9-in. rectangle. Discard scraps.
2. Line bottom of prepared pan with 2 sheets of phyllo dough (sheets will overlap slightly). Brush with butter and sprinkle with 1 Tbsp. Parmesan cheese. Repeat layers 5 times. (Keep the dough covered with a damp towel until ready to use to prevent it from drying out.)
3. Top with layers of remaining phyllo dough; brush with the remaining butter. Sprinkle with mozzarella cheese; arrange onion and tomatoes over cheese. Sprinkle with oregano, thyme, salt, pepper and remaining Parmesan cheese. Bake until edges are golden brown, 20-25 minutes.

1 slice: 54 cal., 3g fat (2g sat. fat), 9mg chol., 87mg sod., 4g carb. (1g sugars, 0 fiber), 2g pro.

EASY CHEESE-STUFFED JALAPENOS

A few years ago, I saw a man in the grocery store buying a big bag of jalapeno peppers. I asked him what he intended to do with them, and right there in the store he gave me this fabulous recipe for stuffed jalapenos!
—Janice Montiverdi, Sugar Land, TX

Prep: 30 min. • **Bake:** 5 min. • **Makes:** 4 dozen

- **24 medium fresh jalapeno peppers**
- **1 pkg. (8 oz.) cream cheese, softened**
- **3 cups finely shredded cheddar cheese**
- **1½ tsp. Worcestershire sauce**
- **4 bacon strips, cooked and crumbled**

1. Preheat oven to 400°. Cut jalapenos in half lengthwise; remove seeds and membranes. In a large saucepan, boil peppers in water for 5-10 minutes (the longer you boil the peppers, the milder they become). Drain and rinse in cold water; set aside.
2. In a small bowl, beat cream cheese, cheddar cheese and Worcestershire sauce until smooth. Spoon 2 teaspoonfuls of the cheese filling into each jalapeno; sprinkle with bacon. Arrange on greased baking sheets. Bake until the filling is warmed, 3-5 minutes.

1 piece: 141 cal., 12g fat (8g sat. fat), 39mg chol., 200mg sod., 3g carb. (0 sugars, 1g fiber), 6g pro.

COLD-BREW COFFEE

Cold brewing reduces the acidity of coffee, enhancing its natural sweetness and complex flavors. Even those who take hot coffee with sugar and cream might find themselves sipping cold brew plain.
—Taste of Home *Test Kitchen*

Prep: 10 min. + chilling • **Makes:** 8 servings

- **1 cup coarsely ground medium-roast coffee**
- **1 cup hot water (205°)**
- **6 to 7 cups cold water**
- **Optional: 2% milk or half-and-half cream**

1. Place the coffee grounds in a clean glass container. Pour hot water over the grounds; let stand 10 minutes. Stir in cold water. Cover and refrigerate 12-24 hours.
2. Strain the coffee through a fine mesh sieve; discard grounds. Strain the coffee again through a coffee filter; discard grounds. Serve over ice, with milk or cream if desired. Store in refrigerator for up to 2 weeks.

1 cup: 2 cal., 0 fat (0 sat. fat), 0 chol., 4mg sod., 0 carb. (0 sugars, 0 fiber), 0 pro.

NEW TO COLD BREW?

Many cold brew recipes don't use any hot water, but we like the way it releases carbon dioxide in the grounds, extracting more flavor from the beans. Some people enjoy a pinch of salt in cold brews to bring out the inherent sweetness of the coffee. Freeze some coffee in ice cube trays. The frozen coffee cubes will chill your beverage without watering it down.

HOT SHRIMP DIP

I came across a recipe for crawfish dip, and it sounded delicious, but we don't have a lot of crawfish available in my area. However, I'm a big fan of shrimp, so I used that instead. The dish has become a family favorite. Increase the heat with your favorite hot sauce or add a bit of acidity with a squeeze of lemon.
—Jill Burwell, Renton, WA

Takes: 25 min. • **Makes:** 4 cups

- ½ **cup butter, cubed**
- 8 **green onions, thinly sliced**
- 1 **small green pepper, finely chopped**
- 1 **lb. peeled and deveined cooked shrimp (61-70 per lb.)**
- 1 **jar (4 oz.) diced pimientos, drained**
- 2 **garlic cloves, minced**
- 2 **tsp. Creole seasoning**
- 1 **pkg. (8 oz.) cream cheese, cubed**
- **Chopped fresh parsley**
- **French bread baguette slices or assorted crackers**

In a Dutch oven, melt butter over medium heat. Add green onions and green pepper; cook and stir until tender, 3-4 minutes. Add the shrimp, pimientos, garlic and Creole seasoning. Cook and stir until heated through. Stir in the cream cheese until melted; sprinkle with parsley. Serve with baguette slices or crackers.

¼ cup: 136 cal., 11g fat (7g sat. fat), 73mg chol., 217mg sod., 2g carb. (1g sugars, 0 fiber), 7g pro.

HOW ELSE CAN I USE CREOLE SEASONING?

Creole seasoning is a blend of pepper, garlic powder, onion powder and dried herbs. It is wonderful on meats, seafood and fish dishes. We love it in jambalaya, in red beans & rice, or for adding a boost of flavor to a sheet-pan dinner of spicy sausage, potatoes and peppers.

CHOCOLATE PECAN PIE SNACK MIX

PICTURED ON P. 4

My crowd-pleasing party mix is buttery, chocolaty and nutty. The recipe yields a party-sized portion, but I recommend keeping it covered so it doesn't disappear before the event.

—Annette Niemiec, Scottsdale, AZ

Takes: 30 min. • **Makes:** 4 qt.

- **4 cups Rice Chex**
- **4 cups Chocolate Chex**
- **4 cups Honey Nut Chex**
- **2 cups coarsely chopped pecans, toasted**
- **1 cup packed brown sugar**
- **½ cup butter, cubed**
- **⅓ cup light corn syrup**
- **½ tsp. baking soda**
- **2 cups semisweet chocolate chips**
- **2 Tbsp. shortening**

1. In a large bowl, combine cereals and pecans. In a small microwave-safe bowl, combine brown sugar, butter and corn syrup. Microwave, uncovered, on high for 2 minutes, stirring once. Whisk in baking soda. Pour over cereal mixture; toss to coat.
2. Cook the cereal mixture in batches on high in a microwave-safe bowl for 3 minutes, stirring every minute. Spread onto waxed paper-lined baking sheets to cool completely.
3. In a microwave, melt chocolate chips and shortening; stir until smooth. Drizzle over cereal mixture; refrigerate until set.
4. Break into pieces. Store in an airtight container at room temperature.

¾ cup: 350 cal., 19g fat (7g sat. fat), 12mg chol., 223mg sod., 47g carb. (30g sugars, 3g fiber), 3g pro.

CHEESY CARAMELIZED ONION SKILLET BREAD

This appetizer is perfect for a football game or informal party, but it came about because I have two sons who are always hungry and I needed to buy some time to get dinner on the table after coming home from work. They love the skillet bread for the flavor, and I love it because it keeps them in the kitchen to chat while I prepare the rest of dinner! If you'd like, you can use homemade biscuits instead of prepared.

—Mary M. Leverette, Columbia, SC

Prep: 45 min. • **Bake:** 20 min.
Makes: 8 servings

- **2 tsp. caraway seeds**
- **1 Tbsp. olive oil**
- **1 large onion, chopped**
- **¼ tsp. salt**
- **1 cup shredded sharp cheddar cheese**
- **½ cup butter, melted**
- **1 tube (16.3 oz.) large refrigerated buttermilk biscuits**
- **1 Tbsp. minced fresh thyme, optional**

1. In a 10-in. cast-iron or other ovenproof skillet, toast caraway seeds until fragrant, about 1 minute. Remove and set aside.
2. In the same skillet, heat the oil over medium heat. Add the onion; cook and stir until softened, 5-6 minutes. Reduce heat to medium-low; cook until deep golden brown, 30-40 minutes, stirring occasionally.
3. Stir in salt; remove from the heat and cool slightly. Sprinkle cheese over onions in skillet.
4. Place melted butter and caraway seeds in a shallow bowl. Cut each biscuit into fourths. Dip the biscuit pieces in butter mixture; place in a single layer over onion mixture in skillet.
5. Bake at 350° until puffed and golden brown, 20-25 minutes. Cool in the skillet 5 minutes before inverting onto a serving plate. If desired, sprinkle with thyme. Serve warm.

1 serving: 352 cal., 25g fat (13g sat. fat), 45mg chol., 874mg sod., 27g carb. (4g sugars, 1g fiber), 7g pro.

BACON-SAUSAGE QUICHE TARTS

As a teacher, I attend many meetings and also have special celebrations with the rest of the staff. The other teachers are very fond of this treat and often request that I bring it to our functions.

—Jackie Milliken, Pittsboro, NC

Prep: 30 min. • **Bake:** 10 min.
Makes: 40 appetizers

- **2 cans (12 oz. each) refrigerated buttermilk biscuits**
- **6 uncooked breakfast sausage links, chopped**
- **2 Tbsp. chopped onion**
- **2 Tbsp. chopped fresh mushrooms**
- **2 Tbsp. chopped green pepper**
- **1 pkg. (8 oz.) cream cheese, softened**
- **2 Tbsp. heavy whipping cream**
- **3 large eggs**
- **1½ cups (6 oz.) finely shredded cheddar cheese, divided**
- **5 bacon strips, cooked and crumbled**

1. Preheat the oven to 375°. Split each biscuit into 2 layers; press each layer into an ungreased miniature muffin cup.
2. In a large skillet, cook sausage, onion, mushrooms and pepper over medium heat until the meat is no longer pink and the vegetables are tender; drain.
3. In a large bowl, beat cream cheese and cream until smooth. Beat in eggs. Fold in ¾ cup cheddar cheese and the sausage mixture. Spoon 1 Tbsp. into each cup. Sprinkle with the bacon and remaining cheese. Bake 10-15 minutes or until golden brown. Serve warm.

1 tart: 97 cal., 5g fat (3g sat. fat), 30mg chol., 245mg sod., 9g carb. (0 sugars, 0 fiber), 4g pro.

SPICE IT UP!

To give these little tarts a spicy southwestern edge, try using chorizo sausage in place of the breakfast sausage.

APPETIZER TOMATO CHEESE BREAD

I found this recipe in a dairy cookbook, and it has become a family favorite. We milk 180 cows and have a large garden, so we welcome dishes that use both dairy and fresh vegetables. My husband and our two children are mostly meat-and-potato eaters, but I don't hear any complaints when I serve this irresistible bread!

—Penney Kester, Springville, NY

Prep: 20 min. • **Bake:** 25 min. + standing
Makes: 12 servings

- **2 Tbsp. butter**
- **1 medium onion, minced**
- **1 cup shredded cheddar cheese**
- **½ cup sour cream**
- **¼ cup mayonnaise**
- **¾ tsp. salt**
- **¼ tsp. pepper**
- **¼ tsp. dried oregano**
- **Pinch rubbed sage**
- **2 cups biscuit/baking mix**
- **⅔ cup 2% milk**
- **3 medium tomatoes, cut into ¼-in. slices**
- **Paprika**

1. Preheat oven to 400°. In a small skillet, heat butter over medium heat. Add the onion and cook until tender. Remove from the heat. Stir in the cheese, sour cream, mayonnaise and seasonings; set aside.
2. In a bowl, combine the baking mix and milk to form a soft dough. Turn dough onto a well-floured surface; knead lightly 10-12 times. Pat into a greased 13x9-in. baking dish, pushing dough up the sides of dish to form a shallow rim. Arrange the tomato slices over top. Spread with topping; sprinkle with paprika.
3. Bake for 25 minutes. Let stand for 10 minutes before cutting.

1 piece: 209 cal., 14g fat (6g sat. fat), 26mg chol., 521mg sod., 17g carb. (3g sugars, 1g fiber), 5g pro.

PIZZA ROLLS

Our family just loves my husband's version of store-bought pizza rolls. They take some time to make, but they freeze well so we get to enjoy the fruits of our labor for a long time!

—Julie Gaines, Normal, IL

Prep: 50 min. • **Cook:** 5 min./batch
Makes: 32 rolls

- **4 cups shredded pizza cheese blend or part-skim mozzarella cheese**
- **1 lb. bulk Italian sausage, cooked and drained**
- **2 pkg. (3 oz. each) sliced pepperoni, chopped**
- **1 medium green pepper, finely chopped**
- **1 medium sweet red pepper, finely chopped**
- **1 medium onion, finely chopped**
- **2 jars (14 oz. each) pizza sauce**
- **32 egg roll wrappers**
- **Oil for frying**
- **Additional pizza sauce for dipping, warmed, optional**

1. In a large bowl, combine the cheese, sausage, pepperoni, peppers and onion. Stir in pizza sauce until combined. Place about ¼ cup filling in the center of each egg roll wrapper. Fold the bottom corner over filling; fold sides toward center over filling. Moisten remaining corner with water and roll up tightly to seal.
2. In a deep-sided cast-iron or another heavy skillet, heat 1 in. of oil to 375°. Fry pizza rolls until golden brown, 1-2 minutes on each side. Drain on paper towels. If desired, serve with additional pizza sauce.

1 roll: 297 cal., 19g fat (5g sat. fat), 28mg chol., 537mg sod., 22g carb. (2g sugars, 1g fiber), 9g pro.

MINI PIZZA CUPS

Served hot or cold, these little pizzas are delightful. Their small size makes them ideal for an after-school snack or a kid-friendly party. Plus, they're so easy to make that little ones can help you in the kitchen!
—Jane Jones, Cedar, MN

Prep: 25 min. • **Bake:** 15 min.
Makes: 32 appetizers

- **2 tubes (8 oz. each) refrigerated round crescent rolls**
- **1 can (8 oz.) pizza sauce**
- **¼ cup finely chopped onion**
- **⅓ cup finely chopped green pepper**
- **2 oz. sliced turkey pepperoni, chopped**
- **1 cup shredded part-skim mozzarella cheese**

1. Preheat oven to 375°. Separate tubes of dough into 8 rolls each; halve the rolls. Press dough onto the bottoms and up the sides of miniature muffin cups coated with cooking spray.
2. Spoon the pizza sauce into each cup. Sprinkle with the onion, green pepper, pepperoni and cheese. Bake until the crusts are browned and the cheese is melted, 15-18 minutes.

1 pizza cup: 75 cal., 4g fat (2g sat. fat), 4mg chol., 193mg sod., 7g carb. (1g sugars, 0 fiber), 3g pro.

WATERMELON-LIME COOLER

When temps heat up, chill some glasses and cool down with a slushy blend of watermelon, lime and ginger ale. Slurp and repeat.
—Taste of Home *Test Kitchen*

Takes: 10 min. • **Makes:** 12 servings

- **12 cups cubed seedless watermelon, frozen, divided**
- **¾ tsp. grated lime zest, divided**
- **6 cups chilled ginger ale, divided**

Place 4 cups frozen watermelon, ¼ tsp. lime zest and 2 cups chilled ginger ale in a blender; cover and process until slushy. Serve immediately. Repeat twice.

1 cup: 82 cal., 0 fat (0 sat. fat), 0 chol., 14mg sod., 24g carb. (23g sugars, 1g fiber), 1g pro.

PEACH-BASIL LEMONADE SLUSH

This chilly slush with peaches, lemon juice and garden-fresh basil is hands-down the best lemonade ever. It tastes just like summer.
—Dana Hinck, Pensacola, FL

Prep: 15 min. • **Cook:** 10 min. + chilling
Makes: 12 servings

- 2 **cups sugar**
- 3 **cups chopped peeled fresh peaches (about 3 medium) or 1 lb. frozen unsweetened sliced peaches**
- 1 **pkg. (¾ oz.) fresh basil leaves or 20 large leaves**
- 4 **cups water**
- 1½ **cups fresh lemon juice**
- 5 **to 8 cups ice cubes**
- **Peach slices and additional fresh basil**

1. In a large saucepan, combine sugar, peaches, basil and water; bring to a boil. Reduce heat; simmer 5 minutes. Remove from heat; let stand 30 minutes. Discard basil; stir in lemon juice. Refrigerate until cooled completely.
2. Process half the peach mixture and 2½ cups ice in a blender; add more ice if desired. Repeat with remaining mixture and ice. Pour into chilled glasses; serve with peach slices and additional basil.

1 cup: 152 cal., 0 fat (0 sat. fat), 0 chol., 1mg sod., 39g carb. (37g sugars, 1g fiber), 1g pro.

MOVIE THEATER PRETZEL RODS

My kids and all their friends clamor for these large, chewy pretzels. These delicious, buttery treats are fantastic fresh from the oven—and you can use as much or as little salt as you like!
—Lisa Shaw, Burnettsville, IN

Prep: 70 min. + rising • **Bake:** 10 min.
Makes: 32 pretzel rods

- 1 **pkg. (¼ oz.) active dry yeast**
- 1½ **cups warm water (110° to 115°)**
- 2 **Tbsp. sugar**
- 2 **Tbsp. butter, melted**
- 1½ **tsp. salt**
- 4 **to 4½ cups all-purpose flour**
- 8 **cups water**
- ⅓ **cup baking soda**
- 1 **large egg yolk**
- 1 **Tbsp. cold water**
- **Optional: Coarse salt and warm cheese sauce**

1. In a large bowl, dissolve yeast in warm water. Add the sugar, butter, salt and 2 cups flour. Beat until smooth. Stir in enough remaining flour to form a soft dough (dough will be sticky).
2. Turn onto a floured surface; knead until smooth and elastic, 6-8 minutes. Place in a greased bowl, turning once to grease top. Cover and let rise in a warm place until doubled, about 1 hour.
3. In a large saucepan, bring 8 cups water and baking soda to a boil. Punch dough down; divide into 32 portions. Roll each into a 5-in. log. Add to boiling water, a few at a time, for 30 seconds. Remove with a slotted spoon; drain on paper towels.
4. Place on greased baking sheets. Lightly beat egg yolk and cold water; brush over pretzels. If desired, sprinkle with coarse salt. Bake at 425° until golden brown, 9-11 minutes. Remove from pans to wire racks. Serve warm with cheese, if desired.

Note: Letting pretzels rest for 30 minutes after forming into logs will help create a fluffier pretzel.

1 pretzel: 69 cal., 1g fat (1g sat. fat), 8mg chol., 156mg sod., 13g carb. (1g sugars, 0 fiber), 2g pro.

CHEWY HONEY GRANOLA BARS

There's sweetness from honey, chewiness from the raisins, hints of chocolate and cinnamon, and a bit of crunch. To save a few for later, wrap individual bars and place them in a resealable freezer container. When you want a satisfying treat on short notice, just grab one and let it thaw for a few minutes.
—Tasha Lehman, Williston, VT

Prep: 10 min. • **Bake:** 15 min. + cooling
Makes: 20 servings

- **3 cups old-fashioned oats**
- **2 cups unsweetened puffed wheat cereal**
- **1 cup all-purpose flour**
- **⅓ cup chopped walnuts**
- **⅓ cup raisins**
- **⅓ cup miniature semisweet chocolate chips**
- **1 tsp. baking soda**
- **1 tsp. ground cinnamon**
- **1 cup honey**
- **¼ cup butter, melted**
- **1 tsp. vanilla extract**

1. Preheat oven to 350°. In a large bowl, combine the first 8 ingredients. In a small bowl, combine the honey, butter and vanilla; pour over the oat mixture and mix well. (Mixture will be sticky.)
2. Press into a 13x9-in. baking pan coated with cooking spray. Bake 14-18 minutes or until set and edges are lightly browned. Cool on a wire rack. Cut into bars.

1 bar: 178 cal., 5g fat (2g sat. fat), 6mg chol., 81mg sod., 32g carb. (17g sugars, 2g fiber), 3g pro. **Diabetic exchanges:** 2 starch, ½ fat.

Contest Winner

CHIPOTLE MEXICAN STREET CORN DIP WITH GOAT CHEESE

I was craving the Mexican street corn that I had during a recent trip to Puerto Vallarta, so I came up with this fabulous dip. It blends the traditional profile of the popular street food with updated flavors for a tasty twist.
—Joseph Sciascia, San Mateo, CA

Prep: 30 min. + cooling • **Bake:** 35 min.
Makes: 3 cups

- **3 medium ears sweet corn**
- **1 Tbsp. olive oil**
- **1 cup crumbled goat cheese**
- **¾ cup mayonnaise**
- **1 can (4 oz.) chopped green chiles**
- **1 jar (4 oz.) diced pimientos, drained**
- **2 green onions, chopped**
- **2 Tbsp. finely chopped chipotle pepper in adobo sauce**
- **1 Tbsp. minced fresh cilantro**
- **1 to 2 Tbsp. lime juice**
- **1½ tsp. grated lime zest**
- **1 tsp. ground cumin**
- **1 tsp. chili powder**
- **Tortilla chips**

1. Brush corn with oil. Grill corn, covered, over medium heat until lightly browned and tender, 10-12 minutes, turning occasionally. Cool slightly.
2. Preheat oven to 350°. Cut corn from cobs; transfer to a large bowl. Stir in the goat cheese, mayonnaise, green chiles, pimientos, green onions, chipotle pepper, cilantro, lime juice and zest, cumin and chili powder.
3. Transfer to a greased 1½-qt. baking dish. Bake until bubbly and golden brown, 35-40 minutes. Serve with tortilla chips.

¼ cup: 157 cal., 14g fat (3g sat. fat), 13mg chol., 182mg sod., 7g carb. (2g sugars, 1g fiber), 3g pro.

CORN EQUIVALENCE

This dip is best when made with fresh corn, but you can use canned or frozen instead. Three medium ears will yield about 2 cups corn kernels.

ICED RASPBERRY TEA

Frozen raspberries lend fruity flavor and lovely color to this pretty iced tea that's good throughout the year. The recipe calls for just a few common ingredients and offers make-ahead convenience.
—Lois McGrady, Hillsville, VA

Prep: 10 min. + chilling
Makes: 16 servings (4 qt.)

- **1½ cups sugar**
- **4 qt. water**
- **1 pkg. (12 oz.) frozen unsweetened raspberries**
- **10 tea bags**
- **¼ cup lemon juice**
- **Optional: Fresh raspberries and lemon slices**

1. In a Dutch oven over high heat, bring sugar and water to a boil. Remove from heat; stir until the sugar is dissolved. Add the raspberries, tea bags and lemon juice. Steep, covered, for 3 minutes. Strain; discard berries and tea bags.

2. Transfer the tea to a large container or pitcher. Refrigerate until chilled. Serve over ice. If desired, serve with raspberries and lemon slices.

1 cup: 87 cal., 0 fat (0 sat. fat), 0 chol., 8mg sod., 22g carb. (20g sugars, 0 fiber), 0 pro.

Touch-of-Mint Iced Tea: Bring 2 qt. of water to a boil. Steep 5 tea bags for 5 minutes and discard; cool for 15 minutes. Add 1⅓ cups packed fresh mint and steep for 5 minutes. Strain and then stir in 1 cup lemonade concentrate. Refrigerate until chilled. Serve over ice.

GARDEN-FRESH SEAFOOD COCKTAIL

For something cool on a hot day, we mix shrimp and crabmeat with crunchy veggies straight from the garden. Look for adobo seasoning in your grocery's international section.
—Teri Rasey, Cadillac, MI

Prep: 15 min. + chilling • **Makes:** 6 cups

- **¾ lb. peeled and deveined cooked shrimp (31-40 per lb.), thawed**
- **1 container (8 oz.) refrigerated jumbo lump crabmeat, drained**
- **3 celery ribs, chopped**
- **1 medium cucumber, peeled, seeded and chopped**
- **1 medium sweet orange pepper, chopped**
- **2 plum tomatoes, seeded and chopped**
- **½ cup red onion, finely chopped**
- **1 to 2 jalapeno peppers, seeded and finely chopped**
- **¼ cup minced fresh cilantro**
- **3 Tbsp. lime juice**
- **1 Tbsp. olive oil**
- **2¼ tsp. adobo seasoning**

Combine the first 9 ingredients. Whisk together the lime juice, oil and adobo seasoning; drizzle over shrimp mixture and toss gently to coat. Refrigerate for at least 1 hour, tossing gently every 20 minutes. Serve shrimp mixture in cocktail glasses.

¾ cup: 103 cal., 3g fat (0 sat. fat), 92mg chol., 619mg sod., 5g carb. (2g sugars, 1g fiber), 15g pro.

ROASTED PUMPKIN NACHOS

I had previously made this dish with black beans and corn off the cob in the summer. Wanting to try it with fresh fall ingredients, I replaced the corn with roasted pumpkin—yum! It's also good with butternut squash.
—Lesle Harwood, Douglassville, PA

Prep: 40 min. • **Bake:** 10 min.
Makes: 12 servings

- **4 cups cubed fresh pumpkin or butternut squash (about 1 lb.)**
- **2 Tbsp. olive oil**
- **¼ tsp. salt**
- **⅛ tsp. pepper**
- **1 pkg. (13 oz.) tortilla chips**
- **1 can (15 oz.) black beans, rinsed and drained**
- **1 jar (16 oz.) salsa**
- **3 cups shredded Mexican cheese blend**
- **Optional: Minced fresh cilantro, sliced green onions and hot pepper sauce**

1. Preheat oven to 400°. Place pumpkin in a greased 15x10x1-in. baking pan. Drizzle with oil; sprinkle with salt and pepper. Toss to coat. Roast until tender, 25-30 minutes, stirring occasionally.
2. Reduce oven setting to 350°. On a greased 15x10x1-in. baking pan, layer half each of the chips, beans, pumpkin, salsa and cheese. Repeat layers. Bake until the cheese is melted, 8-10 minutes. Add the toppings of your choice; serve immediately.

1 serving: 347 cal., 18g fat (6g sat. fat), 25mg chol., 559mg sod., 36g carb. (3g sugars, 4g fiber), 10g pro.

WAFFLE-FRY REUBEN BITES

I love Reubens, so I turned the classic sandwich into a fun appetizer with corned beef and sauerkraut on waffle fries.
—Gloria Bradley, Naperville, IL

Prep: 30 min. • **Bake:** 10 min./batch
Makes: about 4 dozen

- **1 pkg. (22 oz.) frozen waffle-cut fries**
- **4 oz. cream cheese, softened**
- **2 cups shredded fontina cheese, divided**
- **⅓ cup Thousand Island salad dressing**
- **3 Tbsp. chopped sweet onion**
- **1½ tsp. prepared horseradish**
- **12 oz. sliced deli corned beef, coarsely chopped**
- **1 cup sauerkraut, rinsed, well drained and chopped**
- **2 Tbsp. minced fresh chives**

1. Prepare waffle fries according to the package directions for baking. Meanwhile, in a small bowl, beat cream cheese, 1 cup fontina cheese, salad dressing, onion and horseradish until blended.
2. Remove fries from oven; set oven to 400°. Top each waffle fry with about ¼ oz. corned beef and 1 tsp. each cream cheese mixture, sauerkraut and remaining fontina cheese. Bake until the cheese is melted, 8-10 minutes. Sprinkle with chives.

1 appetizer: 62 cal., 4g fat (2g sat. fat), 12mg chol., 168mg sod., 4g carb. (0 sugars, 0 fiber), 3g pro.

FRIED MUSHROOMS MARINARA

Deep-fried breaded mushrooms served on a bed of spaghetti sauce are a sure winner for any party. Get ready to hand out the recipe!
—Barbara McCalley, Allison Park, PA

Prep: 30 min. • **Cook:** 15 min.
Makes: about 2 dozen

- **1 cup all-purpose flour**
- **½ tsp. salt**
- **¼ tsp. pepper**
- **3 large eggs**
- **1 Tbsp. water**
- **1 cup seasoned bread crumbs**
- **1 lb. medium fresh mushrooms, stems removed**
- **Oil for deep-fat frying**
- **1 jar (26 oz.) marinara sauce or meatless spaghetti sauce**
- **1 cup shredded part-skim mozzarella cheese**
- **¼ cup grated Parmesan cheese**

1. In a large shallow dish, combine flour, salt and pepper. In another shallow dish, beat eggs and water. Place bread crumbs in a third shallow dish. Add mushrooms to the flour mixture; turn to coat. Dip them in the egg mixture, then coat with bread crumbs. Let stand for 10 minutes.
2. In a deep saucepan, electric skillet or deep-fat fryer, heat oil to 375°. Fry the mushrooms, 6-8 at a time, until golden brown, 1-2 minutes, turning occasionally. Drain on paper towels.
3. Pour the spaghetti sauce into an ungreased 13x9-in. baking dish. Top with the mushrooms. Sprinkle with cheeses. Bake, uncovered, at 350° for 4-6 minutes or until cheese is melted.

1 mushroom: 111 cal., 6g fat (1g sat. fat), 28mg chol., 310mg sod., 10g carb. (2g sugars, 1g fiber), 4g pro.

Pocket Change: Turnovers & Hand Pies

For quick and tasty snacks, practically everything's better when wrapped in a crust! These scrumptious little bites are hot, delicious and bursting with flavor.

BUFFALO CHICKEN POCKETS

Here is my idea of pub food made easy: biscuits flavored with Buffalo wing sauce and blue cheese. They're my Friday night favorite.
—Maria Regakis, Saugus, MA

Takes: 30 min. • **Makes:** 8 servings

- **¾ lb. ground chicken**
- **⅓ cup Buffalo wing sauce**
- **1 tube (16.3 oz.) large refrigerated buttermilk biscuits**
- **½ cup shredded cheddar cheese**
- **Blue cheese salad dressing, optional**

1. Preheat oven to 375°. In a large skillet, cook chicken over medium heat until no longer pink, 5-7 minutes, breaking into crumbles; drain. Remove from heat; stir in wing sauce.
2. On a lightly floured surface, roll each biscuit into a 6-in. circle and top each with ¼ cup chicken mixture and 2 Tbsp. cheese. Fold dough over filling; pinch edge to seal.
3. Transfer to an ungreased baking sheet. Bake until golden brown, 12-14 minutes. If desired, serve with blue cheese dressing.

Freeze option: Freeze cooled pockets in a freezer container. Reheat on an ungreased baking sheet in a preheated 375° oven.

1 pocket: 258 cal., 12g fat (5g sat. fat), 35mg chol., 987mg sod., 25g carb. (3g sugars, 1g fiber), 12g pro.

CHICKEN SHORTCUTS

You can make an even quicker version of these pockets by using precooked chicken. Start with shredded rotisserie chicken or leftover chicken cut into small pieces, and you never have to get out your skillet!

SPINACH TURNOVERS

Flaky cream cheese pastry adds sensational texture to these hot appetizers—and just wait until you taste the wonderful filling! I usually fix a double batch and freeze some to have on hand in case unexpected guests drop by.
—Jean von Bereghy, Oconomowoc, WI

Prep: 30 min. + chilling • **Bake:** 10 min.
Makes: about 4 dozen

- **2 pkg. (8 oz. each) cream cheese, softened**
- **¾ cup butter, softened**
- **2½ cups all-purpose flour**
- **½ tsp. salt**

FILLING

- **5 bacon strips, diced**
- **¼ cup finely chopped onion**
- **2 garlic cloves, minced**
- **1 pkg. (10 oz.) frozen chopped spinach, thawed and well drained**
- **1 cup 4% cottage cheese**
- **¼ tsp. salt**
- **¼ tsp. pepper**
- **⅛ tsp. ground nutmeg**
- **1 large egg, beaten**
- **Salsa, optional**

1. In a bowl, beat the cream cheese and butter until smooth. Combine flour and salt; gradually add to creamed mixture (dough will be stiff). Turn onto a floured surface; gently knead 10 times. Cover and refrigerate at least 2 hours.
2. In a skillet, cook the bacon until crisp. Remove bacon; reserve 1 Tbsp. drippings. Saute onion and garlic in drippings until tender. Remove from heat; stir in bacon, spinach, cottage cheese and seasonings. Let cool.
3. On a lightly floured surface, roll out the dough to ⅛-in. thickness. Cut into 3-in. circles; brush edges with egg. Place 1 heaping tsp. of filling on each circle. Fold over; seal the edges. Prick the tops with a fork. Brush with egg.
4. Bake at 400° for 10-12 minutes or until golden brown. Serve with salsa if desired.

1 turnover: 103 cal., 8g fat (4g sat. fat), 23mg chol., 129mg sod., 6g carb. (1g sugars, 0 fiber), 2g pro.

CRAB CRESCENT TRIANGLES

When friends who love crab were planning a party, I created this recipe just for them. These comforting baked bundles wrap up a cheesy seafood filling in convenient crescent roll dough.

—Noelle Myers, Grand Forks, ND

Prep: 30 min. • **Bake:** 10 min.
Makes: 40 appetizers

- **1 pkg. (8 oz.) cream cheese, softened**
- **2 tsp. mayonnaise**
- **1½ tsp. Dijon mustard**
- **1½ cups shredded Colby-Monterey Jack cheese**
- **¾ cup shredded carrot (about 1 medium)**
- **¼ cup finely chopped celery**
- **2 green onions, chopped**
- **1 garlic clove, minced**
- **1 can (6 oz.) lump crabmeat, drained**
- **2 tubes (8 oz. each) refrigerated seamless crescent dough sheet**

1. Preheat oven to 375°. In a large bowl, beat cream cheese, mayonnaise and mustard until blended. Stir in cheese, carrot, celery, green onions and garlic. Gently fold in crab.
2. Unroll crescent dough and roll into a 12½x10-in. rectangle. Cut each sheet into twenty 2½-in. squares.
3. Spoon a heaping teaspoonful of the cream cheese mixture diagonally over half of each square to within ½ in. of edges. Fold 1 corner of dough over filling to the opposite corner, forming a triangle. Pinch seams to seal; press edges with a fork. Place on ungreased baking sheets. Bake until golden brown, 8-10 minutes.

1 appetizer: 77 cal., 5g fat (3g sat. fat), 14mg chol., 165mg sod., 6g carb. (1g sugars, 0 fiber), 3g pro.

MINI PARTY BURGERS

We love finger foods here in the South. For parties, I make mini burgers in advance and then wrap them in pastry, bake them and serve them with assorted sauces.

—Monica Flatford, Knoxville, TN

Takes: 30 min. • **Makes:** 8 servings

- **½ lb. ground beef**
- **1 envelope ranch salad dressing mix**
- **1 large egg**
- **1 tsp. water**
- **1 sheet frozen puff pastry, thawed**
- **4 slices Havarti cheese (about 4 oz.), quartered**

1. Preheat oven to 400°. Place beef in a small bowl; sprinkle with the dressing mix and mix lightly but thoroughly. Shape into eight ½-in.-thick patties.
2. In a large nonstick skillet, cook burgers over medium heat 3-4 minutes on each side or until a thermometer reads 160°. Remove from heat.
3. Meanwhile, in a small bowl, whisk egg with water. On a lightly floured surface, unfold the puff pastry; roll into a 12-in. square. Cut pastry into four 6-in. squares; cut squares in half to make 8 rectangles. Place a burger on 1 end of each rectangle; top with cheese. Brush edges of pastry with egg mixture. Fold pastry over burger to enclose; press edges with a fork to seal.
4. Transfer to a parchment-lined baking sheet. Brush tops with egg mixture. Bake 15-20 minutes or until golden brown.

1 appetizer: 271 cal., 16 g fat (6 g sat. fat), 54 mg chol., 488 mg sod., 20 g carb. (0 sugars, 2g fiber), 11 g pro.

Side Dishes & Condiments

No matter the season, veggie sides, casseroles and dressings are a fabulous way to celebrate. On these pages you'll discover 28 hot side dishes, crisp and springy sautes, sun-kissed sweet corn preps and wonderful ways to preserve the abundant produce from your summer garden.

SAUSAGE & CORNBREAD DRESSING

At our house, we add sausage and a little steak sauce to our cornbread dressing. It warms us up on even the coldest days.
—Mandy Nall, Montgomery, AL

Prep: 30 min. • **Bake:** 40 min.
Makes: 12 servings

- **1 pkg. (19½ oz.) Italian turkey sausage links, casings removed**
- **4 medium onions, chopped (about 3 cups)**
- **½ cup chopped celery**
- **6 cups cubed day-old white or French bread**
- **6 cups coarsely crumbled cornbread**
- **2 large eggs**
- **2 Tbsp. steak sauce**
- **2 tsp. onion salt**
- **2 tsp. poultry seasoning**
- **2 tsp. dried parsley flakes**
- **1 tsp. garlic powder**
- **1 tsp. baking powder**
- **2½ to 3 cups reduced-sodium chicken broth**

1. Preheat the oven to 350°. In a 6-qt. stockpot, cook sausage over medium heat 6-8 minutes or until no longer pink, breaking it into crumbles. Remove with a slotted spoon, reserving drippings in pot.
2. Add onions and celery to drippings; cook and stir 6-8 minutes or until tender. Remove from heat; stir in the sausage. Add the cubed bread and cornbread; toss to combine.
3. In a small bowl, whisk the eggs, steak sauce, seasonings and baking powder until blended; stir into the bread mixture. Stir in enough chicken broth to reach desired moistness.
4. Transfer to a greased 13x9-in. or 3-qt. baking dish. Bake 40-50 minutes or until lightly browned.

¾ cup: 240 cal., 6g fat (1g sat. fat), 48mg chol., 1112mg sod., 35g carb. (4g sugars, 3g fiber), 11g pro.

SAVORY BLUEBERRY-ONION JAM

My aunt made this every year. Now I make it and my daughter does, too. Everyone loves the savory jam on hot dogs, meat loaf and scrambled eggs. I even caught my mother eating a spoonful just because!
—Pat Dazis, Charlotte, NC

Prep: 1¾ hours • **Process:** 10 min.
Makes: 6 half-pints

- **¼ cup olive oil**
- **16 cups chopped red onion (about 10 medium)**
- **2 Tbsp. minced fresh tarragon or 2 tsp. dried tarragon**
- **1 Tbsp. minced fresh thyme or 1 tsp. dried thyme**
- **1½ tsp. salt**
- **1 tsp. white pepper**
- **2 cups fresh blueberries**
- **½ cup honey**
- **½ cup balsamic vinegar**
- **2 Tbsp. lemon juice**

1. In a Dutch oven, heat oil over medium heat. Add onions, tarragon, thyme, salt and pepper. Reduce heat to medium-low; cook 30-35 minutes or until the liquid is evaporated, stirring occasionally.
2. Add blueberries, honey, vinegar and lemon juice; bring to a boil. Reduce heat; simmer, uncovered, 50-55 minutes or until the mixture is thickened, stirring occasionally. Remove from heat.
3. Carefully ladle hot mixture into 6 hot half-pint jars, leaving ¼-in. headspace. Remove air bubbles and adjust headspace, if necessary, by adding hot mixture. Wipe rims. Center lids on jars; screw on bands until fingertip tight.
4. Place jars into canner with simmering water, ensuring that they are completely covered with water. Bring to a boil; process for 10 minutes. Remove jars and cool.

2 Tbsp.: 48 cal., 1g fat (0 sat. fat), 0 chol., 76mg sod., 10g carb. (6g sugars, 1g fiber), 1g pro. **Diabetic exchanges:** ½ starch.

ROASTED CARROTS & FENNEL

This addictive combo is a fresh take on one of my mother's standard wintertime dishes. I usually add more carrots—as many as the pans will hold.

—Lily Julow, Lawrenceville, GA

Prep: 15 min. • **Bake:** 40 min.
Makes: 8 servings

- **2½ lbs. medium carrots, peeled and cut in half lengthwise**
- **1 large fennel bulb, cut into ½-in. wedges**
- **1 large red onion, cut into ½-in. wedges**
- **1 medium lemon, thinly sliced**
- **¼ cup olive oil**
- **2 tsp. ground coriander**
- **1 tsp. ground cumin**
- **½ tsp. salt**
- **¼ tsp. pepper**
- **Thinly sliced fresh basil leaves**

1. Preheat oven to 375°. In a large bowl, combine the carrots, fennel, onion and lemon. Mix the oil, coriander, cumin, salt and pepper; drizzle over carrot mixture and toss to coat. Transfer to 2 foil-lined 15x10x1-in. baking pans.
2. Roast the vegetables 40-50 minutes or until tender, stirring occasionally. Sprinkle with basil.

1 serving: 139 cal., 7g fat (1g sat. fat), 0 chol., 262mg sod., 18g carb. (9g sugars, 6g fiber), 2g pro. **Diabetic exchanges:** 2 vegetable, 1½ fat.

❄ SCALLOPED SWEET CORN CASSEROLE

I grew up enjoying my grandmother's sweet corn casserole. Now a grandmother myself, I still serve this comforting, delicious side dish.

—Lonnie Hartstack, Clarinda, IA

Prep: 25 min. • **Bake:** 50 min.
Makes: 8 servings

- **4 tsp. cornstarch**
- **⅔ cup water**
- **¼ cup butter, cubed**
- **3 cups fresh or frozen corn**
- **1 can (5 oz.) evaporated milk**
- **¾ tsp. plus 1½ tsp. sugar, divided**
- **½ tsp. plus ¾ tsp. salt, divided**
- **3 large eggs**
- **¾ cup 2% milk**
- **¼ tsp. pepper**
- **3 cups cubed bread**
- **1 small onion, chopped**
- **1 cup Rice Krispies, slightly crushed**
- **3 Tbsp. butter, melted**

1. Preheat oven to 350°. In a small bowl, mix cornstarch and water until smooth. In a large saucepan, heat the butter over medium heat. Stir in corn, evaporated milk, ¾ tsp. sugar and ½ tsp. salt; bring just to a boil. Stir in cornstarch mixture; return to a boil, stirring constantly. Cook and stir 1-2 minutes or until thickened; cool slightly.
2. In a large bowl, whisk the eggs, milk, pepper and the remaining sugar and salt until blended. Stir in bread, onion and corn mixture. Transfer to a greased 8-in. square or 1½-qt. baking dish.
3. Bake, uncovered, 40 minutes. In a small bowl, toss Rice Krispies with the melted butter; sprinkle over casserole. Bake 10-15 minutes longer or until golden brown.

Freeze option: Cool unbaked casserole, reserving Rice Krispies topping for baking; cover and freeze. To use, partially thaw in the refrigerator overnight. Remove from refrigerator 30 minutes before baking. Preheat oven to 350°. Bake the casserole as directed, increasing time as necessary to heat through and for a thermometer inserted in center to read 165°.

⅔ cup: 258 cal., 15g fat (8g sat. fat), 104mg chol., 604mg sod., 26g carb. (9g sugars, 2g fiber), 8g pro.

CREAMY ROASTED GARLIC & SPINACH ORZO

This side dish brings instant joy. I first made it without spinach so my husband and daughter would like it. The next time, I added spinach for the extra health benefits. They still devoured it! In my book, that's a win-win.

—Dawn Moore, Warren, PA

Prep: 35 min. • **Cook:** 20 min.
Makes: 6 servings

- **1 whole garlic bulb**
- **1 tsp. plus 1 Tbsp. olive oil, divided**
- **1¾ cups uncooked whole wheat orzo pasta**
- **2½ cups chicken stock**
- **3 oz. reduced-fat cream cheese, cubed**
- **1 pkg. (9 oz.) fresh spinach, trimmed and chopped**
- **¼ cup shredded Asiago cheese**
- **¼ cup fat-free milk**
- **1 tsp. salt-free garlic pepper seasoning blend**
- **¼ tsp. salt**
- **2 Tbsp. minced fresh parsley**

1. Preheat oven to 425°. Remove papery outer skin from garlic bulb but do not peel or separate the cloves. Cut off top of garlic bulb, exposing individual cloves. Drizzle cut cloves with 1 tsp. oil. Wrap in foil. Bake 30-35 minutes or until the cloves are soft. Unwrap. When cool enough to handle, squeeze the garlic cloves from skins.
2. In a Dutch oven, heat the remaining oil over medium-high heat. Add pasta; cook and stir 2-3 minutes or until lightly browned. Add the stock; bring to a boil. Reduce the heat; simmer, covered, for 10-12 minutes or until pasta is tender and the liquid is absorbed.
3. Stir in cream cheese until melted. Add spinach, Asiago, milk, seasoning blend, salt and roasted garlic; cook and stir until spinach is wilted. Sprinkle with parsley.

⅔ cup: 271 cal., 8g fat (3g sat. fat), 14mg chol., 422mg sod., 37g carb. (2g sugars, 9g fiber), 12g pro. **Diabetic exchanges:** 2 starch, 1½ fat, 1 vegetable.

FRESH HERBS MADE EASY

To keep parsley fresh for up to a month, trim the stems and place the bunch in a tumbler with an inch of water. Be sure no loose leaves or greenery are in the water. Tie a produce bag around the tumbler to trap humidity; store in the refrigerator. Each time you use the parsley, change the water and turn the produce bag inside out.

CRISPY BAKED ZUCCHINI FRIES

I coat zucchini strips with a mixture of panko bread crumbs, Parmesan cheese and spices. Then I bake them until they're crispy and golden brown. Scrumptious!

—Matthew Hass, Ellison Bay, WI

Prep: 25 min. • **Bake:** 20 min.
Makes: 4 servings

- **2 medium zucchini**
- **1 cup panko bread crumbs**
- **¾ cup grated Parmesan cheese**
- **2 tsp. smoked paprika**
- **½ tsp. garlic powder**
- **¼ tsp. ground chipotle pepper**
- **¼ tsp. salt**
- **¼ tsp. pepper**
- **⅓ cup all-purpose flour**
- **2 large eggs, beaten**
- **3 Tbsp. olive oil**

1. Preheat the oven to 425°. Cut each zucchini in half lengthwise and then in half crosswise. Cut each piece lengthwise into ¼-in. slices.
2. In a shallow bowl, mix bread crumbs, cheese and seasonings. Place the flour and eggs in separate shallow bowls. Dip zucchini slices in flour, then in egg and then in crumb mixture, patting to help the coating adhere. Place on a greased rack in a foil-lined rimmed baking pan. Drizzle with oil. Bake until golden brown, 20-25 minutes.

1 serving: 289 cal., 18g fat (5g sat. fat), 106mg chol., 510mg sod., 21g carb. (3g sugars, 2g fiber), 12g pro.

Contest Winner

CINNAMON BLUEBERRY JAM

Watching my grandmother can hundreds of jars of tomatoes, peaches and pears inspired me to try making jams and jellies myself. I remember going down into her cellar as a girl—all those jars on the shelves gave me such a warm, homey feeling! My family enjoys this jam on warm corn muffins, or blueberry. The cinnamon's a bit of a surprise.

—Barbara Burns, Phillipsburg, NJ

Prep: 15 min. • **Process:** 10 min.
Makes: 4 half-pints

- **1 lb. fresh or frozen blueberries (about 1 qt.)**
- **3½ cups sugar**
- **1 Tbsp. bottled lemon juice**
- **¼ tsp. ground cinnamon**
- **⅛ tsp. ground cloves**
- **1 pouch (3 oz.) liquid fruit pectin**

1. Crush blueberries; measure 2½ cups and place in a large saucepan. Add the sugar, lemon juice, cinnamon and cloves; bring to a rolling boil over high heat, stirring constantly. Quickly stir in the pectin. Return to a full rolling boil; boil for 1 minute, stirring constantly.
2. Remove from the heat; skim off foam. Carefully ladle the hot mixture into hot half-pint jars, leaving ¼-in. headspace. Remove air bubbles; wipe the rims and adjust the lids. Process for 10 minutes in a boiling-water canner.

2 Tbsp.: 93 cal., 0 fat (0 sat. fat), 0 chol., 1mg sod., 24g carb. (23g sugars, 0 fiber), 0 pro.

BOURBON PEACH JAM

Bourbon has been popular at our house since we visited the Kentucky Bourbon Trail a few years ago. Every bite of this jam reminds me of that fun trip.

—Katie Ferrier, Houston, TX

Prep: 70 min. • **Process:** 10 min.
Makes: 3 half-pints

- **4 cups finely chopped peeled fresh peaches (about 6 medium)**
- **1½ cups packed brown sugar**
- **1 cup sugar**
- **1 Tbsp. lemon juice**
- **3 Tbsp. bourbon or 3 tsp. vanilla or bourbon extract**

1. In a large saucepan, combine peaches, sugars and lemon juice; bring to a boil. Reduce heat; simmer, uncovered, until mixture is thick and a thermometer reads 220°, about 60 minutes. Remove from heat; skim off foam. Stir in bourbon.
2. Ladle hot mixture into 3 hot half-pint jars, leaving ¼-in. headspace. Remove air bubbles and adjust the headspace, if necessary, by adding hot mixture. Wipe rims. Center lids on jars; screw on bands until fingertip tight.
3. Place jars in canner, ensuring that they are completely covered with water. Bring to a boil; process for 10 minutes. Remove jars and cool.

2 Tbsp.: 88 cal., 0 fat (0 sat. fat), 0 chol., 4mg sod., 23g carb. (22g sugars, 0 fiber), 0 pro.

CREAMY SWEET POTATOES

I took my mother's yummy sweet potato casserole recipe and gave it a new twist by adding the tempting taste of orange—a fruit very abundant in our state. The flavors are wonderful together and make this dish a family favorite.

—Norma Poole, Auburndale, FL

Prep: 15 min. • **Bake:** 40 min.
Makes: 12 servings

- **5 lbs. sweet potatoes, peeled and cooked**
- **4 large eggs, lightly beaten**
- **½ cup orange juice**
- **½ cup butter, softened**
- **½ cup sugar**
- **1 tsp. vanilla extract**
- **½ tsp. ground nutmeg**
- **Dash salt**
- **1 cup miniature marshmallows**

1. Preheat oven to 350°. In a large bowl, mash sweet potatoes. Add eggs, orange juice, butter, sugar, vanilla, nutmeg and salt; mix well. Transfer to a greased 3-qt. baking dish.
2. Bake until set, 35-40 minutes. Top with marshmallows; return to oven until they just begin to puff and melt, 5-10 minutes.

¾ cup: 312 cal., 10g fat (5g sat. fat), 82mg chol., 266mg sod., 53g carb. (41g sugars, 5g fiber), 4g pro.

GARLIC-ROSEMARY BRUSSELS SPROUTS

This is my go-to Thanksgiving side dish. It is healthy and easy, and it doesn't take very much time or effort to make. I usually use rosemary for my turkey, so this lets me use some of the leftover herbs.

—Elisabeth Larsen, Pleasant Grove, UT

Prep: 15 min. • **Bake:** 25 min.
Makes: 8 servings

- **¼ cup olive oil**
- **4 garlic cloves, minced**
- **1 tsp. salt**
- **½ tsp. pepper**
- **2 lbs. Brussels sprouts (about 8 cups), trimmed and halved**
- **1 cup panko bread crumbs**
- **1 to 2 Tbsp. minced fresh rosemary**

1. Preheat oven to 425°. Place the first 4 ingredients in a small microwave-safe bowl; microwave on high 30 seconds.
2. Place Brussels sprouts in a 15x10x1-in. pan; toss with 3 Tbsp. oil mixture. Roast 10 minutes.
3. Toss bread crumbs with rosemary and remaining oil mixture; sprinkle over sprouts. Bake until crumbs are browned and sprouts are tender, 12-15 minutes. Serve immediately.

¾ cup: 134 cal., 7g fat (1g sat. fat), 0 chol., 342mg sod., 15g carb. (3g sugars, 4g fiber), 5g pro. **Diabetic exchanges:** 1½ fat, 1 vegetable, ½ starch.

REACH FOR THE SPICE JAR

If you don't have fresh rosemary, use 1-2 tsp. dried rosemary that's been crushed with a mortar and pestle or in a dish with the back of a spoon.

DAD'S CREAMED PEAS & PEARL ONIONS

While I was growing up, it was our family tradition to make creamed peas with pearl onions for every Thanksgiving and Christmas dinner. My dad was not a happy camper if he didn't see this dish on the table. It was his favorite! I made it for my own family while our kids were growing up, and now my daughter makes this dish for her family.

—Nancy Heishman, Las Vegas, NV

Takes: 25 min. • **Makes:** 6 servings

- **5 cups frozen peas (about 20 oz.), thawed and drained**
- **2 cups frozen pearl onions (about 9 oz.), thawed and drained**
- **2 celery ribs, finely chopped**
- **¾ cup chicken broth**
- **½ tsp. salt**
- **½ tsp. pepper**
- **½ tsp. dried thyme**
- **½ cup sour cream**
- **10 bacon strips, cooked and crumbled**
- **¾ cup salted cashews**

In a large skillet, combine the first 7 ingredients; bring to a boil. Reduce heat to medium; cook, uncovered, until onions are tender and most of the liquid is evaporated, 8-10 minutes, stirring occasionally. Remove from heat; stir in the sour cream. Top with bacon and cashews.

¾ cup: 322 cal., 18g fat (6g sat. fat), 19mg chol., 783mg sod., 26g carb. (10g sugars, 7g fiber), 14g pro.

GENTLEMAN'S WHISKEY BACON JAM

You can slather this smoky jam on pretty much anything. It lasts only a week in the fridge, so I freeze small amounts for a quick snack with crackers.

—Colleen Delawder, Herndon, VA

Prep: 15 min. • **Cook:** 30 min. • **Makes:** 3 cups

- **1½ lbs. thick-sliced bacon strips, finely chopped**
- **8 shallots, finely chopped**
- **1 large sweet onion, finely chopped**
- **2 garlic cloves, minced**
- **1 tsp. chili powder**
- **½ tsp. paprika**
- **¼ tsp. kosher salt**
- **¼ tsp. pepper**
- **½ cup whiskey**
- **½ cup maple syrup**
- **¼ cup balsamic vinegar**
- **½ cup packed brown sugar**
- **Assorted crackers**

1. In a large skillet, cook the bacon over medium heat until crisp. Drain on paper towels. Discard all but 2 Tbsp. drippings. Add shallots and onion to the drippings; cook over medium heat until caramelized, stirring occasionally.
2. Stir in garlic; cook 30 seconds. Add the seasonings. Remove from heat; stir in whiskey and maple syrup. Increase heat to high; bring to a boil and cook 3 minutes, stirring constantly. Add the vinegar and brown sugar; cook another 3 minutes, continuing to stir constantly.
3. Add crumbled bacon; reduce heat to low and cook 12 minutes, stirring every few minutes. Allow jam to cool slightly. Pulse half the jam in a food processor until smooth; stir puree into remaining jam. Serve with assorted crackers.

2 Tbsp.: 112 cal., 8g fat (3g sat. fat), 10mg chol., 118mg sod., 7g carb. (5g sugars, 0 fiber), 2g pro.

SASSY SAMMIES

Use this bacon jam to step up your grilled cheese game! Add smoky and sweet notes with a few spoonfuls of jam on your next sandwich. It's fantastic alongside Brie, pears and crackers, too.

SWEET ZUCCHINI RELISH

Classic relish is made with cucumbers, but this sweet and tangy topper is packed with zucchini, peppers and onions. I use it on burgers, on sandwiches and in any recipes that normally call for pickle relish.

—Jyl Basinger, Cave City, AR

Prep: 1 hour + chilling • **Process:** 15 min.
Makes: 5 pints

- **10 cups shredded zucchini (about 3½ lbs.)**
- **4 large onions, chopped**
- **2 medium green peppers, chopped**
- **2 medium sweet red peppers, chopped**
- **⅓ cup canning salt**
- **2½ cups sugar**
- **2½ cups cider vinegar**
- **4 tsp. cornstarch**
- **1 tsp. ground turmeric**
- **1 tsp. curry powder**
- **1 tsp. celery seed**
- **½ tsp. pepper**

1. In a large container, combine the zucchini, onions, peppers and salt. Cover and refrigerate overnight. Drain; rinse and drain again.
2. In a stockpot, combine sugar, vinegar, cornstarch and seasonings; bring to a boil. Add the zucchini mixture; return to a boil. Reduce heat; simmer, uncovered, until slightly thickened, 12-15 minutes. Remove from the heat.
3. Carefully ladle the hot mixture into hot 1-pint jars, leaving ½-in. headspace. Remove air bubbles; wipe rims and adjust lids. Process for 15 minutes in a boiling-water canner. Refrigerate remaining relish for up to 1 week.

¼ cup: 67 cal., 0 fat (0 sat. fat), 0 chol., 288mg sod., 16g carb. (14g sugars, 1g fiber), 1g pro.

ROASTED CAULIFLOWER WITH TAHINI YOGURT SAUCE

I created my own cauliflower recipe in honor of my grandma, who taught me to love the delicious and healthy vegetable. She cooked with it all the time.

—Lidia Haddadian, Pasadena, CA

Prep: 15 min. • **Bake:** 40 min.
Makes: 4 servings

- **¼ cup grated Parmesan cheese**
- **3 Tbsp. olive oil**
- **2 garlic cloves, minced**
- **¼ tsp. salt**
- **¼ tsp. pepper**
- **1 small head cauliflower (about 1½ lbs.), cut into 4 wedges**

SAUCE

- **½ cup fat-free plain Greek yogurt**
- **1 Tbsp. lemon juice**
- **1 Tbsp. tahini**
- **¼ tsp. salt**
- **Dash paprika**
- **Dash cayenne pepper**
- **Minced fresh parsley**

1. Preheat oven to 375°. In a small bowl, mix the first 5 ingredients. Rub over the cauliflower; arrange, cut sides up, in a foil-lined 15x10x1-in. baking pan coated with cooking spray. Roast 40-45 minutes or until golden brown and tender.
2. For sauce, in a small bowl, mix the yogurt, lemon juice, tahini, salt, paprika and pepper; serve over the cauliflower. Sprinkle with parsley.

1 cauliflower wedge with about 2 Tbsp. sauce: 177 cal., 14g fat (3g sat. fat), 4mg chol., 421mg sod., 7g carb. (3g sugars, 2g fiber), 7g pro.

BEST EVER SWEET PICKLES

When I was a kid, I always looked forward to the homemade jams and jellies my granny made from her farm-grown berries. Our urban backyard doesn't have room for a berry patch, but we do have a trellis for growing cucumbers. I pack away these sweet pickles every summer.
—Ellie Martin Cliffe, Milwaukee, WI

Prep: 1 hour + standing • **Process:** 10 min.
Makes: 4 pints

- **9 cups sliced pickling cucumbers**
- **1 large sweet onion, halved and thinly sliced**
- **¼ cup canning salt**
- **1 cup sugar**
- **1 cup water**
- **1 cup white vinegar**
- **½ cup cider vinegar**
- **2 Tbsp. mustard seed**
- **1 tsp. celery seed**
- **½ tsp. whole peppercorns**
- **12 garlic cloves, crushed**
- **4 bay leaves**

1. In a large nonreactive bowl, combine the cucumbers, onion and salt. Cover with crushed ice and mix well. Let stand for 3 hours. Drain; rinse and drain thoroughly.
2. In a Dutch oven, combine sugar, water, vinegars, mustard seed, celery seed and peppercorns. Bring to a boil, stirring to dissolve sugar. Add cucumber mixture; return to a boil, stirring occasionally. Reduce the heat; simmer, uncovered, 4-5 minutes or until heated through.
3. Carefully ladle the hot mixture into 4 hot wide-mouth 1-pint jars, leaving ½-in. headspace. Add 3 garlic cloves and 1 bay leaf to each jar. Remove air bubbles and, if necessary, adjust headspace by adding hot pickling liquid. Wipe the rims. Center the lids on the jars; screw on bands until fingertip tight.
4. Place jars into canner with simmering water, ensuring that they are completely covered with water. Bring to a boil; process for 10 minutes. Remove jars and cool.

¼ cup: 35 cal., 0 fat (0 sat. fat), 0 chol., 175mg sod., 8g carb. (7g sugars, 0 fiber), 0 pro.

BRUSSELS SPROUTS & KALE SAUTE

This colorful side dish is filled with healthy greens. It pairs well with turkey, potatoes and other holiday staples. The crispy salami—my kid's favorite ingredient—makes it over-the-top fabulous.
—Jennifer McNabb, Brentwood, TN

Takes: 30 min. • **Makes:** 12 servings

- **¼ lb. thinly sliced hard salami, cut into ¼-in. strips**
- **1½ tsp. olive oil**
- **2 Tbsp. butter**
- **2 lbs. fresh Brussels sprouts, thinly sliced**
- **2 cups shredded fresh kale**
- **1 large onion, finely chopped**
- **½ tsp. kosher salt**
- **⅛ tsp. cayenne pepper**
- **¼ tsp. coarsely ground pepper**
- **1 garlic clove, minced**
- **½ cup chicken broth**
- **½ cup chopped walnuts**
- **1 Tbsp. balsamic vinegar**

1. In a Dutch oven, cook and stir salami in oil over medium-high heat until crisp, 3-5 minutes. Remove to paper towels with a slotted spoon; reserve drippings in pan.
2. Add the butter to drippings; heat over medium-high heat. Add the Brussels sprouts, kale, onion, salt, cayenne and ground pepper; cook and stir until the vegetables are crisp-tender. Add garlic; cook 1 minute longer.
3. Stir in broth; bring to a boil. Reduce heat; cover and cook until the Brussels sprouts are tender, 4-5 minutes. Stir in walnuts and vinegar. Serve with the salami strips.

½ cup: 126 cal., 9g fat (3g sat. fat), 14mg chol., 341mg sod., 9g carb. (3g sugars, 3g fiber), 6g pro. **Diabetic exchanges:** 2 fat, 1 vegetable.

SPRING GREEN RISOTTO

Once a week I create a new recipe for my blog, *An Officer and a Vegan*. I first made this risotto when I needed something cheerful and comforting. It would be perfect with asparagus, zucchini or summer squash, but you can use whatever veggies are in season.
—Deanna Wolfe, Muskegon, MI

Prep: 15 min. • **Cook:** 30 min.
Makes: 8 servings

- **1 carton (32 oz.) vegetable stock**
- **1 to 1½ cups water**
- **1 Tbsp. olive oil**
- **2 cups sliced fresh mushrooms**
- **1 medium onion, chopped**
- **1½ cups uncooked arborio rice**
- **2 garlic cloves, minced**
- **½ cup white wine or additional vegetable stock**
- **1 tsp. dried thyme**
- **3 cups fresh baby spinach**
- **1 cup frozen peas**
- **3 Tbsp. grated Parmesan cheese**
- **1 Tbsp. red wine vinegar**
- **½ tsp. salt**
- **¼ tsp. pepper**

1. In a large saucepan, bring stock and water to a simmer; keep hot. In a Dutch oven, heat the oil over medium-high heat. Add mushrooms and onion; cook and stir 5-7 minutes or until tender. Add rice and garlic; cook and stir 1-2 minutes or until rice is coated.
2. Stir in wine and thyme. Reduce heat to maintain a simmer; cook and stir until wine is absorbed. Add hot stock mixture, ½ cup at a time, cooking and stirring after each addition until stock has been absorbed; continue until the rice is tender but firm to the bite and the mixture is creamy. Stir in spinach, peas, cheese, vinegar, salt and pepper; heat through. Serve immediately.

¾ cup: 198 cal., 3g fat (1g sat. fat), 2mg chol., 477mg sod., 37g carb. (3g sugars, 2g fiber), 5g pro.

PATIENCE PAYS OFF

Low and slow is the name of the game when making risotto. Stirring often is essential to prevent burning and to create the risotto's signature creamy texture. It may take more time, but it's well worth the wait!

PEPPER JACK HASH BROWN CASSEROLE

I found myself in need of an impromptu potato dish, but I had no potatoes. Frozen hash browns and the plethora of cheeses I kept in the freezer offered me the solution to my side-dish dilemma.
—Cyndy Gerken, Naples, FL

Prep: 25 min. • **Bake:** 25 min.
Makes: 12 servings

- **1 pkg. (30 oz.) frozen shredded hash brown potatoes, thawed**
- **1 can (10½ oz.) condensed cream of chicken soup, undiluted**
- **2 cups shredded pepper jack cheese**
- **1½ cups heavy whipping cream**
- **½ cup butter, melted**
- **½ cup sour cream**
- **¼ cup shredded Parmesan cheese**
- **½ tsp. salt**
- **½ tsp. onion powder**
- **¼ tsp. garlic powder**
- **¼ tsp. pepper**

TOPPING
- **1 cup crushed potato chips**
- **5 bacon strips, cooked and crumbled**
- **¾ cup shredded Parmesan cheese**
- **1 tsp. paprika**

1. Preheat oven to 350°. In a large bowl, combine the first 11 ingredients. Transfer to a greased 13x9-in. baking dish. For the topping, combine the potato chips, bacon and Parmesan; sprinkle over casserole. Top with paprika.
2. Bake, uncovered, until the edges are bubbly and the topping is golden brown, 25-30 minutes.

⅔ cup: 416 cal., 33g fat (19g sat. fat), 87mg chol., 682mg sod., 20g carb. (2g sugars, 2g fiber), 12g pro.

FAMILY-FRIENDLY TASTE

If you're making this dish for children or for an adult who doesn't enjoy spicy food, use Monterey Jack cheese instead of the pepper jack.

HONEY GARLIC GREEN BEANS

Green beans are wonderful, but they can seem ordinary on their own. Just a couple of extra ingredients give the mild-mannered veggies a sweet and salty attitude.
—Shannon Dobos, Calgary, AB

Takes: 20 min. • **Makes:** 8 servings

- **4 Tbsp. honey**
- **2 Tbsp. reduced-sodium soy sauce**
- **4 garlic cloves, minced**
- **¼ tsp. salt**
- **¼ tsp. crushed red pepper flakes**
- **2 lbs. fresh green beans, trimmed**

1. Whisk together first 5 ingredients; set aside. In a 6-qt. stockpot, bring 10 cups water to a boil. Add beans in batches; cook, uncovered, just until crisp-tender, 2-3 minutes. Remove the beans and immediately drop into ice water. Drain and pat dry.
2. Coat stockpot with cooking spray. Add beans; cook, stirring constantly, over high heat until slightly blistered, 2-3 minutes. Add sauce; continue stirring until beans are coated and sauce starts to evaporate slightly, 2-3 minutes. Remove from heat.

¾ cup: 72 cal., 0 fat (0 sat. fat), 0 chol., 225mg sod., 18g carb. (12g sugars, 4g fiber), 2g pro.
Diabetic exchanges: 1 vegetable, ½ starch.

SHARP CHEDDAR SCALLOPED POTATOES

Try as I might, I can never follow a recipe exactly! Here's what I came up with when I made a family friend's scalloped potatoes recipe in my own kitchen. These potatoes are so good—you'll just keep going back for more.

—Susan Simons, Eatonville, WA

Prep: 30 min. • **Bake:** 70 min.
Makes: 8 servings

- **¼ cup butter, cubed**
- **⅓ cup all-purpose flour**
- **¾ tsp. salt**
- **½ tsp. ground mustard**
- **½ tsp. white pepper**
- **2 cups half-and-half cream**
- **1½ cups shredded sharp white cheddar cheese**
- **1½ cups shredded sharp yellow cheddar cheese**
- **6 cups thinly sliced peeled Yukon Gold potatoes (about 2 lbs.)**
- **2 small onions, finely chopped**

1. Preheat the oven to 350°. In a large saucepan, heat butter over medium heat. Stir in flour, salt, mustard and pepper until blended; cook and stir 2-3 minutes or until lightly browned. Gradually whisk in cream. Bring to a boil, stirring constantly; cook and stir 1-2 minutes or until thickened. Remove from heat.
2. In a small bowl, combine the cheeses. Layer a third of the potatoes, a third of the onions and ¾ cup cheese mixture in a greased 3-qt. baking dish. Repeat layers twice. Pour sauce over top; sprinkle with remaining cheese.
3. Bake, covered, 45 minutes. Uncover; bake 25-30 minutes longer or until the potatoes are tender and the top is lightly browned.

¾ cup: 436 cal., 26g fat (16g sat. fat), 88mg chol., 576mg sod., 33g carb. (5g sugars, 2g fiber), 15g pro.

LOADED TWICE-BAKED POTATO CASSEROLE

My husband is a meat-and-potatoes guy, so I like to try new combinations for variety. In this dish, twice-baked potatoes and potato skins make a robust casserole.

—Cyndy Gerken, Naples, FL

Prep: 1½ hours • **Bake:** 30 min.
Makes: 8 servings

- **4 large baking potatoes (about 3¼ lbs.)**
- **1 Tbsp. olive oil**
- **¾ tsp. salt, divided**
- **¾ tsp. pepper, divided**
- **¼ cup butter, cubed**
- **⅔ cup heavy whipping cream**
- **¼ cup sour cream**
- **2 cups shredded cheddar cheese, divided**
- **6 bacon strips, cooked and crumbled, divided**
- **2 green onions, sliced, divided**
- **Additional sour cream, optional**

1. Preheat oven to 375°. Scrub potatoes; pierce several times with a fork. Brush with oil; sprinkle with ½ tsp. salt and ¼ tsp. pepper. Place in a foil-lined 15x10x1-in. baking pan; bake 1-1¼ hours or until tender. Cool slightly.
2. In a small saucepan, melt butter over medium heat. Whisk in whipping cream and ¼ cup sour cream. Add 1½ cups cheese; stir until melted. Remove from heat; cover to keep warm.
3. When the potatoes are cool enough to handle, cut each potato lengthwise in half. Scoop out pulp and place in a large bowl. Cut 2 potato skin shells into 1-in. pieces; save remaining skins for another use.
4. Mash pulp with the remaining salt and pepper. Stir in cheese mixture, half the bacon and 2 Tbsp. green onion. Transfer to a greased 1½-qt. baking dish. Top with the cut-up potato skins. Sprinkle with remaining cheese and bacon.
5. Bake until heated through and lightly browned, 30-35 minutes. Sprinkle with remaining green onion. If desired, serve with additional sour cream.

½ cup: 367 cal., 27g fat (16g sat. fat), 84mg chol., 458mg sod., 20g carb. (2g sugars, 2g fiber), 12g pro.

STUFFED BAKED TOMATOES

I make this side dish often—my family really likes it. Besides being flavorful, the tomatoes make a colorful, zesty addition to any dinner.
—Edna Jackson, Kokomo, IN

Prep: 15 min. • **Bake:** 30 min.
Makes: 6 servings

- **6 medium tomatoes**

STUFFING

- **1 cup garlic/cheese croutons, crushed**
- **2 Tbsp. grated Parmesan cheese**
- **2 Tbsp. grated American or cheddar cheese**
- **4 Tbsp. melted butter**
- **½ tsp. salt**
- **¼ tsp. freshly ground pepper**
- **Chopped fresh parsley for garnish**

1. Preheat oven to 350°. Cut a thin slice off the top of each tomato. Scoop out pulp, leaving a ½-in. shell. Invert the shells onto paper towels to drain. Mix stuffing ingredients except parsley; spoon stuffing into tomatoes. Sprinkle with parsley.
2. Place the tomatoes in a baking dish; cover with aluminum foil to prevent over-browning of the stuffing. Bake until the tomatoes are tender and the stuffing is hot, about 30 minutes.

1 serving: 146 cal., 11g fat (6g sat. fat), 24mg chol., 434mg sod., 11g carb. (4g sugars, 2g fiber), 3g pro.

GRILLED VEGGIES WITH MUSTARD VINAIGRETTE

I make this healthy and inviting side dish whenever friends come over for a cookout. The sweet-tangy honeyed vinaigrette lets the veggies shine.
—Shelly Graver, Lansdale, PA

Prep: 20 min. • **Grill:** 15 min.
Makes: 10 servings

- **¼ cup red wine vinegar**
- **1 Tbsp. Dijon mustard**
- **1 Tbsp. honey**
- **½ tsp. salt**
- **⅛ tsp. pepper**
- **¼ cup canola oil**
- **¼ cup olive oil**

VEGETABLES

- **2 large sweet onions**
- **2 medium zucchini**
- **2 yellow summer squash**
- **2 large sweet red peppers, halved and seeded**
- **1 bunch green onions, trimmed**
- **Cooking spray**

1. In a small bowl, whisk the first 5 ingredients. Gradually whisk in the oils until blended.
2. Peel and quarter each sweet onion, leaving the root ends intact. Cut the zucchini and yellow squash lengthwise into ½-in.-thick slices. Lightly spritz onions, zucchini, yellow squash and remaining vegetables with cooking spray, turning to coat all sides.
3. Grill the sweet onions, covered, over medium heat 15-20 minutes until tender, turning occasionally. Grill zucchini, squash and peppers, covered, over medium heat 10-15 minutes or until crisp-tender and lightly charred, turning once. Grill green onions, covered, 2-4 minutes or until lightly charred, turning once.
4. Cut vegetables into bite-sized pieces; place in a large bowl. Add ½ cup of the vinaigrette and toss to coat. Serve with remaining vinaigrette.

¾ cup: 155 cal., 12g fat (1g sat. fat), 0 chol., 166mg sod., 13g carb. (8g sugars, 2g fiber), 2g pro. **Diabetic exchanges:** 2½ fat, 1 vegetable, ½ starch.

The Sweetest Corn

Nothing says summer like ripe, bursting-with-juiciness corn on the cob. Whether you grill the corn in its husk, wrap it in bacon, smear the cobs with street-corn flair or slow-cook the corn in rich coconut milk, here are four enchanting ways to savor the hot-weather staple.

GRILLED CORN IN HUSKS

Seasoned with butter, Parmesan cheese and parsley, grilled corn is especially good. Be sure to give the ears a long soak before putting them on the grill. Hot off the grate, the kernels are moist and tender with a delightful, sweet flavor.

—Nancy Zimmerman, Cape May Court House, NJ

Prep: 20 min. + soaking • **Grill:** 20 min.
Makes: 4 servings

- **4 large ears sweet corn in husks**
- **¼ cup butter, softened**
- **2 Tbsp. minced fresh parsley**
- **¼ cup grated Parmesan cheese**

1. Carefully peel back husks from corn to within 1 in. of bottom; remove silk. Soak in cold water for 20 minutes; drain. Pat corn dry. Combine the butter and parsley; spread over corn. Rewrap corn in husks and secure with string.
2. Grill corn, covered, over medium heat until tender, turning often, 20-25 minutes. Serve with cheese.

1 serving: 196 cal., 9g fat (5g sat. fat), 24mg chol., 186mg sod., 28g carb. (9g sugars, 4g fiber), 8g pro. **Diabetic exchanges:** 2 starch, 1 fat.

SLOW-COOKED CORN ON THE COB

I like to eat corn all year long, so I came up with this recipe. It's my favorite side to serve when I make sloppy joes. You can use a butter substitute for a skinny version of this corn.

—Teresa Flowers, Sacramento, CA

Prep: 10 min. • **Cook:** 2 hours
Makes: 4 servings

- **4 medium ears sweet corn, cut into 2-in. pieces**
- **1 can (15 oz.) coconut milk**
- **1 medium onion, chopped**
- **¼ cup butter, cubed**
- **6 fresh thyme sprigs**
- **2 garlic cloves, minced**
- **1 bay leaf**
- **¾ tsp. salt**
- **¼ tsp. pepper**
- **¼ cup fresh cilantro leaves, chopped**
- **2 green onions, sliced**

In a 5- or 6-qt. slow cooker, combine the first 9 ingredients. Cook, covered, on high for 2-3 hours or until tender. Serve with cilantro and green onions.

4 pieces: 161 cal., 9g fat (6g sat. fat), 8mg chol., 118mg sod., 21g carb. (7g sugars, 2g fiber), 4g pro.

CHOOSE YOUR TEXTURE

Two hours of cooking will produce crisp-tender corn. For softer corn, cook closer to three hours.

BACON-WRAPPED CORN

After one bite of this grilled corn on the cob, you'll never go back to your old way of preparing it. The incredible flavor of roasted corn combined with bacon and chili powder is sure to please your palate and bring rave reviews at your next barbecue.
—Lori Bramble, Omaha, NE

Takes: 30 min. • **Makes:** 8 servings

- **8 large ears sweet corn, husked**
- **8 bacon strips**
- **2 Tbsp. chili powder**

1. Wrap each ear of corn with a bacon strip; place on a piece of heavy-duty foil. Sprinkle with chili powder. Wrap securely, twisting ends to make handles for turning.
2. Grill corn, covered, over medium heat 20-25 minutes or until the corn is tender and the bacon is cooked, turning once.

1 ear of corn: 210 cal., 14g fat (5g sat. fat), 15mg chol., 199mg sod., 18g carb. (5g sugars, 3g fiber), 5g pro.

BAKED CHILI-LIME CORN

Tart lime and spicy chili powder offer vibrant flavor contrasts in this easy baked corn dish.
—Lawrence Davis, Saint Louis, MO

Prep: 10 min. • **Bake:** 35 min.
Makes: 4 servings

- **¼ cup butter, melted**
- **2 Tbsp. lime juice**
- **1½ tsp. grated lime zest**
- **1 tsp. chili powder**
- **¾ tsp. seasoned pepper**
- **¼ tsp. salt**
- **4 medium ears sweet corn, cut into 3-in. pieces**

1. Preheat oven to 400°. In a small bowl, combine the first 6 ingredients. Place corn in a greased 13x9-in. baking dish. Brush corn with half the butter mixture. Cover and bake for 30 minutes.
2. Uncover; brush corn with remaining butter mixture. Bake, uncovered, for 5-10 minutes or until tender.

2 pieces: 182 cal., 13g fat (7g sat. fat), 30mg chol., 248mg sod., 19g carb. (3g sugars, 3g fiber), 3g pro.

SPICY CORN KABOBS

Corn on the cob becomes a tangy delight when grilled, dotted with sour cream and cheese, and zinged with a splash of lime.
—Leah Lenz, Los Angeles, CA

Prep: 10 min. • **Grill:** 25 min.
Makes: 6 servings

- **6 medium ears sweet corn, husked and halved**
- **¼ cup sour cream**
- **¼ cup mayonnaise**
- **½ cup grated Cotija cheese or Parmesan cheese**
- **2 tsp. chili powder**
- **¼ tsp. cayenne pepper, optional**
- **6 lime wedges**

1. Insert a metal or soaked wooden skewer into the cut end of each piece of corn. Grill, covered, over medium heat until tender, 25-30 minutes, turning often.
2. In a small bowl, combine sour cream and mayonnaise; spread over the corn. Sprinkle with cheese, chili powder and, if desired, cayenne. Serve with lime wedges.

2 kabobs: 205 cal., 13g fat (4g sat. fat), 20mg chol., 222mg sod., 19g carb. (3g sugars, 3g fiber), 6g pro.

Soups, Salads & Sandwiches

Combine fresh garden ingredients in a gorgeous salad. Create a tasty sandwich for lunch on the go. Simmer a pot of comforting soup. Serve each on its own, or mix and match them for a complete meal—there's a reason soups, salads and sandwiches make for classic combinations!

YUMMY CORN CHIP SALAD

Corn chips give a special crunch and an unexpected flavor to this potluck favorite. Bacon adds a hint of smokiness, while the cranberries bring a touch of sweetness. It's the perfect picnic companion!
—Nora Friesen, Aberdeen, MS

Takes: 25 min. • **Makes:** 12 servings

- ¾ cup canola oil
- ¼ cup cider vinegar
- ¼ cup mayonnaise
- 2 Tbsp. yellow mustard
- ½ tsp. salt
- ¾ cup sugar
- ½ small onion
- ¾ tsp. poppy seeds

SALAD

- 2 bunches leaf lettuce, chopped (about 20 cups)
- 1 pkg. (9¼ oz.) corn chips
- 8 bacon strips, cooked and crumbled
- 1 cup shredded part-skim mozzarella cheese
- 1 cup dried cranberries

1. For dressing, place first 7 ingredients in a blender. Cover; process until smooth. Stir in poppy seeds.
2. Place salad ingredients in a large bowl; toss with dressing. Serve immediately.

1⅓ cups: 436 cal., 30g fat (4g sat. fat), 12mg chol., 456mg sod., 38g carb. (24g sugars, 2g fiber), 7g pro.

PORK & CHEESY MACARONI SLIDERS

I love sliders! This sweet and savory recipe was created out of leftover ingredients I had in my fridge. It is perfect for a weeknight meal or a special-occasion potluck.
—Rashanda Cobbins, Milwaukee, WI

Prep: 30 min. • **Bake:** 10 min.
Makes: 12 servings

- 1 cup uncooked cavatappi pasta
- 1 Tbsp. butter
- 1½ tsp. all-purpose flour
- ¼ tsp. pepper
- ½ cup 2% milk
- ¾ cup shredded sharp cheddar cheese
- 1 pkg. (18 oz.) Hawaiian sweet rolls
- 1 carton (16 oz.) refrigerated fully cooked barbecue shredded pork, warmed
- 2 Tbsp. melted butter
- 1 Tbsp. honey
- ½ tsp. ground mustard
- 1 jalapeno pepper, sliced, optional

1. Preheat oven to 375°. Cook pasta according to package directions.
2. Meanwhile, in a small saucepan, melt butter over medium heat. Stir in flour and pepper until smooth; gradually whisk in milk. Bring to a boil, stirring constantly; cook and stir until thickened, 3-5 minutes. Stir in cheese until melted. Drain pasta; stir into the cheese sauce. Set aside.
3. Place the roll bottoms in a greased 13x9-in. baking dish. Layer with the pork, pasta mixture and roll tops. Whisk together the melted butter, honey and mustard. Brush over roll tops.
4. Bake until the tops are golden brown and the filling is hot, 10-12 minutes. If desired, top with jalapeno pepper slices.

1 slider: 305 cal., 10g fat (6g sat. fat), 48mg chol., 466mg sod., 39g carb. (17g sugars, 2g fiber), 14g pro.

BUTTERNUT SQUASH & PEAR SOUP

The pears in this harvest soup create a pleasant sweetness and a nice velvety finish, while curry and ginger provide delightful flavor.

—Sarah Vasques, Milford, NH

Contest Winner

Prep: 1¼ hours
Cook: 45 min.
Makes: 9 servings

- **1 medium butternut squash (about 3 lbs.)**
- **1 medium onion, chopped**
- **2 Tbsp. canola oil**
- **1 Tbsp. curry powder**
- **2 garlic cloves, minced**
- **2 tsp. minced fresh gingerroot**
- **1 tsp. salt**
- **4 cups reduced-sodium chicken broth**
- **4 medium pears, peeled and chopped**
- **½ cup heavy whipping cream**
- **Optional: Balsamic vinegar and snipped chives**

1. Cut squash in half; discard seeds. Place the squash cut side down in a 15x10x1-in. baking pan coated with cooking spray. Bake at 400° for 40-50 minutes or until tender. Cool slightly; scoop out flesh and set aside.
2. In a Dutch oven, saute the onion in oil until tender. Add the curry, garlic, ginger and salt; cook 1 minute longer. Stir in the broth, pears and squash. Bring to a boil. Reduce heat; simmer, uncovered, for 30 minutes. Cool slightly.
3. Puree the soup using an immersion blender. Or cool slightly and puree the soup in batches in a blender until smooth. Return all to the pan; add cream and heat through. Top with balsamic vinegar and chives if desired.

¾ cup: 190 cal., 8g fat (3g sat. fat), 18mg chol., 527mg sod., 29g carb. (12g sugars, 7g fiber), 4g pro. **Diabetic exchanges:** 2 starch, 1 fat.

LISA'S ALL-DAY SUGAR & SALT PORK ROAST

My family loves this tender and juicy roast, so we eat it a lot. The salty crust is so delicious—be sure to mix it into the pulled pork!

—Lisa Allen, Joppa, AL

Prep: 15 min. + marinating • **Cook:** 6¼ hours
Makes: 12 servings

- **1 cup plus 1 Tbsp. sea salt, divided**
- **1 cup sugar**
- **1 bone-in pork shoulder butt roast (6 to 8 lbs.)**
- **¼ cup barbecue seasoning**
- **½ tsp. pepper**
- **½ cup packed brown sugar**
- **12 hamburger buns or kaiser rolls, split**

1. Combine 1 cup sea salt and granulated sugar; rub onto all sides of roast. Place in a shallow dish; refrigerate, covered, overnight.
2. Preheat oven to 300°. Using a kitchen knife, scrape the salt and sugar coating from roast; discard any accumulated juices. Transfer pork to a large shallow roasting pan. Rub with the barbecue seasoning; sprinkle with pepper. Roast until tender, 6-8 hours.
3. Increase oven temperature to 500°. Combine brown sugar and 1 Tbsp. sea salt; sprinkle over cooked pork. Return the pork to oven and roast until a crisp crust forms, 10-15 minutes. Remove; when cool enough to handle, shred the meat with 2 forks. Serve warm on fresh buns or rolls.

Freeze option: Freeze cooled meat with some of the juices in freezer containers. To use, partially thaw in refrigerator overnight. Heat through in a saucepan, stirring occasionally; add water if necessary.

1 sandwich: 534 cal., 24g fat (9g sat. fat), 135mg chol., 2240mg sod., 33g carb. (14g sugars, 1g fiber), 43g pro.

HEARTY SPLIT PEA SOUP

For a different spin on traditional split pea soup, try this recipe. The flavor is peppery rather than smoky, and the corned beef is a tasty change of pace.
—Barbara Link, Alta Loma, CA

Prep: 15 min. • **Cook:** 1½ hours
Makes: 12 servings (3 qt.)

- **1 pkg. (16 oz.) dried split peas**
- **8 cups water**
- **2 medium potatoes, peeled and cubed**
- **2 large onions, chopped**
- **2 medium carrots, chopped**
- **2 cups cubed cooked corned beef or ham**
- **½ cup chopped celery**
- **5 tsp. chicken bouillon granules**
- **1 tsp. dried marjoram**
- **1 tsp. poultry seasoning**
- **1 tsp. rubbed sage**
- **½ to 1 tsp. pepper**
- **½ tsp. dried basil**
- **½ tsp. salt, optional**

In a Dutch oven, combine all ingredients; bring to a boil. Reduce heat; cover and simmer for 1¼-1½ hours or until the peas and vegetables are tender.
½ cup: 199 cal., 2g fat (0 sat. fat), 11mg chol., 352mg sod., 32g carb. (0 sugars, 0 fiber), 15g pro. **Diabetic exchanges:** 2 starch, 1 lean meat.

BRUSCHETTA CHICKEN WRAPS

As an Italian American, I love, love, love garlic, tomatoes and basil, all of which are musts for good bruschetta. This recipe was created in celebration of the first tomatoes to come out of our home garden this year.
—Gina Rine, Canfield, OH

Takes: 30 min. • **Makes:** 4 servings

- **2 plum tomatoes, finely chopped (about 1 cup)**
- **1 cup fresh baby spinach, coarsely chopped**
- **¼ cup finely chopped red onion**
- **1 Tbsp. shredded Parmesan or Romano cheese**
- **1 Tbsp. minced fresh basil**
- **1 tsp. olive oil**
- **1 tsp. balsamic vinegar**
- **⅛ tsp. plus ¼ tsp. pepper, divided**
- **Dash garlic powder**
- **4 boneless skinless chicken breast halves (4 oz. each)**
- **½ tsp. salt**
- **2 oz. fresh mozzarella cheese, cut into 4 slices**
- **4 whole wheat tortillas (8 in.)**

1. In a small bowl, mix the tomatoes, spinach, onion, Parmesan cheese, basil, olive oil, vinegar, ⅛ tsp. pepper and the dash of garlic powder.
2. Sprinkle the chicken with salt and the remaining pepper; place on lightly oiled grill rack. Grill, covered, over medium heat 4-6 minutes on each side or until a thermometer reads 165°.
3. Top each chicken breast with 1 cheese slice; cover and grill 1-2 minutes longer or until cheese is melted. Grill tortillas over medium heat 20-30 seconds or until heated through.
4. Place a chicken breast half on the center of each tortilla; top with about ¼ cup of the tomato mixture. Fold bottom of tortilla over filling; fold both sides to close.
1 wrap: 330 cal., 10g fat (3g sat. fat), 75mg chol., 569mg sod., 25g carb. (3g sugars, 3g fiber), 31g pro. **Diabetic exchanges:** 3 lean meat, 2 starch, 1 fat.

LAMB PITAS WITH YOGURT SAUCE

The spiced lamb in these stuffed pita pockets goes perfectly with the cool cucumber and yogurt. It's like having your own Greek gyro stand in the kitchen!

—Angela Leinenbach, Mechanicsville, VA

Prep: 35 min. • **Cook:** 6 hours
Makes: 8 servings

- **2 Tbsp. olive oil**
- **2 lbs. lamb stew meat (¾-in. pieces)**
- **1 large onion, chopped**
- **1 garlic clove, minced**
- **⅓ cup tomato paste**
- **½ cup dry red wine**
- **1¼ tsp. salt, divided**
- **1 tsp. dried oregano**
- **½ tsp. dried basil**
- **1 medium cucumber**
- **1 cup plain yogurt**
- **16 pita pocket halves, warmed**
- **4 plum tomatoes, sliced**

1. In a large skillet, heat the oil over medium-high heat; brown lamb in batches. Transfer lamb to a 3- or 4-qt. slow cooker, reserve drippings in skillet.
2. Over medium heat, saute onion in the drippings until tender, 4-6 minutes. Add garlic and tomato paste; cook and stir 2 minutes. Stir in wine, 1 tsp. salt, the oregano and basil. Add to lamb. Cook, covered, on low until the lamb is tender, 6-8 hours.
3. To serve, dice enough cucumber to measure 1 cup; thinly slice the remaining cucumber. Combine diced cucumber with yogurt and the remaining ¼ tsp. salt. Fill pita halves with lamb mixture, tomatoes, sliced cucumbers and yogurt mixture.

Freeze option: Freeze cooled lamb mixture in freezer containers. To use, partially thaw in refrigerator overnight. Heat through in a saucepan, stirring occasionally; add a little broth or water if necessary.

2 filled pita halves: 383 cal., 11g fat (3g sat. fat), 78mg chol., 766mg sod., 39g carb. (5g sugars, 3g fiber), 31g pro. **Diabetic exchanges:** 3 lean meat, 2½ starch, 1 fat.

KALE CAESAR SALAD

I love Caesar salads, so I created this blend of kale and romaine with a creamy Caesar dressing. Pair it with chicken or steak for a light weeknight meal.

—Rashanda Cobbins, Milwaukee, WI

Takes: 15 min. • **Makes:** 8 servings

- **4 cups chopped fresh kale**
- **4 cups torn romaine**
- **1 cup Caesar salad croutons**
- **½ cup shredded Parmesan cheese**
- **½ cup mayonnaise**
- **2 Tbsp. lemon juice**
- **1 Tbsp. Worcestershire sauce**
- **2 tsp. Dijon mustard**
- **2 tsp. anchovy paste**
- **1 garlic clove, minced**
- **¼ tsp. salt**
- **¼ tsp. pepper**

In a large salad bowl, toss kale, romaine, croutons and cheese. For the dressing, combine remaining ingredients in a small bowl; pour over salad and toss to coat. Serve immediately.

1 cup: 148 cal., 13g fat (3g sat. fat), 10mg chol., 417mg sod., 6g carb. (1g sugars, 1g fiber), 3g pro. **Diabetic exchanges:** 2½ fat, 1 vegetable.

GRANDMA'S BAKED HAM SANDWICHES

This is another tried-and-true recipe I found in my grandma's recipe box. I love seeing her handwriting on faded notecards.
—Crystal Jo Bruns, Iliff, CO

Takes: 30 min. • **Makes:** 6 servings

- **2 cups cubed fully cooked ham**
- **½ cup sliced sweet pickles**
- **4 hard-boiled large eggs, finely chopped**
- **¾ cup finely chopped celery**
- **½ cup finely chopped sweet onion**
- **¼ cup mayonnaise**
- **6 onion rolls, split**

Preheat oven to 350°. Place ham and pickles in a food processor; pulse until almost smooth. Transfer to a small bowl; stir in eggs, celery, onion and mayonnaise. Spread ½ cup over each roll bottom; replace the tops. Wrap each in foil and place on a baking sheet. Bake until heated through, 10-15 minutes.

1 sandwich: 338 cal., 15g fat (4g sat. fat), 153mg chol., 971mg sod., 30g carb. (6g sugars, 2g fiber), 21g pro.

RICH SEAFOOD CHOWDER

This creamy, delectable soup is even better the next day. It also works well with scallops or a flaky whitefish. Substitute half-and-half or heavy cream for all or part of the milk to make this soup even richer.
—Anita Culver, Royersford, PA

Prep: 30 min. • **Cook:** 25 min.
Makes: 8 servings (2 qt.)

- **2 Tbsp. butter**
- **1 small onion, chopped**
- **1 celery rib, chopped**
- **1 medium carrot, shredded**
- **2 Tbsp. all-purpose flour**
- **½ cup 2% milk**
- **3 cups seafood stock**
- **1 medium potato, peeled and diced**
- **1 Tbsp. Worcestershire sauce**
- **1 tsp. salt**
- **½ tsp. pepper**
- **1 lb. uncooked shrimp (41-50 per lb.), peeled and deveined**
- **2 cans (6½ oz. each) chopped clams, drained**
- **2 cans (6 oz. each) lump crabmeat, drained**
- **1 pkg. (8 oz.) cream cheese, cubed**
- **Minced fresh parsley**

1. In a Dutch oven, heat the butter over medium-high heat. Add onion, celery and carrot; cook and stir until crisp-tender, 2-3 minutes. Stir in flour until blended; gradually add milk. Bring to a boil; cook and stir until thickened, about 2 minutes.
2. Add stock, potato, Worcestershire sauce, salt and pepper; return to a boil. Reduce heat; cover and simmer until potato is tender, 10-15 minutes.
3. Add shrimp, clams, crab and cream cheese; cook and stir until the shrimp turn pink and the cheese is melted, 4-5 minutes. Garnish with parsley.

1 cup: 272 cal., 15g fat (8g sat. fat), 164mg chol., 1076mg sod., 11g carb. (3g sugars, 1g fiber), 24g pro.

CHICKEN CUCUMBER PITAS

I wanted a good recipe for stuffing pitas. Seeing the large stack of garden-fresh cucumbers on my counter, I decided to improvise and create my own recipe. It was a huge hit.

—Sheena Wellard, Nampa, ID

Takes: 25 min. • **Makes:** 6 servings

- **2 cups cubed cooked chicken breast**
- **1 large cucumber, quartered, seeded and sliced**
- **1 can (2¼ oz.) sliced ripe olives, drained**
- **1 medium tomato, seeded and chopped**
- **1 small sweet red pepper, chopped**
- **½ cup cubed cheddar cheese**
- **¼ cup chopped red onion**

DRESSING

- **½ cup ranch salad dressing**
- **¼ cup mayonnaise**
- **1 Tbsp. Italian salad dressing**
- **¼ tsp. garlic powder**
- **¼ tsp. pepper**
- **12 pita pocket halves**

In a large bowl, combine the first 7 ingredients. In a small bowl, combine ranch dressing, mayonnaise, Italian dressing, garlic powder and pepper; pour over chicken mixture and toss to coat. Fill each pita half with a scant ½ cup of the chicken mixture.

2 filled pita halves: 445 cal., 22g fat (5g sat. fat), 49mg chol., 747mg sod., 37g carb. (4g sugars, 2g fiber), 22g pro.

RED, WHITE & BLUE SUMMER SALAD

Caprese and fresh fruit always remind me of summer. In this salad, I combine traditional Caprese flavors with summer blueberries and peaches. I also add prosciutto for saltiness, creating a balanced, flavor-packed side dish.

—Emily Falke, Santa Barbara, CA

Takes: 25 min. • **Makes:** 12 servings

- **⅔ cup extra virgin olive oil**
- **½ cup julienned fresh basil**
- **⅓ cup white balsamic vinegar**
- **¼ cup julienned fresh mint leaves**
- **2 garlic cloves, minced**
- **2 tsp. Dijon mustard**
- **1 tsp. sea salt**
- **1 tsp. sugar**
- **1 tsp. pepper**
- **2 cups cherry tomatoes**
- **8 cups fresh arugula**
- **1 carton (8 oz.) fresh mozzarella cheese pearls, drained**
- **2 medium peaches, sliced**
- **2 cups fresh blueberries**
- **6 oz. thinly sliced prosciutto, julienned**
- **Additional mint leaves**

1. In a small bowl, whisk together the first 9 ingredients. Add tomatoes; let stand while preparing salad.
2. In a large bowl, combine the arugula, mozzarella, peach slices, blueberries and prosciutto. Pour the tomato mixture over top; toss to coat. Garnish with additional mint leaves. Serve immediately.

1 cup: 233 cal., 18g fat (5g sat. fat), 27mg chol., 486mg sod., 10g carb. (8g sugars, 2g fiber), 8g pro.

KEEPING IT LIGHT

White balsamic vinegar keeps the colors bright in this sweet, salty salad. If you can't find it in your market and you're not fussy about the color, you can use regular balsamic. Otherwise, use a rice wine vinegar instead.

CHEESY HAM & EGG SANDWICHES

I turned classic breakfast sandwiches into something heartier that you could even enjoy for dinner. We pile toppings like salsa and avocado—mayo and ketchup, too—on the homemade biscuits.
—Fay Moreland, Wichita Falls, TX

Takes: 30 min. • **Makes:** 10 servings

- **4 cups biscuit/baking mix**
- **1 cup shredded cheddar cheese**
- **1 cup finely chopped fully cooked ham**
- **1 tsp. coarsely ground pepper, divided**
- **1 cup 2% milk**
- **3 Tbsp. butter, melted**

EGGS

- **8 large eggs**
- **½ cup 2% milk**
- **¼ tsp. coarsely ground pepper**
- **⅛ tsp. salt**
- **2 Tbsp. butter**
- **1 cup shredded cheddar cheese**
  Optional: Salsa, sliced tomato, red onion and avocado

1. Preheat oven to 425°. In a large bowl, combine biscuit mix, cheese, ham and ½ tsp. pepper. Add milk; mix just until moistened.
2. Turn onto a lightly floured surface; knead gently 8-10 times. Pat or roll the dough to 1-in. thickness; cut with a floured 2½-in. biscuit cutter. Place 2 in. apart on an ungreased baking sheet. Brush with the melted butter; sprinkle with remaining ½ tsp. pepper. Bake 12-14 minutes or until golden brown.
3. Meanwhile, for eggs, in a bowl, whisk the eggs, milk, pepper and salt. In a large nonstick skillet, heat butter over medium heat. Pour in the egg mixture; cook and stir until the eggs are thickened and no liquid egg remains. Stir in cheese; remove from heat.
4. Split warm biscuits in half. Layer the bottoms with egg mixture and toppings as desired. Replace tops.

1 sandwich: 430 cal., 25g fat (12g sat. fat), 198mg chol., 1058mg sod., 34g carb. (3g sugars, 1g fiber), 18g pro.

HEARTY BEEF & VEGETABLE SOUP

When you need to feed a crowd, consider this beefy favorite loaded with veggies.
—Sue Straughan, Prattville, AL

Prep: 1¾ hours • **Cook:** 2¼ hours
Makes: 26 servings

- **2 to 4 Tbsp. canola oil**
- **4 lbs. beef stew meat**
- **8 medium onions (2¼ lbs.), halved and thinly sliced**
- **12 cups water**
- **1 can (28 oz.) diced tomatoes, undrained**
- **1 can (15 oz.) tomato sauce**
- **1⅓ cups Worcestershire sauce**
- **½ cup beef bouillon granules**
- **12 medium red potatoes (about 3½ lbs.), cubed**
- **½ large head cabbage, chopped**
- **1 lb. carrots, thinly sliced**
- **6 celery ribs, thinly sliced (3 cups)**
- **3 cups (about 15 oz.) frozen corn**
- **3 cups (about 12 oz.) frozen peas**
- **3 cups (about 12 oz.) frozen cut green beans**
- **1½ cups (about 15 oz.) frozen lima beans**
- **1 bay leaf**
- **3 tsp. dried marjoram**
- **3 tsp. dried thyme**
- **1 tsp. salt**
- **1 tsp. pepper**
- **1½ cups (6 oz.) frozen sliced okra**

1. In a large stockpot, heat 1 Tbsp. oil over medium heat. Brown beef in batches, adding oil as necessary. Remove with a slotted spoon. Add onions to the drippings; cook and stir until tender. Discard drippings; return beef to pot . Stir in water, tomatoes, tomato sauce, Worcestershire sauce and bouillon. Bring to a boil. Reduce heat; simmer, covered, 45 minutes.
2. Stir in potatoes, cabbage, carrots, celery, corn, peas, green beans, lima beans and seasonings. Return to a boil. Reduce the heat; simmer, covered, for 35 minutes.
3. Stir in okra; cook 15-20 minutes longer or until beef and vegetables are tender. Discard bay leaf.

1½ cups: 245 cal., 6g fat (2g sat. fat), 42mg chol., 1090mg sod., 31g carb. (9g sugars, 6g fiber), 18g pro.

BEST CURRIED PUMPKIN SOUP

I whipped up this satisfying soup last Thanksgiving for my family, and everyone was crazy about it! Even my brother, who is one of the pickiest eaters I know, asked for seconds.

—Kimberly Knepper, Euless, TX

Takes: 20 min. • **Makes:** 7 servings

- **½ lb. fresh mushrooms, sliced**
- **½ cup chopped onion**
- **2 Tbsp. butter**
- **2 Tbsp. all-purpose flour**
- **½ to 1 tsp. curry powder**
- **3 cups vegetable broth**
- **1 can (15 oz.) pumpkin**
- **1 can (12 oz.) evaporated milk**
- **1 Tbsp. honey**
- **½ tsp. salt**
- **¼ tsp. pepper**
- **¼ tsp. ground nutmeg**
- **Minced chives**

In a large saucepan, saute mushrooms and onion in butter until tender. Stir in the flour and curry powder until blended. Gradually add broth. Bring to a boil; cook and stir for 2 minutes or until thickened. Add the pumpkin, milk, honey, salt, pepper and nutmeg; heat through. Garnish with chives if desired.

1 cup: 157 cal., 8g fat (5g sat. fat), 26mg chol., 686mg sod., 18g carb. (12g sugars, 3g fiber), 7g pro.

BASIL & HEIRLOOM TOMATO TOSS

I came up with this fresh salad to showcase the heirloom tomatoes and peppers we raised for our stall at the farmers market.

—Sue Gronholz, Beaver Dam, WI

Takes: 15 min. • **Makes:** 4 servings

- **¼ cup olive oil**
- **3 Tbsp. red wine vinegar**
- **2 tsp. sugar**
- **1 garlic clove, minced**
- **¾ tsp. salt**
- **¼ tsp. ground mustard**
- **¼ tsp. pepper**
- **2 large heirloom tomatoes, cut into ½-in. pieces**
- **1 medium sweet yellow pepper, cut into ½-in. pieces**
- **½ small red onion, thinly sliced**
- **1 Tbsp. chopped fresh basil**

In a large bowl, whisk together the first 7 ingredients until blended. Add remaining ingredients; toss to combine.

1 cup: 162 cal., 14g fat (2g sat. fat), 0 chol., 449mg sod., 10g carb. (5g sugars, 2g fiber), 1g pro. **Diabetic exchanges:** 3 fat, 1 vegetable.

TRY A NEW BASIL

There are lots of different varieties of basil—each one will give this salad a slightly different spin. Try making this using lemon, lime, licorice or cinnamon basil instead of the classic sweet basil.

TURKEY FOCACCIA CLUB

My family thinks this sandwich is pure heaven thanks to the cranberry-pecan mayo. It's so good that I'm asked to make it all year long.
—Judy Wilson, Sun City West, AZ

Takes: 20 min. • **Makes:** 4 servings

- **½ cup mayonnaise**
- **½ cup whole-berry cranberry sauce**
- **2 Tbsp. chopped pecans, toasted**
- **2 Tbsp. Dijon mustard**
- **1 Tbsp. honey**
- **1 loaf (8 oz.) focaccia bread**
- **3 lettuce leaves**
- **½ lb. thinly sliced cooked turkey**
- **¼ lb. sliced Gouda cheese**
- **8 slices tomato**
- **6 bacon strips, cooked**

In a small bowl, mix the first 5 ingredients until blended. Using a long serrated knife, cut focaccia horizontally in half. Spread cut sides with the mayonnaise mixture. Layer bottom half with lettuce, turkey, cheese, tomato and bacon; replace bread top. Cut into wedges.
1 wedge: 707 cal., 41g fat (10g sat. fat), 96mg chol., 1153mg sod., 53g carb. (17g sugars, 2g fiber), 32g pro.

HONEY-ORANGE BROCCOLI SLAW

PICTURED ON P. 40

When you need coleslaw quickly, here's a fantastic choice. Hints of honey and citrus make it feel special.
—Debbie Cassar, Rockford, MI

Takes: 15 min. • **Makes:** 6 servings

- **1 pkg. (12 oz.) broccoli coleslaw mix**
- **⅓ cup sliced almonds**
- **⅓ cup raisins**
- **2 to 3 Tbsp. honey**
- **2 Tbsp. olive oil**
- **2 Tbsp. orange juice**
- **4 tsp. grated orange zest**
- **¼ tsp. salt**

In a large bowl, combine the coleslaw mix, almonds and raisins. In a small bowl, whisk the remaining ingredients. Pour over the salad; toss to coat.
⅔ cup: 136 cal., 7g fat (1g sat. fat), 0 chol., 103mg sod., 18g carb. (13g sugars, 3g fiber), 3g pro. **Diabetic exchanges:** 1½ fat, 1 starch.

SOUTHWESTERN BEAN CHOWDER

Even though there is a bit of heat from the spices and green chiles, my young children love this soup as much as my husband does. I like using white kidney beans—they have a terrific texture.
—Juli Meyers, Hinesville, GA

Prep: 20 min. • **Cook:** 35 min.
Makes: 8 servings (2 qt.)

- **2 cans (15 oz. each) cannellini beans, rinsed and drained, divided**
- **1 medium onion, chopped**
- **¼ cup chopped celery**
- **¼ cup chopped green pepper**
- **1 Tbsp. olive oil**
- **2 garlic cloves, minced**
- **3 cups vegetable broth**
- **1½ cups frozen corn, thawed**
- **1 medium carrot, shredded**
- **1 can (4 oz.) chopped green chiles**
- **1 Tbsp. ground cumin**
- **½ tsp. chili powder**
- **4½ tsp. cornstarch**
- **2 cups 2% milk**
- **1 cup shredded cheddar cheese**
- **Optional: Minced fresh cilantro and additional shredded cheddar cheese**

1. In a small bowl, mash 1 can beans with a fork; set aside.
2. In a Dutch oven, saute onion, celery and pepper in oil until tender. Add garlic; cook 1 minute longer. Stir in the mashed beans, broth, corn, carrot, chiles, cumin, chili powder and the remaining beans. Bring to a boil. Reduce heat; simmer, uncovered, for 20 minutes.
3. Combine the cornstarch and milk until smooth. Stir into bean mixture. Bring to a boil; cook and stir for 2 minutes or until thickened. Stir in the cheese until melted. Serve with cilantro and additional cheese if desired.

1 cup: 236 cal., 8g fat (4g sat. fat), 20mg chol., 670mg sod., 31g carb. (6g sugars, 6g fiber), 11g pro. **Diabetic exchanges:** 2 starch, 1 lean meat, ½ fat.

MINI CHICKEN & BISCUIT SANDWICHES

My 11-year-old son, Jake, invented these sliders at dinner one night when he plunked his chicken on a biscuit. The rest of us tried it his way, and now we have them all the time!
—Jodie Kolsan, Palm Coast, FL

Takes: 30 min. • **Makes:** 5 servings

- **1 tube (12 oz.) refrigerated buttermilk biscuits**
- **5 boneless skinless chicken breasts (4 oz. each)**
- **½ tsp. salt**
- **½ tsp. dried thyme**
- **¼ tsp. pepper**
- **1 Tbsp. canola oil**
- **1 Tbsp. butter**
- **Optional: Cranberry chutney, lettuce leaves, sliced tomato and red onion**

1. Bake biscuits according to package directions. Meanwhile, cut chicken crosswise in half. Pound with a meat mallet to ¼-in. thickness. Sprinkle with salt, thyme and pepper.
2. In a large skillet, heat oil and butter over medium-high heat. Add chicken in batches; cook until no longer pink, 2-3 minutes on each side.
3. Split biscuits in half; top with chicken and toppings as desired. Replace tops.

2 mini sandwiches: 367 cal., 16g fat (4g sat. fat), 69mg chol., 1029mg sod., 28g carb. (4g sugars, 0 fiber), 27g pro.

Contest
Winner

BACON & DATE GOAT CHEESE BURGERS

Every bite of this burger is a rich and decadent combination of sweet and savory. If you can't find maple bacon in your local store, you can add 1½ tablespoons maple syrup to the spinach-goat cheese mixture in the food processor and use regular bacon.
—Sharon Michelle Anglin, Livingston, MT

Prep: 30 min. • **Grill:** 10 min.
Makes: 6 servings

- **2¾ cups fresh baby spinach, divided**
- **1 pkg. (8 oz.) pistachios, shelled**
- **2 Tbsp. lemon juice**
- **2 garlic cloves, halved**
- **½ to 1½ tsp. crushed red pepper flakes**
- **¼ tsp. salt**
- **¼ tsp. pepper**
- **1 pkg. (5.3 oz.) fresh goat cheese, crumbled**
- **¼ cup olive oil**
- **1½ lbs. ground beef**
- **1 pkg. (8 oz.) pitted dates, chopped**
- **6 brioche hamburger buns, split**
- **1 medium red onion, sliced**
- **½ lb. maple-flavored bacon strips, cooked**

1. Place 2 cups spinach, pistachios, lemon juice, garlic, pepper flakes, salt and pepper in a food processor; pulse until chopped. Add goat cheese; process until blended. Continue processing while gradually adding oil in a steady stream to reach a spreadable consistency. Refrigerate until serving.
2. Meanwhile, in a large bowl, combine the beef and dates, mixing lightly but thoroughly. Shape into six ½-in.-thick patties. Place the burgers on an oiled grill rack or in a greased 15x10x1-in. pan. Grill, covered, over medium heat or broil 4-5 in. from heat until a thermometer reads 160°, 4-5 minutes per side. Grill buns, cut sides down, over medium heat until toasted.
3. Top bun bottoms with remaining spinach, burgers, red onion and bacon. Spread 4 tsp. goat cheese mixture over cut side of each bun top; place on burger. Cover and refrigerate remaining goat cheese mixture; save for another use.

1 burger: 804 cal., 45g fat (11g sat. fat), 118mg chol., 788mg sod., 67g carb. (34g sugars, 9g fiber), 39g pro.

OPEN-FACED TURKEY SANDWICH

It doesn't get much cozier than these fantastic suppertime sandwiches. They are an easy way to use up leftover turkey, and I love the way the thick toast soaks up the creamy sauce.
—Carol Hull, Hermiston, OR

Takes: 30 min. • **Makes:** 4 servings

- **2 Tbsp. butter**
- **½ cup finely chopped onion**
- **¼ cup finely chopped celery**
- **2 Tbsp. all-purpose flour**
- **1 cup chicken stock**
- **1 cup evaporated milk**
- **4 oz. cream cheese, cubed**
- **1 cup frozen peas**
- **2 cups chopped cooked turkey (about 10 oz.)**
- **½ tsp. salt**
- **¼ tsp. pepper**
- **4 slices Texas toast or other thick-sliced bread, toasted**
- **Optional: Chopped tomato and minced fresh parsley**

1. In a large saucepan, heat butter over medium-high heat; saute onion and celery until tender, 4-6 minutes. Stir in flour until blended; cook and stir until golden brown. Gradually stir in stock and milk. Bring to a boil, stirring constantly; cook and stir until thickened, 4-6 minutes.
2. Add cream cheese, peas, turkey, salt and pepper; cook and stir until blended and heated through. Serve over toast. If desired, top with tomato and parsley.

1 serving: 488 cal., 24g fat (13g sat. fat), 135mg chol., 917mg sod., 35g carb. (11g sugars, 3g fiber), 32g pro.

USE YOUR LEFTOVERS

One 12-oz. can of evaporated milk contains a little more than 1½ cups. The leftover milk can be refrigerated for up to five days. Stir evaporated milk into your morning coffee or add it to mashed potatoes or macaroni and cheese for a richer flavor.

SESAME, SUNFLOWER & CARROT SALAD

I love the harmonizing colors of the ingredients that make this a beautiful salad to serve and a super healthy salad to eat. It's a versatile side that goes with everything!
—Jessica Gerschitz, Jericho, NY

Prep: 20 min. + chilling • **Makes:** 8 servings

- **6 medium carrots**
- **½ cup sesame seeds, toasted**
- **½ cup sunflower kernels, toasted**
- **½ cup sliced almonds, toasted**
- **½ cup golden raisins**

DRESSING

- **¼ cup reduced-fat mayonnaise**
- **¼ cup lemon juice**
- **¼ cup olive oil**
- **2 Tbsp. honey mustard**
- **½ tsp. salt**

Shred carrots with a hand grater or in a food processor fitted with grating attachment. Place carrots in a large bowl with next 4 ingredients. In a small bowl, whisk dressing ingredients until blended. Pour dressing over the carrot mixture; toss to coat. Cover and refrigerate for at least 1 hour before serving.

½ cup: 283 cal., 21g fat (3g sat. fat), 3mg chol., 335mg sod., 22g carb. (11g sugars, 5g fiber), 6g pro.

HAM, POTATO & PEPPER CHOWDER

I have been serving this chowder for years now. When I'm feeding family members who don't eat dairy, I substitute oil for the butter and use coconut milk or soy creamer instead of heavy cream. It still turns out wonderful.

—Eileen Stefanski, Wales, WI

Prep: 20 min. • **Cook:** 30 min.
Makes: 6 servings (2 qt.)

- **1½ lbs. potatoes (about 2 large), peeled and cut into 1-in. cubes**
- **1 carton (32 oz.) chicken broth, divided**
- **2 Tbsp. butter**
- **1 large sweet red pepper, coarsely chopped**
- **1 large green pepper, coarsely chopped**
- **1 large onion, finely chopped**
- **1 large carrot, chopped**
- **1½ cups cubed fully cooked ham (about 8 oz.)**
- **2 Tbsp. chopped seeded jalapeno pepper**
- **¼ tsp. white pepper**
- **¼ tsp. cayenne pepper**
- **1 large egg yolk**
- **¼ cup heavy whipping cream**
- **Optional: Shredded cheddar cheese, cooked and crumbled bacon, minced fresh chives and sour cream**

1. Place potatoes and 2 cups broth in a Dutch oven; bring to a boil. Reduce the heat; simmer, covered, until the potatoes are tender, 10-15 minutes. Cool slightly. Transfer to a food processor; cover and process until smooth.
2. In same pot, heat butter over medium heat; saute the red and green peppers, onion and carrot until carrot is tender, 8-10 minutes. Add ham, jalapeno and seasonings; cook and stir 1 minute.
3. Stir in the pureed potatoes and the remaining broth; bring just to a boil. In a small bowl, whisk a small amount of hot soup into egg yolk and cream; return all to the pot, whisking constantly. Bring to a gentle boil; cook and stir until thickened, 1-2 minutes. Serve with toppings as desired.

1⅓ cups: 226 cal., 10g fat (6g sat. fat), 76mg chol., 1124mg sod., 23g carb. (6g sugars, 3g fiber), 11g pro.

BARLEY CORN SALAD

A terrific alternative to pasta salad, this fresh, fast dish adds summery flavor to barley and sweet corn. Take it to your next get-together and see how fast it disappears!
—Mary Ann Kieffer, Lawrence, KS

Prep: 15 min. + chilling • **Makes:** 6 servings

- **2 cups cooked medium pearl barley**
- **2 cups frozen corn, thawed**
- **½ cup chopped sweet red pepper**
- **½ cup chopped green pepper**
- **3 green onions, chopped**
- **1 Tbsp. minced fresh cilantro**
- **2 Tbsp. lemon juice**
- **2 Tbsp. canola oil**
- **½ tsp. salt**
- **½ tsp. dried thyme**
- **⅛ tsp. pepper**

In a large bowl, combine the first 6 ingredients. In a jar with a tight-fitting lid, combine lemon juice, oil, salt, thyme and pepper; shake well. Drizzle over salad and toss to coat. Cover and refrigerate for at least 2 hours before serving.

Freeze option: Prepare salad without onions and cilantro. Transfer to freezer containers; freeze. To use, thaw completely in refrigerator. Gently stir in onions, cilantro and a little oil if necessary.

⅔ cup: 156 cal., 5g fat (0 sat. fat), 0 chol., 202mg sod., 26g carb. (2g sugars, 4g fiber), 3g pro. **Diabetic exchanges:** 1½ starch, 1 fat.

CHIPOTLE PULLED CHICKEN

I love chicken that has a chipotle kick to it. This is a go-to meal when I'm looking for something extra tasty.
—Tamra Parker, Manlius, NY

Prep: 15 min. • **Cook:** 3 hours
Makes: 12 servings

- **2 cups ketchup**
- **1 small onion, finely chopped**
- **¼ cup Worcestershire sauce**
- **3 Tbsp. reduced-sodium soy sauce**
- **2 Tbsp. brown sugar**
- **2 Tbsp. cider vinegar**
- **3 garlic cloves, minced**
- **1 Tbsp. molasses**
- **2 tsp. dried oregano**
- **2 tsp. minced chipotle pepper in adobo sauce plus 1 tsp. sauce**
- **1 tsp. ground cumin**
- **1 tsp. smoked paprika**
- **¼ tsp. salt**
- **¼ tsp. crushed red pepper flakes**
- **2½ lbs. boneless skinless chicken breasts**
- **12 sesame seed hamburger buns, split and toasted**

1. In a 3-qt. slow cooker, combine the first 14 ingredients; add chicken. Cook, covered, on low 3-4 hours or until the chicken is tender (a thermometer should read at least 165°).
2. Remove the chicken from slow cooker. Shred with 2 forks; return to slow cooker. Using tongs, place chicken mixture on bun bottoms. Replace tops.

Freeze option: Freeze cooled meat mixture and sauce in freezer containers. To use, partially thaw in refrigerator overnight. Heat through in a saucepan, stirring occasionally.

1 sandwich: 298 cal., 5g fat (2g sat. fat), 52mg chol., 1031mg sod., 39g carb. (18g sugars, 1g fiber), 24g pro.

Ultimate Comfort—Chicken Noodle Soups

Wherever there is chicken and some form of pasta, there is bound to be a recipe for chicken noodle soup! It's a worldwide constant for comfort food, and wherever you go, there's nothing that makes you feel more at home.

THE ULTIMATE CHICKEN NOODLE SOUP

My first Wisconsin winter was so cold, all I wanted to eat was soup. Colorado isn't much warmer, so when I moved, this recipe came with me!
—Gina Nistico, Denver, CO

Prep: 15 min, • **Cook:** 45 min. + standing
Makes: 10 servings (about 3½ qt.)

- **2½ lbs. bone-in chicken thighs**
- **½ tsp. salt**
- **½ tsp. pepper**
- **1 Tbsp. canola oil**
- **1 large onion, chopped**
- **1 garlic clove, minced**
- **10 cups chicken broth**
- **4 celery ribs, chopped**
- **4 medium carrots, chopped**
- **2 bay leaves**
- **1 tsp. minced fresh thyme or ¼ tsp. dried thyme**
- **3 cups uncooked kluski or other egg noodles (about 8 oz.)**
- **1 Tbsp. chopped fresh parsley**
- **1 Tbsp. lemon juice**
- **Optional: Additional salt and pepper**

1. Pat chicken dry with paper towels; sprinkle with salt and pepper. In a 6-qt. stockpot, heat oil over medium-high heat. Add chicken in batches, skin side down; cook until dark golden brown, 3-4 minutes. Remove chicken from pot; remove and discard skin. Discard drippings, reserving 2 Tbsp.
2. Add onion to drippings; cook and stir over medium-high heat until tender, 4-5 minutes. Add garlic; cook 1 minute longer. Add broth, stirring to loosen browned bits from pot. Bring to a boil. Return the chicken to pot. Add celery, carrots, bay leaves and thyme. Reduce heat; simmer, covered, until chicken is tender, 25-30 minutes.
3. Transfer chicken to a plate. Remove soup from heat. Add noodles; let stand, covered, until the noodles are tender, 20-22 minutes.
4. Meanwhile, when the chicken is cool enough to handle, remove meat from bones; discard bones. Shred meat into bite-sized pieces. Return meat to pot. Stir in parsley and lemon juice. If desired, adjust seasoning with additional salt and pepper. Discard bay leaves.

1⅓ cups: 239 cal., 12g fat (3g sat. fat), 68mg chol., 1176mg sod., 14g carb. (3g sugars, 2g fiber), 18g pro.

PREFER WHITE MEAT?

If you'd like, replace the chicken thighs in this soup with bone-in chicken breast. Once it reaches an internal temperature of 165°, set the chicken breast on a plate, let it cool and shred it, then return the meat to the pot as directed.

CEYLON CHICKEN CURRY & RICE NOODLE SOUP

Whenever cold or flu season hit, my mom always made a curried chicken rice noodle soup that was comforting and cozy. This turmeric lemongrass soup is a take on that curry soup I ate during childhood. It is loaded with ingredients to boost immunity and can easily be made vegan or vegetarian.
—Sarita Gelner, Chesterfield, MO

Prep: 25 min. • **Cook:** 25 min.
Makes: 8 servings (2½ qt.)

- **6 oz. uncooked wide rice noodles**
- **2 Tbsp. ghee or olive oil, divided**
- **1 lb. boneless chicken breasts, thinly sliced and cut into ½-in. pieces**
- **1 medium onion, chopped**
- **⅔ cup sliced fresh carrots**
- **3 bay leaves**
- **2 Tbsp. minced fresh gingerroot**
- **1 stalk lemongrass**
- **1 whole star anise**
- **1 Tbsp. curry powder**
- **2 tsp. ground turmeric**
- **1 garlic clove, minced**
- **½ tsp. salt**
- **¼ tsp. cayenne pepper**
- **2 anchovy fillets, minced, optional**
- **2 Tbsp. white wine vinegar**
- **1 carton (32 oz.) chicken broth**
- **1 can (13.66 oz.) coconut milk**
- **2 Tbsp. jaggery or dark brown sugar**
- **1½ cups chopped fresh kale**
- **½ cup cherry tomatoes, halved**

1. Cook noodles according to package directions for al dente. Meanwhile, in a Dutch oven, heat 1 Tbsp. ghee over medium-high heat. Add chicken; cook and stir until no longer pink, 4-5 minutes. Remove from pot. Cook and stir onion and carrots in the remaining 1 Tbsp. ghee until tender, 12-15 minutes. Add bay leaves, ginger, lemongrass, star anise, curry powder, turmeric, garlic, salt, cayenne and, if desired, minced anchovy fillets; cook 1 minute longer.
2. Add vinegar to pot; increase heat to medium-high. Cook 30 seconds, stirring to loosen browned bits from pot. Add broth, coconut milk and jaggery. Bring to a boil; reduce heat. Add the kale and tomatoes; simmer until tender, 6-8 minutes. Remove and discard bay leaves, lemongrass and star anise. Drain noodles; stir into soup. Add the chicken; heat through.

1¼ cups: 316 cal., 16g fat (11g sat. fat), 46mg chol., 758mg sod., 26g carb. (6g sugars, 2g fiber), 15g pro.

GRANDMA'S PRESSURE-COOKER CHICKEN NOODLE SOUP

I've made this soup weekly since I modified my grandma's recipe for the pressure cooker. Chicken soup, especially this one, is quick to make and budget-friendly for any large family.
—Tammy Stanko, Greensburg, PA

Prep: 10 min. • **Cook:** 25 min.
Makes: 8 servings

- **2 tsp. olive oil**
- **4 bone-in chicken thighs**
- **2 medium carrots, peeled, sliced into ½-in. pieces**
- **1½ celery ribs, sliced into ½-in. pieces**
- **6 cups reduced-sodium chicken broth**
- **½ tsp. salt**
- **⅛ tsp. pepper**
- **½ pkg. (8 oz.) fine egg noodles, cooked**
- **Chopped fresh parsley, optional**

1. Select saute setting on a 3- or 6-qt. electric pressure cooker and adjust for normal heat; add oil. Brown the chicken thighs. Add carrots, celery and broth to pressure cooker. Lock lid; close pressure-release valve. Adjust to pressure-cook on high for 10 minutes. Allow pressure to release naturally for 10 minutes, then quick-release any remaining pressure.
2. Stir in salt and pepper. Evenly divide the noodles among serving bowls; top with 1 chicken thigh and top with broth. If desired, sprinkle with parsley.

2 cups soup with 1 chicken thigh: 195 cal., 15g fat (2g sat. fat), 56mg chol., 631mg sod., 13g carb. (2g sugars, 1g fiber), 16g pro.

Breads, Rolls & More

Sweet pastries in the morning, soft loaves for sandwiches, fresh rolls and biscuits with dinner—there's just nothing like home-baked bread. Let the unmatched aromas and flavors of these treats show loved ones how much you care!

SOUTHERN BRUNCH PASTRY PUFF

My family just about jumps out of bed when the smell of eggs, sausage and buttery pastry hits their noses. This recipe is morning magic.
—Misty Leddick, Chester, SC

Prep: 30 min. • **Bake:** 30 min. + standing
Makes: 8 servings

- **2 cups plus 1 Tbsp. water, divided**
- **½ cup quick-cooking grits**
- **1 cup shredded cheddar cheese**
- **¼ cup butter, cubed**
- **2 Tbsp. prepared pesto**
- **½ tsp. salt, divided**
- **¼ tsp. coarsely ground pepper, divided**
- **½ lb. bulk pork sausage**
- **¼ cup finely chopped sweet red pepper**
- **7 large eggs, divided use**
- **1 pkg. (17.3 oz.) frozen puff pastry, thawed**

1. Preheat oven to 375°. In a small saucepan, bring 2 cups water to a boil. Slowly stir in grits. Reduce heat to medium-low; cook, covered, about 5 minutes or until thickened, stirring occasionally. Remove from heat. Stir in cheese, butter, pesto, ¼ tsp. salt and ⅛ tsp. pepper until blended.
2. Meanwhile, in a large skillet, cook sausage and red pepper over medium heat 4-6 minutes or until sausage is no longer pink and red pepper is tender, breaking up sausage into crumbles; drain.
3. In a small bowl, whisk 6 eggs and the the remaining salt and pepper until blended. Return sausage to skillet. Pour in egg mixture; cook and stir until eggs are thickened and no liquid egg remains.
4. Unfold each puff pastry sheet onto a 12x10-in. sheet of parchment. Spread the grits to within ½ in. of edges. Spoon sausage mixture over half of grits on each pastry. Fold pastries over sausage mixture to enclose; press edges with a fork to seal. Transfer to a baking sheet.
5. In a small bowl, whisk remaining egg and water; brush over pastries. If desired, top with additional ground pepper. Bake until golden brown. Let stand 10 minutes. Cut each pastry into 4 pieces.

1 piece: 587 cal., 39g fat (14g sat. fat), 208mg chol., 766mg sod., 43g carb. (1g sugars, 5g fiber), 18g pro.

SOUR CREAM CUT-OUT BISCUITS

After trying different ways to make biscuits without being completely satisfied, I decided to incorporate sour cream. Success! Split while warm, spread with butter and enjoy.
—Lorraine Caland, Shuniah, ON

Takes: 30 min. • **Makes:** 10 biscuits

- **2 cups all-purpose flour**
- **2 Tbsp. sugar**
- **3 tsp. baking powder**
- **½ tsp. salt**
- **½ tsp. baking soda**
- **1 cup sour cream**
- **1 Tbsp. butter, melted**

1. Preheat oven to 425°. In a large bowl, whisk flour, sugar, baking powder, salt and baking soda. Stir in the sour cream just until moistened.
2. Turn dough onto a lightly floured surface; knead gently 8-10 times. Pat or roll to ½-in. thickness; cut with a floured 2¼-in. biscuit cutter. Place 1 in. apart on an ungreased baking sheet. Bake until golden brown, 10-12 minutes. Brush biscuits with butter; serve warm.

1 biscuit: 159 cal., 6g fat (4g sat. fat), 9mg chol., 343mg sod., 22g carb. (3g sugars, 1g fiber), 3g pro.

PEPPERONI CHEESE BREAD

As a stay-at-home mother of two little girls, I pack a lot of activity into my days. The bread machine makes it a snap for me to turn out this attractive loaf that get plenty of zip from cayenne pepper, pepperoni and Mexican cheese.
—Dusti Christensen, Goodridge, MN

Prep: 10 min. • **Bake:** 4 hours
Makes: 1 loaf (16 slices)

- **1 cup water (70° to 80°)**
- **1 Tbsp. butter**
- **2 Tbsp. sugar**
- **2 tsp. ground mustard**
- **½ tsp. salt**
- **½ tsp. cayenne pepper**
- **¼ tsp. garlic powder**
- **3 cups bread flour**
- **2¼ tsp. active dry yeast**
- **1½ cups shredded Mexican cheese blend**
- **1 cup chopped pepperoni**

In bread machine pan, place the first 9 ingredients in order suggested by manufacturer. Select basic bread setting. Choose crust color and loaf size if available. Bake according to bread machine directions. Check dough after 5 minutes of mixing; add 1-2 Tbsp. water or flour if needed. Just before the final kneading (your machine may audibly signal this), add cheese and pepperoni.

Freeze option: Securely wrap and freeze cooled loaf in foil and place in freezer bag. To use, thaw at room temperature.

1 slice: 177 cal., 8g fat (4g sat. fat), 19mg chol., 329mg sod., 19g carb. (2g sugars, 1g fiber), 7g pro.

SWEDISH RYE BREAD

This recipe came from my mother, and it's long been a family favorite. You can make a meal of it with soup and a salad.
—Mary Ann Ross, Crown Point, IN

Prep: 25 min. + rising • **Bake:** 30 min.
Makes: 4 loaves (8 slices each)

- **1 pkg. (¼ oz.) active dry yeast**
- **1¾ cups warm water (110° to 115°), divided**
- **¼ cup packed brown sugar**
- **¼ cup molasses**
- **2 Tbsp. shortening**
- **2 tsp. salt**
- **2½ cups rye flour**
- **3¾ to 4¼ cups all-purpose flour**
- **2 Tbsp. butter, melted**

1. In a bowl, dissolve yeast in ¼ cup water. Add sugar, molasses, shortening, salt and the remaining water; stir well. Add rye flour; beat until smooth. Add enough all-purpose flour to form a soft dough.
2. Turn onto a floured surface; knead until smooth and elastic, 6-8 minutes. Place in a greased bowl, turning once to grease top. Cover and let rise in a warm place until doubled, about 1½ hours. Punch dough down.
3. Shape into 4 round loaves. Place on greased baking sheets. Cover and let rise until doubled, 45-60 minutes. Bake at 350° until golden brown, 30-35 minutes. Brush with butter.

1 slice: 109 cal., 2g fat (1g sat. fat), 2mg chol., 155mg sod., 21g carb. (4g sugars, 1g fiber), 2g pro.

CHANGE YOUR YEAST

Active dry yeast is the most commonly used type of yeast. You can use instant yeast instead; just use 25% less of it than the recipe calls for. Likewise, in recipes that call for instant yeast, you can use active dry yeast—just increase the amount by 25%.

RHUBARB BREAD

This is quite a good bread—our family really enjoys it! It's also very quick and easy to prepare, once you have the rhubarb diced.
—Grace Capen, Sacramento, CA

Prep: 15 min. • **Bake:** 45 min. + cooling
Makes: 2 loaves (16 slices each)

- **1⅓ cups packed brown sugar**
- **⅔ cup vegetable oil**
- **1 large egg, room temperature, beaten**
- **1 tsp. vanilla extract**
- **1 cup buttermilk**
- **2½ cups all-purpose flour**
- **¾ tsp. salt**
- **½ tsp. ground cinnamon**
- **1 tsp. baking soda**
- **1½ to 2 cups finely diced rhubarb, ¼-in. cuts**
- **½ cup chopped nuts**

1. Combine the sugar and oil; blend in egg, vanilla and milk. In a second bowl, combine flour, salt, cinnamon and baking soda; add to moist ingredients. Stir in rhubarb and nuts. Transfer to 2 well-greased 8x4-in. loaf pans.
2. Bake at 350° until a toothpick inserted in the center comes out clean, about 45 minutes. Cool for 10 minutes before removing from pans to wire racks.

1 slice: 129 cal., 6g fat (1g sat. fat), 7mg chol., 109mg sod., 17g carb. (10g sugars, 0 fiber), 2g pro.

SKILLET APPLE MUFFIN BREAD

Instead of sprinkling cinnamon sugar over this bread before baking, you could use your favorite streusel topping to make it more like coffee cake. I like to serve it warm with applesauce.

—Donna Goutermont, Sequim, WA

Prep: 20 min. • **Bake:** 35 min. + cooling
Makes: 12 servings

- **2 large eggs, room temperature**
- **1 cup 2% milk**
- **½ cup plus 1 Tbsp. sugar, divided**
- **3 Tbsp. canola oil**
- **2 cups all-purpose flour**
- **3 tsp. baking powder**
- **½ tsp. salt**
- **½ tsp. plus ⅛ tsp. ground cinnamon, divided**
- **¼ tsp. ground allspice**
- **3 medium tart apples, peeled and finely chopped**

1. Preheat oven to 350°. In a large bowl, beat eggs, milk, ½ cup sugar and canola oil until well blended. Combine the flour, baking powder, salt, ½ tsp. cinnamon and allspice; gradually beat into sugar mixture until blended. Fold in apples.
2. Transfer to a well-seasoned 10-in. cast-iron or other ovenproof skillet. Sprinkle with remaining 1 Tbsp. sugar and ⅛ tsp. cinnamon. Bake until until a toothpick inserted in the center comes out clean, 35-40 minutes. Let cool for 10 minutes; serve warm.

1 piece: 181 cal., 5g fat (1g sat. fat), 33mg chol., 240mg sod., 31g carb. (14g sugars, 1g fiber), 4g pro. **Diabetic exchanges:** 2 starch, 1 fat.

CREAMY LEMON ALMOND PASTRIES

I love lemon-filled doughnuts when I can find them. This recipe brings the concept to a new level by placing the filling into a baked beignet and enhancing it with a bit of almond flavoring and toasted almonds. The result? Sunshine in a bite.

—Arlene Erlbach, Morton Grove, IL

Prep: 30 min. + chilling • **Bake:** 15 min.
Makes: 9 servings

- **½ cup plus 1 Tbsp. cream cheese, softened (4½ oz.)**
- **⅔ cup confectioners' sugar, divided**
- **2 Tbsp. lemon curd**
- **2 tsp. grated lemon zest**
- **¼ tsp. almond extract**
- **1 sheet frozen puff pastry, thawed**
- **1 large egg, beaten**
- **2 Tbsp. water**
- **2 tsp. lemon juice**
- **2 tsp. 2% milk**
- **3 Tbsp. sliced almonds, toasted**

1. Beat the cream cheese, 3 Tbsp. confectioners' sugar, the lemon curd, lemon zest and almond extract on medium until combined. Refrigerate, covered, for 30 minutes.
2. Preheat oven to 400°. On a lightly floured surface, unfold puff pastry. Roll into a 12x9-in. rectangle. Using a pastry cutter or sharp knife, cut pastry into 9 rectangles. Spoon a rounded tablespoonful of the cream cheese mixture in the center of each rectangle. In a small bowl, whisk egg with water. Brush edges of pastry with egg mixture.
3. Wrap puff pastry around filling to cover completely. Pinch edges together to form a ball. Place seam side down, 2 in. apart, on a parchment-lined baking sheet. Brush pastries with remaining egg mixture. Pierce each once with a fork. Bake until golden brown, 15-18 minutes. Cool on wire rack for 5 minutes. Loosen pastries from the parchment.
4. Meanwhile, combine lemon juice, milk and the remaining confectioners' sugar. Brush each pastry with lemon glaze. Top with almonds. When glaze is set, in 1-2 minutes, peel off parchment. Serve warm.

1 pastry: 255 cal., 14g fat (5g sat. fat), 39mg chol., 148mg sod., 29g carb. (12g sugars, 2g fiber), 4g pro.

DUTCH-OVEN BREAD

Crusty homemade bread makes an average day extraordinary. Enjoy this beautiful bread recipe as is, or stir in a few of your favorites like cheese, garlic, herbs and dried fruits. You can also double this recipe to make a loaf that will fill your Dutch oven.

—Catherine Ward, Mequon, WI

Prep: 15 min. + rising • **Bake:** 45 min. + cooling
Makes: 1 loaf (16 slices)

- **3 to 3½ cups all-purpose flour**
- **1 tsp. active dry yeast**
- **1 tsp. salt**
- **1½ cups water (70° to 75°)**

1. In a large bowl, whisk 3 cups flour, yeast and salt. Stir in water and enough remaining flour to form a moist, shaggy dough. Do not knead. Cover and let rise in a cool place until doubled, 7-8 hours. Preheat oven to 450°; place a Dutch oven with lid onto center rack and heat for at least 30 minutes. Once Dutch oven is heated, turn dough onto a generously floured surface. Using a metal scraper or spatula, quickly shape into a round loaf. Gently place on top of a piece of parchment.
2. Using a sharp knife, make a slash (¼ in. deep) across top of loaf. Using the parchment, immediately lower bread into heated Dutch oven. Cover; bake for 30 minutes. Uncover and bake until top is deep golden brown and bread sounds hollow when tapped, 15-20 minutes longer, partially covering if browning too much. Remove loaf from pan and cool completely on wire rack.

1 piece: 86 cal., 0 fat (0 sat. fat), 0 chol., 148mg sod., 18g carb. (0 sugars, 1g fiber), 3g pro.

WORK FAST!

This is a soft, gentle dough that should be baked immediately after shaping. Working quickly and preheating the Dutch oven prior to shaping are keys to success.

WHOLESOME WHEAT BREAD

My sister and I were in 4-H, and Mom was our breads project leader for years. Because of that early training, fresh homemade bread like this is a staple in my own kitchen.
—Karen Wingate, Coldwater, KS

Prep: 30 min. + rising • **Bake:** 55 min. + cooling
Makes: 2 loaves (16 slices each)

- **2 pkg. (¼ oz. each) active dry yeast**
- **2¼ cups warm water (110° to 115°)**
- **⅓ cup butter, softened**
- **⅓ cup honey**
- **3 Tbsp. sugar**
- **1 Tbsp. salt**
- **½ cup nonfat dry milk powder**
- **4½ cups whole wheat flour**
- **2¾ to 3½ cups all-purpose flour**

1. In a large bowl, dissolve yeast in warm water. Add butter, honey, sugar, salt, milk powder and 3 cups whole wheat flour; beat on medium speed until smooth. Stir in the remaining whole wheat flour and enough all-purpose flour to form a soft dough.
2. Turn dough onto a floured surface; knead until smooth and elastic, about 10 minutes. Place in a greased bowl, turning once to grease the top. Cover and let rise in a warm place until doubled, about 1 hour.
3. Punch down dough. Turn onto a lightly floured surface; divide the dough into 4 portions. Roll each into a 15-in. rope. For each loaf, twist 2 ropes together; pinch ends to seal. Place in greased 9x5-in. loaf pans. Cover with kitchen towels; let rise in a warm place until doubled, about 30 minutes.
4. Bake at 375° until golden brown, 25-30 minutes. Remove from pans to wire racks to cool.

1 slice: 134 cal., 2g fat (1g sat. fat), 5mg chol., 243mg sod., 25g carb. (5g sugars, 2g fiber), 4g pro. **Diabetic exchanges:** 2 starch.

COMBINING FLOURS

Whole wheat and rye flours are "soft" flours, meaning they contain less gluten, and make an extremely dense loaf if used alone. They're usually used in combination with higher-gluten "hard" flours, like all-purpose and bread flour.

SAVORY SKILLET POPOVER

This showstopping recipe delivers comfort and flavor, and it brings a smile. It's the perfect vehicle for using up little bits of leftovers, as long as they are fully cooked and heated in the bottom of the skillet prior to adding the batter and cheese.

—Susan Anderson, Helena, MT

Prep: 25 min. • **Bake:** 20 min.
Makes: 6 servings

- **6 Tbsp. butter**
- **2 Tbsp. chopped shallot**
- **8 large eggs, room temperature**
- **¾ cup 2% milk**
- **1 cup plus 2 Tbsp. all-purpose flour**
- **½ tsp. kosher salt**
- **½ tsp. pepper**
- **1 Tbsp. minced fresh thyme or 1 tsp. dried thyme**
- **¾ cup grated Parmesan cheese**

1. Preheat oven to 425°. In a 12-in. cast-iron or other ovenproof skillet, melt butter over medium-high heat. Add shallot; cook and stir until tender, 1-2 minutes.
2. In a large bowl, whisk eggs and milk until blended. Whisk in flour, salt and pepper until smooth; stir in thyme. Pour batter into hot pan; sprinkle with Parmesan cheese.
3. Bake until top is puffed and sides are golden brown and crisp, 20-25 minutes. Serve immediately.

1 slice: 343 cal., 21g fat (11g sat. fat), 290mg chol., 542mg sod., 22g carb. (2g sugars, 1g fiber), 15g pro.

SOUR CREAM ROLLS WITH WALNUT FILLING

When I was little, my grandmother taught me how to make these rolls. I remember feeling so special when we served them. This is a great recipe if you have never worked with yeast before, so it's a good one to share with young bakers.

—Nadine Mesch, Mount Healthy, OH

Prep: 1 hour + rising • **Bake:** 20 min.
Makes: 8 loaves (6 slices each)

- **4 cups ground walnuts (about 14 oz.)**
- **1 cup sugar**
- **¾ cup butter, melted**
- **½ cup 2% milk**
- **⅓ cup honey**

DOUGH

- **2 pkg. (¼ oz. each) active dry yeast**
- **1 tsp. plus ⅓ cup sugar, divided**
- **½ cup warm 2% milk (110° to 115°)**
- **1 cup butter, melted**
- **1 cup sour cream**
- **4 large eggs, room temperature, divided use**
- **1 tsp. salt**
- **5¼ to 5¾ cups all-purpose flour**

1. In a large bowl, mix first 5 ingredients until blended. In a small bowl, dissolve yeast and 1 tsp. sugar in warm milk; let stand for 15 minutes. In a large bowl, combine melted butter, sour cream, 3 eggs, salt, remaining sugar, the yeast mixture and 2 cups flour; beat on medium speed 3 minutes. Stir in enough of the remaining flour to form a soft dough (dough will be sticky).
2. Turn dough onto a floured surface; knead until smooth and elastic, 6-8 minutes. Place in a greased bowl, turning once to grease the top. Cover and let rise in a warm place until doubled, about 1 hour.
3. Punch down dough. Turn onto a lightly floured surface; divide and shape into 8 portions. Roll each into a 12x8-in. rectangle (dough will be very thin). Spread each with ½ cup walnut mixture to within ¾ in. of edges. Carefully roll up each rectangle jelly-roll style, starting with a long side; pinch seam and ends to seal.
4. Place rolls 2 in. apart on parchment-lined baking sheets, seam side down. Prick tops with a fork. Cover; let rise in a warm place until almost doubled, about 1 hour. Preheat oven to 350°.
5. Lightly beat the remaining egg; brush over the rolls. Bake until golden brown, 20-25 minutes, switching position of pans halfway through baking (filling may leak during baking). Remove loaves to wire racks to cool. To serve, cut into slices.

1 slice: 201 cal., 13g fat (5g sat. fat), 37mg chol., 113mg sod., 20g carb. (8g sugars, 1g fiber), 3g pro.

OATMEAL ROLLS

I grew up on oatmeal and still love it, so these soft rolls really appeal to me. They are simple to make and freeze well.

—Jeanette Fuehring, Concordia, MO

Prep: 20 min. + rising • **Bake:** 20 min.
Makes: 24 rolls

- **2⅓ cups water, divided**
- **1 cup dry oatmeal**
- **3 Tbsp. butter**
- **2 pkg. (¼ oz. each) active dry yeast**
- **⅔ cup packed brown sugar**
- **1 Tbsp. sugar**
- **1½ tsp. salt**
- **5 to 5¾ cups all-purpose flour**

1. In a saucepan, bring 2 cups water to a boil. Add oatmeal and butter; simmer 1 minute. Remove to a large bowl and let cool to 110°-115°.

2. Heat the remaining water to 110°-115°; add yeast. To the oatmeal mixture, add sugars, salt, the yeast mixture and half the flour. Mix well. Add enough remaining flour to make a soft dough.

3. Turn dough out onto a floured surface; knead 6-8 minutes or until smooth and elastic. Add more flour if necessary. Place dough in a greased bowl, turning once to grease the top. Cover and let rise until doubled, about 1 hour.

4. Punch down dough; divide in half and shape each half into 12 balls. Place balls 1 in. apart on greased baking sheets. Cover and let rise until doubled, 45-60 minutes. Bake at 350° for 20-30 minutes.

1 roll: 146 cal., 2g fat (1g sat. fat), 4mg chol., 165mg sod., 29g carb. (7g sugars, 1g fiber), 3g pro.

HAM & GREEN ONION BISCUITS

I started with my grandmother's biscuits and added a bit of my personality. When I make them with my kids, it feels as if she's with us.
—Amy Chase, Vanderhoof, BC

Prep: 20 min. • **Bake:** 10 min.
Makes: about 1 dozen

- **2 cups all-purpose flour**
- **3 tsp. baking powder**
- **1 tsp. sugar**
- **¼ tsp. garlic salt**
- **Dash pepper**
- **6 Tbsp. cold butter, cubed**
- **1 cup finely chopped fully cooked ham**
- **2 green onions, chopped**
- **¾ cup 2% milk**

1. Preheat oven to 450°. In a large bowl, whisk the first 5 ingredients. Cut in butter until mixture resembles coarse crumbs. Stir in ham and green onions. Add milk; stir just until moistened.
2. Turn dough onto a lightly floured surface; knead gently 8-10 times. Pat or roll dough to ½-in. thickness; cut with a floured 2½-in. biscuit cutter. Place 2 in. apart on an ungreased baking sheet. Bake 10-12 minutes or until golden brown. Serve warm.

1 biscuit: 151 cal., 7g fat (4g sat. fat), 23mg chol., 315mg sod., 17g carb. (1g sugars, 1g fiber), 5g pro.

COUNTRY CRUST SOURDOUGH BREAD

For many years, I've been making 45 loaves of this bread for an annual Christmas bazaar, where we feed bread and soup to over 300 folks.
—Beverley Whaley, Camano Island, WA

Prep: 20 min. + rising • **Bake:** 30 min.
Makes: 2 loaves (16 slices each)

- **2 pkg. (¼ oz. each) active dry yeast**
- **1¼ cups warm water (110° to 115°)**
- **1 cup Sourdough Starter**
- **2 large eggs. room temperature**
- **¼ cup sugar**
- **¼ cup vegetable oil**
- **1 tsp. salt**
- **6 to 6½ cups all-purpose flour**
- **Melted butter**

1. In a large bowl, dissolve yeast in warm water. Add the Sourdough Starter, eggs, sugar, oil, salt and 3 cups flour. Beat until smooth. Stir in enough remaining flour to form a soft dough.
2. Turn onto a floured surface; knead until smooth and elastic, 6-8 minutes. Place in a greased bowl, turning once to grease top. Cover and let rise in a warm place until doubled, about 1 hour.
3. Punch dough down. Turn onto a lightly floured surface; divide in half. Shape into loaves. Place in 2 greased 8x4-in. loaf pans. Cover and let rise until doubled, about 45 minutes.
4. Bake at 375° for 30-35 minutes or until golden brown. Remove from pans to wire racks to cool. Brush with butter.

1 slice: 113 cal., 2g fat (0 sat. fat), 12mg chol., 79mg sod., 20g carb. (2g sugars, 1g fiber), 3g pro.

Sourdough starter: In a covered 4-qt. glass or ceramic container, mix 2 cups all-purpose flour and 1 package (¼ oz.) active dry yeast. Gradually stir in 2 cups warm (110° to 115°) water until smooth. Cover loosely with a kitchen towel; let stand in a warm place 2-4 days or until mixture is bubbly and sour smelling and a clear liquid has formed on top. (Starter may darken, but if it turns another color or develops an offensive odor or mold, discard it and start over.) Cover tightly and refrigerate starter until ready to use.

SPICED SWEET POTATO DOUGHNUTS

These sweet potato treats are easy to prepare—and no one minds eating the nutritious spuds when they're inside doughnuts! Serve them up for breakfast, or with your midday coffee break.
—Jan Valdez, Lombard, IL

Prep: 15 min. • **Cook:** 5 min./batch
Makes: 1 dozen

- **3 Tbsp. butter, softened**
- **1 cup sugar**
- **3 large eggs, room temperature**
- **1 cup mashed sweet potatoes**
- **½ cup buttermilk**
- **1 tsp. vanilla extract**
- **3½ cups self-rising flour**
- **2 Tbsp. pumpkin pie spice**
- **¾ tsp. salt**
- **Oil for deep-fat frying**

TOPPING

- **1 cup sugar**
- **4 tsp. ground cinnamon**

1. In a large bowl, beat the butter and sugar until blended. Beat in eggs, sweet potatoes, buttermilk and vanilla. In another bowl, whisk flour, pie spice and salt; gradually beat into creamed mixture.
2. Turn onto a well-floured surface; pat to ½-in. thickness. Cut with a floured 3-in. doughnut cutter. In an electric skillet or deep fryer, heat oil to 375°. Fry doughnuts, a few at a time, until golden brown, 2-3 minutes on each side. Drain on paper towels. In a small bowl, mix sugar and cinnamon; dip warm doughnuts in topping mixture to coat both sides.

1 doughnut: 383 cal., 14g fat (3g sat. fat), 55mg chol., 651mg sod., 59g carb. (27g sugars, 2g fiber), 6g pro.

JALAPENO CORNBREAD FILLED WITH BLUEBERRY QUICK JAM

Fresh jalapenos and blueberry quick jam make the perfect blend of sweet and spicy in this special cornbread. Once you eat one piece, you won't be able to resist going back for another.

—Colleen Delawder, Herndon, VA

Prep: 20 min. + chilling
Bake: 30 min. + cooling • **Makes:** 12 servings

- **2 cups fresh blueberries**
- **1 cup sugar**
- **1 Tbsp. cider vinegar**
- **¼ tsp. kosher salt**

CORNBREAD

- **½ cup 2% milk**
- **1 Tbsp. lemon juice**
- **1½ cups all-purpose flour**
- **½ cup yellow cornmeal**
- **½ cup sugar**
- **3 tsp. baking powder**
- **½ tsp. kosher salt**
- **2 Tbsp. unsalted butter**
- **1 Tbsp. honey**
- **2 large eggs, room temperature**
- **⅓ cup canola oil**
- **2 jalapeno peppers, seeded and minced**

1. In a large heavy saucepan, combine blueberries, sugar, vinegar and kosher salt. Bring to a boil over high heat. Cook, stirring constantly, 5 minutes. Cool completely. Refrigerate, covered, overnight.
2. For cornbread, preheat oven to 350°. Combine milk and lemon juice; let stand briefly. In another bowl, whisk the next 5 ingredients. In a small bowl, microwave butter and honey on high for 30 seconds; cool slightly. Whisk eggs and oil into milk mixture (mixture may appear curdled). Add the butter mixture; whisk until well combined. Add flour mixture; whisk just until combined. Fold in jalapenos.
3. Pour 2 cups batter into a well-buttered 10-in. fluted tube pan. Spoon half to three-fourths of the blueberry quick jam over batter. Cover with remaining batter. Bake until a toothpick inserted in center comes out clean, 30-35 minutes. Cool 10 minutes; invert onto a cake plate or serving platter. Drizzle with the remaining blueberry quick jam.

1 slice: 289 cal., 10g fat (2g sat. fat), 37mg chol., 258mg sod., 48g carb. (30g sugars, 1g fiber), 4g pro.

BLUEBERRY-ORANGE MUFFINS

This recipe was given to me years ago, and I've used it often since. In fact, it's so good that it won first prize at a county fair! Blueberries are plentiful in the Midwest, and this is a fragrant and fruity way to prepare them.

—Irene Parry, Kenosha, WI

Takes: 30 min. • **Makes:** 2 dozen

- **1 cup quick-cooking oats**
- **1 cup orange juice**
- **1 tsp. grated orange zest**
- **1 cup canola oil**
- **3 large eggs, room temperature, beaten**
- **3 cups all-purpose flour**
- **1 cup sugar**
- **4 tsp. baking powder**
- **1 tsp. salt**
- **½ tsp. baking soda**
- **3 to 4 cups fresh blueberries**

TOPPING

- **½ cup finely chopped nuts**
- **3 Tbsp. sugar**
- **½ tsp. ground cinnamon**

1. Preheat oven to 400°. Mix oats, orange juice and zest. Blend in oil and eggs; set aside. Stir together flour, sugar, baking powder, salt and baking soda. Add oat mixture; mix lightly. Fold in blueberries.
2. Spoon batter into 24 paper-lined muffin tins, filling cups two-thirds full. Combine the topping ingredients; sprinkle over batter. Bake for 15-18 minutes or until lightly browned. Cool for 5 minutes before removing to a wire rack.

1 muffin: 228 cal., 12g fat (2g sat. fat), 27mg chol., 200mg sod., 28g carb. (13g sugars, 1g fiber), 4g pro.

PUMPKIN EGG BRAID

I developed this bread to celebrate our two favorite holidays—Thanksgiving and Hanukkah. Try it with flavored butters, and use leftovers for French toast or sandwiches.
—Sara Mellas, Hartford, CT

Prep: 30 min. + rising • **Bake:** 20 min.
Makes: 1 loaf (12 slices)

- **1 pkg. (¼ oz.) active dry yeast**
- **3 Tbsp. warm water (110° to 115°)**
- **½ cup canned pumpkin**
- **1 large egg, room temperature**
- **2 Tbsp. light brown sugar**
- **2 Tbsp. butter, softened**
- **1 tsp. pumpkin pie spice**
- **½ tsp. salt**
- **2 to 2½ cups bread flour**

EGG WASH

- **1 large egg**
- **1 Tbsp. water**

1. In a small bowl, dissolve yeast in warm water. In a large bowl, combine pumpkin, egg, brown sugar, butter, pie spice, salt, yeast mixture and 1 cup flour; beat on medium speed until smooth. Stir in enough remaining flour to form a soft dough (dough will be sticky).
2. Turn the dough onto a floured surface; knead until smooth and elastic, 6-8 minutes. Place in a greased bowl, turning once to grease the top. Cover and let rise in a warm place until doubled, about 1 hour.
3. Punch down dough. Turn onto a lightly floured surface; divide into thirds. Roll each into a 16-in. rope. Place ropes on a greased baking sheet and braid. Pinch ends to seal; tuck under.
4. Cover with a kitchen towel; let rise in a warm place until almost doubled, about 45 minutes. Preheat oven to 350°.
5. For egg wash, in a small bowl, whisk the egg and water until blended; brush over loaf. Bake until golden brown, 20-25 minutes. Remove from pan to a wire rack to cool.

1 slice: 126 cal., 3g fat (2g sat. fat), 36mg chol., 129mg sod., 20g carb. (3g sugars, 1g fiber), 4g pro. **Diabetic exchanges:** 1 starch, ½ fat.

SLOW-COOKER PUMPKIN YEAST BREAD

Savor the rich flavors of fall with this homey loaf you can bake up in the slow cooker. Butterscotch adds a sweet surprise.
—Erica Polly, Sun Prairie, WI

Prep: 20 min. • **Cook:** 2½ hours + cooling
Makes: 1 loaf (12 slices)

- **⅓ cup packed brown sugar**
- **1 pkg. (¼ oz.) quick-rise yeast**
- **2 tsp. pumpkin pie spice**
- **¾ tsp. salt**
- **3½ to 4 cups all-purpose flour**
- **¾ cup 2% milk**
- **2 Tbsp. butter, cubed**
- **¾ cup canned pumpkin**
- **1 large egg, lightly beaten**
- **⅓ cup raisins**
- **⅓ cup chopped pecans, toasted**
- **⅓ cup butterscotch chips, optional**

1. In a large bowl, mix brown sugar, yeast, pumpkin pie spice, salt and 1½ cups flour. In a small saucepan, heat milk and butter to 120°-130°; stir into dry ingredients. Stir in pumpkin, egg and enough remaining flour to form a soft dough (dough will be sticky).
2. Turn the dough onto a floured surface; knead until smooth and elastic, 6-8 minutes. During the last few minutes of kneading, add raisins, pecans and, if desired, butterscotch chips. Shape into a 6-in. round loaf; transfer to a greased double thickness of heavy-duty foil (about 12 in. square). Lifting with foil, place in a 6-qt. slow cooker. Press foil against bottom and sides of slow cooker.
3. Cook, covered, on high 2½-3 hours or until a thermometer reads 190°-200°. Remove to a wire rack; cool completely before slicing.

1 slice: 228 cal., 5g fat (2g sat. fat), 22mg chol., 180mg sod., 40g carb. (10g sugars, 2g fiber), 6g pro.

KEEPING BREAD FRESH

Homemade bread lasts 3-4 days when stored in a bread box. For long-term storage, freeze it—bread lasts for up to 6 months in the freezer.

GREEN CHILE CORN FRITTERS

This is a crispy side dish, appetizer or snack to add to a Mexican meal. The fritters also go well with chili or soup. I usually have all the ingredients on hand.
—Johnna Johnson, Scottsdale, AZ

Prep: 20 min. • **Cook:** 5 min./batch
Makes: 2 dozen

- **1 cup yellow cornmeal**
- **½ cup all-purpose flour**
- **1½ tsp. baking powder**
- **¾ tsp. salt**
- **½ tsp. garlic powder**
- **½ tsp. onion powder**
- **½ tsp. paprika**
- **½ tsp. pepper**
- **1 large egg, room temperature**
- **⅔ cup whole milk**
- **1 can (8¾ oz.) whole kernel corn, drained**
- **1 can (4 oz.) chopped green chiles, drained**
- **Oil for deep-fat frying**
- **Sriracha mayonnaise or condiment of your choice, optional**

1. In a large bowl, whisk the first 8 ingredients. In another bowl, whisk the egg and milk until blended. Add to the dry ingredients, stirring just until moistened. Let stand 5 minutes. Fold in corn and green chiles.
2. In a deep cast-iron or electric skillet, heat oil to 375°. Drop the batter by tablespoonfuls, a few at a time, into hot oil. Fry until golden brown, 1-1½ minutes on each side. Drain on paper towels. Serve with desired condiments.

1 fritter: 74 cal., 4g fat (0 sat. fat), 8mg chol., 159mg sod., 9g carb. (1g sugars, 1g fiber), 1g pro.

WHOLE WHEAT BUTTERHORNS

I take these to potluck suppers and serve them to guests—they've always brought many requests for the recipe. They're a favorite at home, too. The rolls don't take long to make, and they freeze very well for future use.

—Mary Jane Mullins, Livonia, MO

Prep: 30 min. + rising • **Bake:** 10 min.
Makes: 24 rolls

- **2¾ cups all-purpose flour**
- **2 pkg. (¼ oz. each) active dry yeast**
- **1¾ cups water**
- **⅓ cup packed brown sugar**
- **½ cup butter, divided**
- **2 Tbsp. honey**
- **2 tsp. salt**
- **2 cups whole wheat flour**

1. In a large bowl, combine 1½ cups all-purpose flour and yeast.
2. Combine water, brown sugar, 3 Tbsp. butter, honey and salt; heat to 120°-130°. Add to flour mixture. Beat on low for 30 seconds with electric mixer; increase speed to high and continue beating 3 minutes. Stir in the whole wheat flour and enough of the remaining all-purpose flour to form a soft dough.
3. Turn dough out onto a lightly floured surface and knead until smooth and elastic, 6-8 minutes. Place in a greased bowl, turning once to grease the top. Cover and let rise in a warm place until doubled, about 1½ hours.
4. Punch dough down and divide into thirds. Shape each into a ball; cover and let rest 10 minutes.
5. On a lightly floured surface, roll the balls into three 12-in. circles. Cut each circle into 8 wedges. Roll wedges into crescent shapes, starting at the wide end. Place on greased baking sheets. Cover and let rise in a warm place until doubled, about 1 hour.
6. Melt the remaining butter and brush some on each crescent. Bake at 400° until golden brown, 10-15 minutes. Brush again with butter while hot.

1 serving: 137 cal., 4g fat (2g sat. fat), 10mg chol., 237mg sod., 23g carb. (5g sugars, 2g fiber), 3g pro.

SWEET POTATO DUTCH BABY WITH PRALINE SYRUP

This recipe reminds me of my favorite breakfast from when I was a child. It's a perfect comfort dish morning or evening.

—Angela Spengler, Niceville, FL

Prep: 10 min. • **Cook:** 30 min.
Makes: 6 servings

- **4 Tbsp. butter, divided**
- **3 large eggs, room temperature**
- **½ cup 2% milk**
- **¼ cup mashed canned sweet potatoes in syrup**
- **½ cup all-purpose flour**
- **¼ tsp. salt**
- **½ cup maple syrup**
- **¼ cup chopped pecans**

1. Preheat oven to 400°. Place 2 Tbsp. butter in a 10-in. cast-iron or other ovenproof skillet. Place in oven until butter is melted, 4-5 minutes; carefully swirl to coat evenly.
2. Meanwhile, in a large bowl, whisk the eggs, milk and sweet potatoes until blended. Whisk in flour and salt. Pour into the hot skillet. Bake until puffed and the sides are golden brown and crisp, 20-25 minutes.
3. In a small saucepan, combine syrup, pecans and remaining 2 Tbsp. butter. Cook and stir over medium heat until butter is melted. Remove pancake from oven; serve immediately with syrup.

1 serving: 261 cal., 14g fat (6g sat. fat), 115mg chol., 210mg sod., 30g carb. (19g sugars, 1g fiber), 5g pro.

GINGERBREAD CINNAMON ROLLS

These cinnamon rolls are sure to please anyone who has a sweet tooth. The gingerbread flavor makes them perfect for the holiday season, but why wait when you can enjoy them year-round?

—Andrea Price, Grafton, WI

Prep: 30 min. + rising • **Bake:** 25 min.
Makes: 1 dozen

- **1 pkg. (¼ oz.) active dry yeast**
- **½ cup warm 2% milk (110° to 115°)**
- **¼ cup warm water (110° to 115°)**
- **⅓ cup molasses**
- **¼ cup packed brown sugar**
- **1 large egg, room temperature**
- **2 Tbsp. canola oil**
- **½ tsp. salt**
- **3½ to 4 cups all-purpose flour**

FILLING

- **¼ cup packed brown sugar**
- **2 Tbsp. sugar**
- **1 tsp. ground cinnamon**
- **½ tsp. ground ginger**
- **¼ tsp. ground cloves**
- **2 Tbsp. butter, softened**

SPICED GLAZE

- **1½ cups confectioners' sugar**
- **½ tsp. ground cinnamon**
- **½ tsp. vanilla extract**
- **6 to 7 tsp. 2% milk**

1. In a small bowl, dissolve yeast in warm milk and water. In a large bowl, combine molasses, brown sugar, egg, oil, salt, the yeast mixture and 1½ cups flour; beat on medium speed until smooth. Stir in enough remaining flour to form a soft dough (dough will be sticky).
2. Turn dough onto a floured surface; knead 6-8 minutes (dough will be sticky). Place in a greased bowl, turning once to grease the top. Cover and let rise in a warm place until doubled, about 1 hour.
3. For filling, mix sugars and spices. Punch down dough. Turn dough onto a lightly floured surface and press into a 12x8-in. rectangle. Brush with butter to within ½ in. of edges; sprinkle with the sugar mixture. Roll up jelly-roll style, starting with a long side; pinch seam to seal. Cut into 12 slices.
4. Place slices in a greased 13x9-in. baking pan, cut side down. Cover; let rise in a warm place until almost doubled, about 1 hour.
5. Preheat oven to 350°. Bake until golden brown, 20-25 minutes. In a small bowl, mix confectioners' sugar, cinnamon, vanilla and enough milk to reach desired consistency; spread over warm rolls.

Note: The dough does not need to be made in a bread machine, but it can be. Dissolve the yeast in warm water for 5 minutes. Then add the remaining ingredients. Knead dough to form a ball. Cover and let rise until doubled in size. Punch down and allow to rise again until doubled in size. Proceed with the instructions for assembly.

1 roll: 315 cal., 5g fat (2g sat. fat), 22mg chol., 133mg sod., 62g carb. (33g sugars, 2g fiber), 5g pro.

Holiday Celebration Breads

Part of making the season bright is bringing out the traditional recipes that your family looks forward to all year! These flavors are just right for the holidays, and might just launch a new tradition in your home.

CRANBERRY EGGNOG MUFFINS

No one in my house wants to be the one to finish the leftover eggnog or cranberry sauce, so I use those ingredients to make warm muffins that quickly vanish.
—Nancy Mock, Colchester, VT

Takes: 30 min. • **Makes:** 1 dozen

- **2 cups all-purpose flour**
- **¾ cup sugar**
- **3 tsp. baking powder**
- **½ tsp. salt**
- **¼ tsp. ground cinnamon**
- **1 large egg, room temperature**
- **1 cup eggnog**
- **¼ cup butter, melted**
- **¾ cup whole-berry cranberry sauce**

1. Preheat oven to 400°. In a large bowl, whisk the first 5 ingredients. In another bowl, whisk egg, eggnog and melted butter until blended. Add to the flour mixture; stir just until moistened.
2. Spoon 1 Tbsp. batter in bottom of each of 12 greased or paper-lined muffin cups. Drop 1 tsp. cranberry sauce into center of each; top with remaining batter and cranberry sauce. Cut through batter with a knife to swirl.
3. Bake 15-18 minutes or until a toothpick inserted in center comes out clean. Cool 5 minutes before removing from pan to a wire rack. Serve warm.

1 muffin: 208 cal., 5g fat (3g sat. fat), 38mg chol., 275mg sod., 37g carb. (19g sugars, 1g fiber), 4g pro.

STOLLEN BUTTER ROLLS

Our family enjoys my stollen so much they say it's just too good to be served only as a sweet bread. So I created these buttery, less-sweet dinner rolls as an alternative to the whole loaf.
—Mindy White, Nashville, TN

Prep: 45 min. + rising • **Bake:** 15 min.
Makes: 2 dozen

- **1 pkg. (¼ oz.) active dry yeast**
- **¼ cup warm water (110° to 115°)**
- **1 cup 2% milk**
- **2 large eggs, room temperature**
- **½ cup butter, softened**
- **1 Tbsp. sugar**
- **1 tsp. salt**
- **4¼ to 4¾ cups all-purpose flour**
- **¾ cup chopped mixed candied fruit**
- **¾ cup dried currants**
- **½ cup cold butter, cut into 24 pieces (1 tsp. each)**

1. In a small bowl, dissolve yeast in warm water. In a large bowl, combine milk, eggs, butter, sugar, salt, the yeast mixture and 3 cups flour; beat on medium speed until smooth. Stir in enough remaining flour to form a soft dough (dough will be sticky).
2. Turn onto a floured surface; knead until smooth and elastic, 6-8 minutes. Place in a greased bowl, turning once to grease the top. Cover and let rise in a warm place until doubled, about 1 hour.
3. Punch dough down; turn onto a floured surface. Knead candied fruit and currants into dough (knead in more flour if necessary). Divide and shape into 24 balls; flatten slightly. Place 1 tsp. cold butter in center of each circle. Fold circles in half over butter; press edges to seal. Place in a greased 15x10x1-in. baking pan. Cover and let rise in a warm place until doubled, about 45 minutes.
4. Bake at 375° until golden brown, 15-20 minutes. Cool in pan 5 minutes; serve warm.

Freeze option: Freeze cooled rolls in airtight containers. To use, microwave each roll on high until warmed, 30-45 seconds.

1 roll: 198 cal., 9g fat (5g sat. fat), 37mg chol., 178mg sod., 28g carb. (9g sugars, 1g fiber), 4g pro.

CHAI-SPICED STAR BREAD

My chai star bread is great for potlucks or parties because it's easy to share and looks beautiful. I make this with pears, but you can try using this recipe with other fruits, too, like persimmons or apples.

—Elizabeth Ding, El Cerrito, CA

Prep: 45 min. + rising • **Bake:** 20 min. + cooling
Makes: 16 servings

- **2 tsp. active dry yeast**
- **½ cup warm water (110° to 115°)**
- **½ cup warm whole milk (110° to 115°)**
- **¼ cup sugar**
- **2¾ to 3¼ cups all-purpose flour**

FILLING

- **5 Tbsp. butter, softened**
- **¾ cup packed brown sugar**
- **2 tsp. vanilla extract**
- **1 tsp. ground ginger**
- **1 tsp. ground cinnamon**
- **½ tsp. ground nutmeg**
- **½ tsp. ground allspice**
- **¼ tsp. ground cloves**
- **1 medium Bartlett pear, peeled and chopped**
- **1 large egg, beaten**

1. In a small bowl, dissolve the yeast in warm water. In a large bowl, combine milk, sugar, yeast mixture and 1½ cups flour; beat on medium speed until smooth. Stir in enough of the remaining flour to form a soft dough (dough will be sticky).
2. Turn onto a floured surface; knead until smooth and elastic, 6-8 minutes. Place in a greased bowl, turning once to grease top. Cover and let rise in a warm place until doubled, about 1 hour.
3. Punch down dough. Turn onto a lightly floured surface; divide into 4 portions. Roll each into a 12-in. circle. Place 1 circle on a parchment-lined 14-in. pizza pan. For the filling, combine butter, brown sugar, vanilla and spices. Spread circle with a third of the filling. Repeat twice, layering dough and filling; top with pears. Top with final portion of dough.
4. Place a 2½-in. round cutter on top of the dough in center of circle (do not press down). With a sharp knife, make 16 evenly spaced cuts from round cutter to edge of dough, forming a starburst. Remove cutter; grasp 2 strips and rotate twice outward. Pinch ends together. Repeat with remaining strips.
5. Cover with a kitchen towel; let rise until almost doubled, about 30 minutes. Preheat oven to 375°. Brush with beaten egg. Bake until golden brown, 20-25 minutes. Cool completely on a wire rack.

1 piece: 178 cal., 4g fat (3g sat. fat), 13mg chol., 37mg sod., 32g carb. (15g sugars, 1g fiber), 3g pro.

EGGNOG BREAD

It just wouldn't be Christmas if I didn't bake my traditional loaf of eggnog bread. It's quite the hit during the holidays.

—Ruth Bickel, Hickory, NC

Prep: 15 min. • **Bake:** 50 min.
Makes: 1 loaf (16 slices)

- **2 large eggs, room temperature**
- **¾ cup sugar**
- **¼ cup butter, melted**
- **2¼ cups all-purpose flour**
- **2 tsp. baking powder**
- **¾ tsp. salt**
- **1 cup eggnog**
- **½ cup chopped red and green candied cherries**
- **½ cup chopped pecans**
- **½ cup raisins**

1. Preheat oven to 350°. Grease an 8x4-in. loaf pan.
2. In a large bowl, beat the eggs, sugar and melted butter until well blended. In another bowl, whisk flour, baking powder and salt; beat into egg mixture alternately with the eggnog, beating well after each addition. Fold in candied cherries, pecans and raisins.
3. Transfer to prepared pan. Bake until a toothpick inserted in the center comes out clean, 50-60 minutes. Cool in pan for 10 minutes before removing to a wire rack to cool.

1 slice: 202 cal., 7g fat (3g sat. fat), 40mg chol., 206mg sod., 32g carb. (17g sugars, 1g fiber), 4g pro.

Main Dishes

When your family sits down to dinner, the main course is the main event! Savory and satisfying, an ideal entree is a dish that you can build a meal around and that will keep your loved ones coming back for more. The 35 recipes in this chapter include speedy weeknight dinners, make-ahead casseroles, Sunday roasts and more!

PORK CHOPS WITH APPLES & STUFFING

The heartwarming taste of apples with cinnamon is the perfect accompaniment to tender pork chops. This dish is always a winner with my family. Because it calls for only four ingredients, it's a main course that I can serve with little preparation.
—Joan Hamilton, Worcester, MA

Prep: 15 min. • **Bake:** 45 min.
Makes: 6 servings

- **6 boneless pork loin chops (6 oz. each)**
- **1 Tbsp. canola oil**
- **1 pkg. (6 oz.) crushed stuffing mix**
- **1 can (21 oz.) apple pie filling with cinnamon**
- **Minced fresh parsley, optional**

1. In a large skillet, brown the pork chops in oil over medium-high heat. Meanwhile, prepare the stuffing according to package directions. Spread pie filling into a greased 13x9-in. baking dish. Place the pork chops on top; spoon stuffing over chops.
2. Cover and bake at 350° for 35 minutes. Uncover; bake until a thermometer reads 145°, about 10 minutes longer. If desired, sprinkle with parsley.

1 serving: 527 cal., 21g fat (9g sat. fat), 102mg chol., 550mg sod., 48g carb. (15g sugars, 3g fiber), 36g pro.

TEXAS-STYLE BRISKET

This is the quintessential Texas-style brisket. Even my husband's six-generation Texas family is impressed by it! Grilling with wood chips takes a little extra effort, but I promise you'll be glad you did. Each bite tastes like heaven on a plate.
—Renee Morgan, Taylor, TX

Prep: 35 min. + chilling
Cook: 6 hours + standing • **Makes:** 20 servings

- **1 whole fresh beef brisket (12 to 14 lbs.)**
- **½ cup pepper**
- **¼ cup kosher salt**
- **Large disposable foil pan**
- **About 6 cups wood chips, preferably oak**

1. Trim fat on brisket to ½-in. thickness. Rub brisket with pepper and salt; place in a large disposable foil pan, fat side up. Refrigerate, covered, several hours or overnight. Meanwhile, soak wood chips in water.
2. To prepare grill for slow indirect cooking, adjust the grill vents so top vent is half open and bottom vent is open only a quarter of the way. Make 2 arrangements of 45 unlit coals on opposite sides of the grill, leaving the center of the grill open. Light 20 additional coals until ash-covered; distribute over the unlit coals. Sprinkle 2 cups soaked wood chips over lit coals.
3. Replace grill rack. Close grill and allow temperature in grill to reach 275°, about 15 minutes.
4. Place foil pan with brisket in center of grill rack; cover grill and cook 3 hours (do not open grill). Check temperature of grill periodically to maintain a temperature of 275° throughout cooking. Heat level may be adjusted by opening vents to raise temperature and closing vents partway to decrease temperature.
5. Add another 10 unlit coals and 1 cup wood chips to each side of the grill. Cook the brisket, covered, 3-4 hours longer or until fork-tender (a thermometer inserted in the brisket should read about 190°); add coals and wood chips as needed to maintain a grill temperature of 275°.
6. Remove brisket from grill. Cover tightly with foil; let stand 30-60 minutes. Cut the brisket across the grain into slices.

Note: If your charcoal grill does not have a built-in thermometer, the grill temperature may be checked by inserting the stem of a food thermometer through the top vent.

5 oz. cooked beef: 351 cal., 12g fat (4g sat. fat), 116mg chol., 1243mg sod., 2g carb. (0 sugars, 1g fiber), 56g pro.

ABERDEEN BEEF PIE

When set in the middle of the table, this hearty beef pie is the center of attention. With chunks of tender beef and tasty vegetables under a flaky pastry crust, this pure comfort food will welcome your family home.

—Peggy Goodrich, Enid, OK

Prep: 1½ hours • **Bake:** 35 min. + standing
Makes: 12 servings

- **¼ lb. sliced bacon, diced**
- **3 lbs. beef stew meat, cut into 1-in. cubes**
- **1 cup chopped onion**
- **1½ cups halved fresh baby carrots**
- **6 Tbsp. all-purpose flour**
- **1 cup beef broth**
- **1 Tbsp. Worcestershire sauce**
- **1 pkg. (10 oz.) frozen peas**
- **½ tsp. salt**
- **½ tsp. pepper**
- **1 sheet refrigerated pie crust**
- **1 large egg, lightly beaten, optional**

1. Preheat oven to 375°. In a Dutch oven, cook bacon over medium heat until crisp. Remove to paper towels to drain. Brown the beef in drippings in batches; drain and set beef aside. Add onion to the pan; saute until crisp-tender. Add the carrots, bacon and beef.
2. Meanwhile, in a small bowl, combine the flour, broth and Worcestershire sauce until smooth; add to beef mixture. Bring to a boil. Reduce heat; cover and simmer until meat is tender, 1-1½ hours. Stir in peas, salt and pepper. Transfer to an ungreased 11x7-in. baking dish.
3. On a lightly floured surface, roll out crust into a 12x8-in. rectangle. Cut slits in crust. Place over filling; trim and seal the edges. If desired, brush with beaten egg. Bake until the crust is golden and the filling is bubbly, 35-40 minutes. Let stand for 15 minutes before serving. Refrigerate any leftovers.

1 serving: 308 cal., 14g fat (6g sat. fat), 76mg chol., 389mg sod., 18g carb. (3g sugars, 2g fiber), 25g pro.

BOURBON-SPICED GLAZED HAM

This amazing bourbon-spiked ham makes a wonderful main course for a holiday feast. And the leftovers (if there are any!) make fantastic sandwiches.

—Karen Sublett-Young, Princeton, IN

Prep: 20 min. + marinating • **Bake:** 3 hours
Makes: 16 servings

- **1 cup packed brown sugar**
- **1 cup orange juice**
- **1 cup bourbon**
- **1½ tsp. ground cloves**
- **7 to 9 lbs. fully cooked bone-in ham**

1. In a large bowl, whisk the first 4 ingredients. Add the ham; turn to coat. Cover and refrigerate 8 hours or overnight, turning occasionally.
2. Preheat oven to 325°. Remove the ham from the marinade and place on a rack in a roasting pan; reserve remaining marinade, placing it in the refrigerator until ready to baste.
3. Using a sharp knife, score surface of ham with ¼-in.-deep cuts in a diamond pattern. Bake, covered, 2 hours.
4. Baste the ham with about half the reserved marinade. Bake, uncovered, for 1-1½ hours, basting the ham twice more during the first half hour, until a thermometer reads 140°.

4 oz. cooked ham: 182 cal., 5g fat (2g sat. fat), 87mg chol., 1043mg sod., 4g carb. (3g sugars, 0 fiber), 29g pro.

BAKED SIMPLE MEATBALL STROGANOFF

If you enjoy meatball subs, you'll love this tangy casserole that has all the rich flavor of the popular sandwiches with none of the mess. Italian bread is spread with a cream cheese mixture, then topped with meatballs, spaghetti sauce and cheese. Bravo!

—Gina Harris, Seneca, SC

Prep: 40 min. • **Bake:** 30 min.
Makes: 6 servings

- **⅓ cup chopped green onions**
- **¼ cup seasoned bread crumbs**
- **3 Tbsp. grated Parmesan cheese**
- **1 lb. ground beef**
- **1 loaf (1 lb.) Italian bread, cut into 1-in. slices**
- **1 pkg. (8 oz.) cream cheese, softened**
- **½ cup mayonnaise**
- **1 tsp. Italian seasoning**
- **¼ tsp. pepper**
- **2 cups shredded part-skim mozzarella cheese, divided**
- **3½ cups spaghetti sauce**
- **1 cup water**
- **2 garlic cloves, minced**

1. In a large bowl, combine the onions, bread crumbs and Parmesan cheese. Crumble beef over mixture and mix well. Shape into 1-in. balls; place on a greased rack in a shallow baking pan. Bake at 400° until no longer pink, 15-20 minutes.
2. Meanwhile, arrange the bread in a single layer in an ungreased 13x9-in. baking dish. Combine the cream cheese, mayonnaise, Italian seasoning and pepper; spread over the bread. Sprinkle with ½ cup mozzarella.
3. Combine the spaghetti sauce, water and garlic; add the meatballs. Pour over cheese mixture; sprinkle with remaining mozzarella. Bake, uncovered, at 350° until heated through, about 30 minutes.

1 serving: 641 cal., 39g fat (15g sat. fat), 94mg chol., 1234mg sod., 43g carb. (9g sugars, 3g fiber), 29g pro.

PORCINI MAC & CHEESE

This recipe was inspired by a mushroom mac and cheese I had at a local restaurant. I incorporated the fall flavor of a pumpkin ale, and it turned out better than the original.
—Laura Davis, Chincoteague, VA

Prep: 30 min. + standing • **Bake:** 35 min.
Makes: 6 servings

- **1 pkg. (1 oz.) dried porcini mushrooms**
- **1 cup boiling water**
- **1 pkg. (16 oz.) small pasta shells**
- **6 Tbsp. butter, cubed**
- **1 cup chopped baby portobello mushrooms**
- **1 shallot, finely chopped**
- **1 garlic clove, minced**
- **3 Tbsp. all-purpose flour**
- **2½ cups 2% milk**
- **½ cup pumpkin or amber ale**
- **2 cups shredded sharp white cheddar cheese**
- **1 cup shredded fontina cheese**
- **1 tsp. salt**
- **1 cup soft bread crumbs**

1. Preheat oven to 350°. In a small bowl, combine dried porcini mushrooms and boiling water; let stand 15-20 minutes or until the mushrooms are softened. Remove with a slotted spoon; rinse and finely chop. Discard the liquid. Set aside mushrooms. Cook the pasta according to package directions for al dente.
2. Meanwhile, in a Dutch oven, heat the butter over medium-high heat. Add the portobello mushrooms and shallot; cook and stir 2-3 minutes or until tender. Add garlic; cook 1 minute longer. Stir in flour until blended; gradually stir in milk and beer. Bring to a boil, stirring constantly; cook and stir 3-4 minutes or until slightly thickened. Stir in the cheeses, salt and reserved porcini mushrooms.
3. Drain pasta; add to the mushroom mixture and toss to combine. Transfer to a greased 13x9-in. baking dish. Top with bread crumbs. Bake, uncovered, 35-40 minutes or until golden brown.

1½ cups: 723 cal., 33g fat (19g sat. fat), 97mg chol., 968mg sod., 74g carb. (9g sugars, 4g fiber), 30g pro.

SKILLET-ROASTED LEMON CHICKEN WITH POTATOES

I have my students make this meal in our nutrition unit. It has a delicious lemon-herb flavor and is simple to make.
—Mindy Rottmund, Lancaster, PA

Prep: 20 min. • **Bake:** 25 min.
Makes: 4 servings

- **1 Tbsp. olive oil, divided**
- **1 medium lemon, thinly sliced**
- **4 garlic cloves, minced and divided**
- **¼ tsp. grated lemon zest**
- **½ tsp. salt, divided**
- **¼ tsp. pepper, divided**
- **8 boneless skinless chicken thighs (4 oz. each)**
- **¼ tsp. dried rosemary, crushed**
- **1 lb. fingerling potatoes, halved lengthwise**
- **8 cherry tomatoes**
- **Minced fresh parsley, optional**

1. Preheat oven to 450°. Grease a 10-in. cast-iron or other ovenproof skillet with 1 tsp. oil. Arrange lemon slices in a single layer in skillet.
2. Combine 1 tsp. oil, 2 minced garlic cloves, lemon zest, ¼ tsp. salt and ⅛ tsp. pepper; rub over the chicken. Place over lemon slices.
3. In a large bowl, combine rosemary and the remaining oil, garlic, salt and pepper. Add potatoes and tomatoes; toss to coat. Arrange over chicken. Bake, uncovered, for 25-30 minutes or until chicken is no longer pink and the potatoes are tender. If desired, sprinkle with minced parsley before serving.

2 chicken thighs with 4 oz. potatoes and 2 tomatoes: 446 cal., 20g fat (5g sat. fat), 151mg chol., 429mg sod., 18g carb. (2g sugars, 3g fiber), 45g pro.

CRAWFISH ETOUFFEE

I like to serve this Cajun sensation when I entertain. Etouffee is typically served with shellfish over rice and is similar to gumbo. This dish has its roots in New Orleans and the bayou country of Louisiana.
—Tamra Duncan, Lincoln, AR

Prep: 15 min. • **Cook:** 50 min.
Makes: 8 servings

- **½ cup butter, cubed**
- **½ cup plus 2 Tbsp. all-purpose flour**
- **1¼ cups chopped celery**
- **1 cup chopped green pepper**
- **½ cup chopped green onions**
- **1 can (14½ oz.) chicken broth**
- **1 cup water**
- **¼ cup minced fresh parsley**
- **1 Tbsp. tomato paste**
- **1 bay leaf**
- **½ tsp. salt**
- **¼ tsp. pepper**
- **¼ tsp. cayenne pepper**
- **2 lbs. frozen cooked crawfish tail meat, thawed**
- **Hot cooked rice**

1. In a large heavy skillet, melt butter; stir in flour. Cook and stir over low heat for about 20 minutes until mixture is a caramel-colored paste. Add the celery, pepper and onions; stir until coated. Add the broth, water, parsley, tomato paste, bay leaf, salt, pepper and cayenne pepper. Bring to a boil.

2. Reduce heat; cover and simmer for 30 minutes, stirring occasionally. Discard bay leaf. Add crawfish and heat through. Serve with rice.

1 cup: 250 cal., 13g fat (7g sat. fat), 187mg chol., 579mg sod., 10g carb. (1g sugars, 1g fiber), 22g pro.

PICK PENNE INSTEAD!

If you prefer, you can serve this with cooked penne pasta instead of rice—mix everything together or just serve the etouffee over the pasta. Also, you can add a bit more tomato paste for a deeper color and more cayenne pepper to raise the heat level.

SLOW-COOKER MEATBALL STEW

This recipe was a lifesaver when I worked full time and needed a dinner for us all to enjoy when we got home. And your young ones can help prepare it! They can chop, peel, mix and pour. It doesn't matter if the veggies are all different sizes—your children will still devour this fun, tasty stew.
—Kallee Krong-Mccreery, Escondido, CA

Prep: 20 min. • **Cook:** 6 hours
Makes: 8 servings

- **4 peeled medium potatoes, cut into ½-in. cubes**
- **4 medium carrots, cut into ½-in. cubes**
- **2 celery ribs, cut into ½-in. cubes**
- **1 medium onion, diced**
- **¼ cup frozen corn**
- **1 pkg. (28 to 32 oz.) frozen fully cooked home-style meatballs**
- **1½ cups ketchup**
- **1½ cups water**
- **1 Tbsp. white vinegar**
- **1 tsp. dried basil**
- **Optional: Biscuits or dinner rolls**

In a 5-qt. slow cooker, combine potatoes, carrots, celery, onion, corn and meatballs. In a bowl, mix ketchup, water, vinegar and basil; pour over meatballs. Cook, covered, on low for 6-8 hours, until meatballs are cooked through. If desired, serve with biscuits or dinner rolls.

1 cup: 449 cal., 26g fat (12g sat. fat), 41mg chol., 1322mg sod., 40g carb. (17g sugars, 4g fiber), 16g pro.

CHICKEN POTPIE GALETTE WITH CHEDDAR-THYME CRUST

This gorgeous galette takes traditional chicken potpie and gives it an open-faced spin. The rich filling and flaky cheddar-flecked crust makes it taste so homey.
—Elisabeth Larsen, Pleasant Grove, UT

Prep: 45 min. + chilling
Bake: 30 min. + cooling
Makes: 8 servings

- 1¼ **cups all-purpose flour**
- ½ **cup shredded sharp cheddar cheese**
- 2 **Tbsp. minced fresh thyme**
- ¼ **tsp. salt**
- ½ **cup cold butter, cubed**
- ¼ **cup ice water**

FILLING

- 3 **Tbsp. butter**
- 2 **large carrots, sliced**
- 1 **celery rib, diced**
- 1 **small onion, diced**
- 8 **oz. sliced fresh mushrooms**
- 3 **cups julienned Swiss chard**
- 3 **garlic cloves, minced**
- 1 **cup chicken broth**
- 3 **Tbsp. all-purpose flour**
- ½ **tsp. salt**
- ¼ **tsp. pepper**
- 2 **cups shredded cooked chicken**
- ½ **tsp. minced fresh oregano**
- 2 **Tbsp. minced fresh parsley**

1. Combine flour, cheese, thyme and salt; cut in butter until crumbly. Gradually add ice water, tossing with a fork until dough holds together when pressed. Shape into a disk; refrigerate 1 hour.
2. For filling, melt the butter in a large saucepan over medium-high heat. Add carrots, celery and onion; cook and stir until slightly softened, 5-7 minutes. Add the mushrooms; cook 3 minutes longer. Add Swiss chard and garlic; cook until chard is wilted, 2-3 minutes.
3. Whisk together broth, flour, salt and pepper; slowly pour over the vegetables, stirring constantly. Cook until thickened, 2-3 minutes. Stir in chicken and oregano.
4. Preheat oven to 400°. On a floured sheet of parchment, roll dough into a 12-in. circle. Transfer to a baking sheet. Spoon filling over crust to within 2 in. of edge. Fold crust edge over filling, pleating as you go, leaving the center uncovered. Bake on a lower oven rack until the crust is golden brown and the filling is bubbly, 30-35 minutes. Cool 15 minutes before slicing. Sprinkle with parsley.

1 piece: 342 cal., 21g fat (12g sat. fat), 81mg chol., 594mg sod., 22g carb. (2g sugars, 2g fiber), 16g pro.

CHOOSE YOUR TOPPINGS

Fill this potpie with any meat/cheese/veggie combo you like. It would be just as amazing, for example, with sausage, golden beets and kale. The filling may start to bubble a bit toward the end of the bake time, so be sure to use parchment or a silicone mat.

CAST-IRON FAVORITE PIZZA

Cast-iron skillets are the perfect vessel for a crisp, deep-dish pizza without needing any extra cookware. Our team developed this meaty pizza that is fabulous any time of year.
—Taste of Home *Test Kitchen*

Prep: 30 min. + rising • **Bake:** 30 min.
Makes: 8 slices

- **1 pkg. (¼ oz.) active dry yeast**
- **½ cup warm water (110° to 115°)**
- **½ cup butter, melted and cooled**
- **3 large eggs**
- **¼ cup grated Parmesan cheese**
- **1 tsp. salt**
- **3 to 3½ cups bread flour**
- **2 Tbsp. yellow cornmeal**
- **½ lb. ground beef**
- **½ lb. bulk Italian sausage**
- **1 small onion, chopped**
- **1 can (8 oz.) pizza sauce**
- **1 jar (4½ oz.) sliced mushrooms, drained**
- **1 pkg. (3 oz.) sliced pepperoni**
- **½ lb. deli ham, cubed**
- **½ cup chopped pitted green olives**
- **1 can (4¼ oz.) chopped ripe olives, drained**
- **1½ cups shredded part-skim mozzarella cheese**
- **½ cup shredded Parmesan cheese**
- **Additional pizza sauce**

1. In a small bowl, dissolve yeast in warm water. In a large bowl, combine butter, eggs, grated Parmesan, salt, yeast mixture and 2 cups flour; beat on medium speed until smooth. Stir in enough remaining flour to form a soft dough.
2. Turn the dough onto a floured surface; knead until smooth and elastic, 6-8 minutes. Place in a greased bowl, turning once to grease top. Cover and let rise in a warm place until doubled, about 1 hour.
3. Punch dough down; let rest for 5 minutes. Grease a 12-in. deep-dish cast-iron skillet or other ovenproof skillet; sprinkle with cornmeal. Press dough into pan; build up edges slightly.
4. Preheat oven to 400°. In a large skillet, cook the beef, sausage and onion over medium heat until meat is no longer pink and onion is tender, breaking meat into crumbles, 8-10 minutes; drain. Spread pizza sauce over dough to within 1 in. of edges; sprinkle with meat mixture. Top with mushrooms, pepperoni, ham, olives, mozzarella and shredded Parmesan.
5. Bake until crust is golden brown and cheese is melted, 30-35 minutes. Serve with additional pizza sauce.

1 slice: 712 cal., 42g fat (19g sat. fat), 184mg chol., 1865mg sod., 48g carb. (3g sugars, 3g fiber), 36g pro.

BBQ COUNTRY-STYLE RIBS

Quick to prep for the slow cooker, this dinner is terrific with a salad and a fresh side. My family practically cheers whenever I make it!
—Cheryl Mann, Winside, NE

Prep: 10 min. • **Cook:** 6 hours
Makes: 6 servings

- **3 lbs. boneless country-style pork ribs**
- **½ tsp. salt**
- **½ tsp. pepper**
- **1 large onion, cut into ½-in. rings**
- **1 bottle (18 oz.) hickory smoke-flavored barbecue sauce**
- **⅓ cup maple syrup**
- **¼ cup spicy brown mustard**
- **Thinly sliced green onions, optional**

1. Sprinkle ribs with salt and pepper. Place the onion in a 6-qt. slow cooker. Top with ribs. In a large bowl, combine the barbecue sauce, maple syrup and mustard; pour over ribs. Cook, covered, on low 6-8 hours or until meat is tender.
2. Transfer the meat to a serving platter; keep warm. Pour cooking liquid into a large saucepan; bring to a boil. Reduce heat; simmer, uncovered, 10 minutes or until sauce is thickened. Serve with pork. If desired, sprinkle with onions.

6 oz. cooked pork with ⅓ cup sauce: 598 cal., 21g fat (8g sat. fat), 131mg chol., 1443mg sod., 56g carb. (46g sugars, 1g fiber), 41g pro.

CHICKEN & CHEDDAR BISCUIT CASSEROLE

I always get rave reviews when I bring this casserole to my son's Cub Scouts meetings. It's a delightful comfort meal after a long day.
—Sarah Phillips, East Lansing, MI

Prep: 40 min. • **Bake:** 35 min.
Makes: 12 servings

- **⅓ cup butter, cubed**
- **1 large onion, chopped**
- **2 celery ribs, chopped**
- **2 medium carrots, chopped**
- **2 garlic cloves, minced**
- **½ cup all-purpose flour**
- **1 tsp. salt**
- **½ tsp. pepper**
- **4 cups chicken broth or stock**
- **5 cups cubed cooked chicken**
- **3 cups biscuit/baking mix**
- **¾ cup 2% milk**
- **1 cup shredded cheddar cheese**
- **1 cup roasted sweet red peppers, drained and chopped**

1. Preheat the oven to 425°. In a 6-qt. stockpot, heat butter over medium-high heat. Add onion, celery and carrots; cook and stir 3-5 minutes or until tender. Add garlic; cook and stir 1 minute longer. Stir in flour, salt and pepper until blended; gradually whisk in broth. Bring to a boil, stirring constantly; cook and stir over medium heat 4-6 minutes or until thickened. Add chicken.
2. Transfer to a greased 13x9-in. baking dish. Bake, uncovered, 20 minutes.
3. Meanwhile, in a large bowl, combine biscuit mix and milk just until moistened. Turn onto a lightly floured surface; knead gently 8-10 times. Roll the dough into a 12x8-in. rectangle. Sprinkle with cheese and peppers. Roll up jelly-roll style, starting with a long side; pinch seam to seal. Cut crosswise into 1-in.-thick slices.
4. Place slices on top of the hot chicken mixture. Bake, uncovered, 15-20 minutes or until biscuits are golden brown.

Freeze option: Cool baked casserole; cover and freeze. To use, partially thaw in refrigerator overnight. Remove from the refrigerator 30 minutes before baking. Preheat oven to 425°. Bake casserole, covered, 40 minutes or until heated through and a thermometer inserted in center reads 165°.

1 serving: 357 cal., 16g fat (7g sat. fat), 78mg chol., 1081mg sod., 29g carb. (4g sugars, 2g fiber), 23g pro.

CHICKEN & SWISS CASSEROLE

It's nice to have an alternative to traditional baked ham on Easter. This comforting casserole is always a crowd pleaser. Using rotisserie chicken from the deli makes prep simple.

—Christina Petri, Alexandria, MN

Prep: 30 min. • **Bake:** 10 min.
Makes: 8 servings

- **5½ cups uncooked egg noodles (about ½ lb.)**
- **3 Tbsp. olive oil**
- **3 shallots, chopped**
- **3 small garlic cloves, minced**
- **⅓ cup all-purpose flour**
- **2 cups chicken broth**
- **¾ cup 2% milk**
- **1½ tsp. dried thyme**
- **¾ tsp. grated lemon zest**
- **½ tsp. salt**
- **¼ tsp. ground nutmeg**
- **¼ tsp. pepper**
- **5 cups cubed rotisserie chicken**
- **1½ cups frozen peas**
- **2 cups shredded Swiss cheese**
- **¾ cup dry bread crumbs**
- **2 Tbsp. butter, melted**

1. Preheat oven to 350°. Cook noodles according to package directions; drain. In a large skillet, heat oil over medium heat. Add shallots and garlic; cook and stir 45 seconds. Stir in flour; cook and stir 1 minute. Add broth, milk, thyme, lemon zest, salt, nutmeg and pepper. Stir in chicken and peas; heat through. Stir in noodles and cheese.
2. Transfer to a greased 13x9-in. baking dish. In a small bowl, mix bread crumbs and butter; sprinkle over top. Bake for 8-10 minutes or until top is browned.

1¼ cups: 551 cal., 25g fat (10g sat. fat), 136mg chol., 661mg sod., 38g carb. (4g sugars, 3g fiber), 41g pro.

HOMEMADE APPLE CIDER BEEF STEW

It's especially nice to use this recipe in fall when the weather gets crisp and Nebraska's apple orchards start selling fresh apple cider. This entree's subtle sweetness is a welcome change from other savory stews. Enjoy it with biscuits and slices of apple and cheddar cheese.

—Joyce Glaesemann, Lincoln, NE

Prep: 30 min. • **Cook:** 1¾ hours
Makes: 8 servings

- **2 lbs. beef stew meat, cut into 1-in. cubes**
- **2 Tbsp. canola oil**
- **3 cups apple cider or juice**
- **1 can (14½ oz.) reduced-sodium beef broth**
- **2 Tbsp. cider vinegar**
- **1½ tsp. salt**
- **¼ to ½ tsp. dried thyme**
- **¼ tsp. pepper**
- **3 medium potatoes, peeled and cubed**
- **4 medium carrots, cut into ¾-in. pieces**
- **3 celery ribs, cut into ¾-in. pieces**
- **2 medium onions, cut into wedges**
- **¼ cup all-purpose flour**
- **¼ cup water**
- **Fresh thyme sprigs, optional**

1. In a Dutch oven, brown the beef on all sides in oil over medium-high heat; drain. Add the cider, broth, vinegar, salt, thyme and pepper; bring to a boil. Reduce heat; cover and simmer for 1¼ hours.
2. Add the potatoes, carrots, celery and onions; return to a boil. Reduce the heat; cover and simmer for 30-35 minutes or until beef and vegetables are tender.
3. Combine flour and water until smooth; stir into stew. Bring to a boil; cook and stir for 2 minutes or until thickened. If desired, serve with fresh thyme.

1 cup: 330 cal., 12g fat (3g sat. fat), 72mg chol., 628mg sod., 31g carb. (14g sugars, 2g fiber), 24g pro. **Diabetic exchanges:** 3 lean meat, 1½ starch, 1 vegetable.

CONTEST-WINNING EGGPLANT PARMESAN

Because my recipe calls for baking the eggplant instead of frying it, it is much healthier than other parmesans! The prep time is a little longer than for some recipes, but the Italian flavors and rustic elegance are well worth it.

—Laci Hooten, McKinney, TX

Prep: 40 min. • **Bake:** 25 min.
Makes: 8 servings

- **3 large eggs, beaten**
- **2½ cups panko bread crumbs**
- **3 medium eggplants, cut into ¼-in. slices**
- **2 jars (4½ oz. each) sliced mushrooms, drained**
- **½ tsp dried basil**
- **⅛ tsp. dried oregano**
- **2 cups shredded part-skim mozzarella cheese**
- **½ cup grated Parmesan cheese**
- **1 jar (28 oz.) spaghetti sauce**

1. Preheat oven to 350°. Place eggs and bread crumbs in separate shallow bowls. Dip eggplant slices in the eggs, then coat in crumbs. Place on baking sheets coated with cooking spray. Bake until tender and golden brown, 15-20 minutes; turn once.
2. In a small bowl, combine the sliced mushrooms, basil and oregano. In another small bowl, combine the mozzarella and Parmesan cheeses.
3. Spread ½ cup sauce into a 13x9-in. baking dish coated with cooking spray. Layer with a third of the mushroom mixture, a third of the eggplant, ¾ cup sauce and a third of the cheese mixture. Repeat layers twice.
4. Bake, uncovered, until heated through and cheese is melted, 25-30 minutes.

1 serving: 305 cal., 12g fat (5g sat. fat), 102mg chol., 912mg sod., 32g carb. (12g sugars, 9g fiber), 18g pro.

Contest
Winner

ROADSIDE DINER CHEESEBURGER QUICHE

Here is an unforgettable quiche that tastes just like its burger counterpart. Easy and appealing, it's perfect for guests and fun for the whole family.
—Barbara J. Miller, Oakdale, MN

Prep: 20 min. • **Bake:** 50 min. + standing
Makes: 8 servings

- **1 sheet refrigerated pie crust**
- **¾ lb. ground beef**
- **2 plum tomatoes, seeded and chopped**
- **1 medium onion, chopped**
- **½ cup dill pickle relish**
- **½ cup crumbled cooked bacon**
- **5 large eggs**
- **1 cup heavy whipping cream**
- **½ cup 2% milk**
- **2 tsp. prepared mustard**
- **1 tsp. hot pepper sauce**
- **½ tsp. salt**
- **¼ tsp. pepper**
- **1½ cups shredded cheddar cheese**
- **½ cup shredded Parmesan cheese**
- **Optional: Mayonnaise, additional pickle relish, crumbled cooked bacon, chopped onion and chopped tomato**

1. Preheat oven to 375°. Unroll crust into a 9-in. deep-dish pie plate; flute edges and set aside. In a large skillet, cook the beef over medium heat until no longer pink, breaking into crumbles; drain. Stir in the tomatoes, onion, relish and bacon. Transfer to prepared crust.
2. In a large bowl, whisk the eggs, cream, milk, mustard, pepper sauce, salt and pepper. Pour over the beef mixture. Sprinkle with cheeses.
3. Bake until a knife inserted in the center comes out clean, 50-60 minutes. If necessary, cover the edges with foil during the last 15 minutes to prevent overbrowning. Let stand for 10 minutes before cutting. Garnish with optional ingredients as desired.

1 piece: 502 cal., 35g fat (19g sat. fat), 236mg chol., 954mg sod., 24g carb. (8g sugars, 1g fiber), 23g pro.

RHUBARB-APRICOT BARBECUED CHICKEN

Springtime brings back memories of the rhubarb that grew beside my childhood home. When I found rhubarb in the store, I created this recipe for my family.
—Laurie Hudson, Westville, FL

Prep: 30 min. • **Grill:** 30 min.
Makes: 6 servings

- **1 Tbsp. olive oil**
- **1 cup finely chopped sweet onion**
- **1 garlic clove, minced**
- **2 cups chopped fresh or frozen rhubarb**
- **¾ cup ketchup**
- **⅔ cup water**
- **⅓ cup apricot preserves**
- **¼ cup cider vinegar**
- **¼ cup molasses**
- **1 Tbsp. honey Dijon mustard**
- **2 tsp. finely chopped chipotle pepper in adobo sauce**
- **5 tsp. barbecue seasoning, divided**
- **1¼ tsp. salt, divided**
- **¾ tsp. pepper, divided**
- **12 chicken drumsticks (about 4 lbs.)**

1. In a large saucepan, heat the oil over medium heat. Add onion; cook and stir until tender, 4-6 minutes. Add garlic; cook 1 minute longer. Stir in rhubarb, ketchup, water, preserves, vinegar, molasses, mustard, chipotle pepper, 1 tsp. barbecue seasoning, ¼ tsp. salt and ¼ tsp. pepper. Bring to a boil. Reduce heat; simmer, uncovered, until rhubarb is tender, 8-10 minutes. Puree rhubarb mixture using an immersion blender, or cool slightly and puree in a blender. Reserve 2 cups sauce for serving.
2. Meanwhile, in a small bowl, mix the remaining 4 tsp. barbecue seasoning, 1 tsp. salt and ½ tsp. pepper; sprinkle over the chicken. On a lightly oiled grill rack, grill chicken, covered, over indirect medium heat 15 minutes. Turn; grill until a thermometer reads 170°-175°, 15-20 minutes longer, brushing meat occasionally with remaining sauce. Serve with reserved sauce.

2 drumsticks with ⅓ cup sauce: 469 cal., 19g fat (5g sat. fat), 126mg chol., 1801mg sod., 35g carb. (28g sugars, 1g fiber), 39g pro.

GERMAN BRATWURST WITH SAUERKRAUT & APPLES

I created this Old World favorite based on a dish I had during my travels. The flavorful entree is perfect for weeknights or special occasions. I like to serve it with pasta.
—Gerald Hetrick, Erie, PA

Prep: 15 min. • **Cook:** 6 hours
Makes: 15 servings

- **4 lbs. uncooked bratwurst links**
- **3 bottles (12 oz. each) German-style beer or 4½ cups reduced-sodium chicken broth**
- **1 jar (32 oz.) sauerkraut, rinsed and well drained**
- **4 medium Granny Smith apples (about 1¼ lbs.), cut into wedges**
- **1 medium onion, halved and thinly sliced**
- **1½ tsp. caraway seeds**
- **¼ tsp. pepper**

1. In batches, in a large nonstick skillet, brown bratwursts over medium-high heat. Transfer to a 7-qt. slow cooker. Add the remaining ingredients.
2. Cook, covered, on low 6-8 hours or until a thermometer inserted in the sausage reads at least 160°.

1 serving: 445 cal., 35g fat (12g sat. fat), 90mg chol., 1424mg sod., 13g carb. (6g sugars, 3g fiber), 17g pro.

OKTOBERFEST CASSEROLE

In northeast Ohio, we love German flavors. This delicious casserole is a trifecta mashup of my favorite dishes. It combines the flavors of classic cheesy hash brown casserole with bratwursts and sauerkraut, pretzels and beer cheese. It takes less than 10 minutes to mix and takes only one bowl. It's sure to please everyone any time of the year.

—Sarah Markley, Ashland, OH

Prep: 15 min. • **Bake:** 1½ hours
Makes: 12 servings

- **2 cans (10½ oz. each) condensed cheddar cheese soup, undiluted**
- **1 cup beer or chicken broth**
- **1 cup sour cream**
- **1 pkg. (32 oz.) frozen cubed hash brown potatoes, thawed**
- **1 pkg. (14 oz.) fully cooked bratwurst links, chopped**
- **1 can (14 oz.) sauerkraut, rinsed and well drained**
- **2 cups shredded cheddar cheese**
- **2 cups pretzel pieces**

1. Preheat oven to 350°. In a large bowl, whisk soup, beer and sour cream until combined. Stir in potatoes, chopped bratwurst, sauerkraut and cheese. Transfer to a greased 13x9-in. baking dish. Cover and bake for 45 minutes.
2. Uncover; bake 30 minutes longer. Top with the pretzel pieces. Bake until bubbly and heated through, 12-15 minutes longer. Let stand 10 minutes before serving.

1 serving: 356 cal., 21g fat (10g sat. fat), 49mg chol., 884mg sod., 29g carb. (4g sugars, 3g fiber), 13g pro.

WHICH BEER? WHICH BRAT?

Choose a beer you enjoy drinking to use in this recipe. Substitute any flavor of brats or pretzel pieces to add more flavor.

SUNDAY BEST STUFFED PORK CHOPS

When we are having our most-loved stuffed pork chops for Sunday dinner, we pass around potatoes, a green salad and steamed broccoli on the side.
—Lorraine Smith, Carpenter, WY

Prep: 30 min. • **Cook:** 35 min.
Makes: 8 servings

- **1 pkg. (6 oz.) pork stuffing mix**
- **¾ tsp. seasoned salt**
- **½ tsp. garlic powder**
- **½ tsp. coarsely ground pepper**
- **1 can (10¾ oz.) condensed cream of mushroom soup, undiluted**
- **¼ cup 2% milk**
- **1 cup shredded smoked Gouda cheese**
- **1 small apple, finely chopped**
- **½ cup chopped pecans, toasted**
- **8 boneless pork loin chops (6 oz. each)**
- **2 Tbsp. olive oil, divided**
- **Optional: Minced fresh chives or parsley**

1. Prepare stuffing according to package directions; cool slightly. In a small bowl, mix seasonings. In another bowl, whisk soup and milk until blended.
2. Stir cheese, apple and pecans into the cooled stuffing. Cut a pocket horizontally in the thickest part of each chop. Fill with stuffing mixture. Brush the outsides of the chops with 1 Tbsp. oil; sprinkle with seasoning mixture.
3. In a Dutch oven, heat the remaining 1 Tbsp. oil over medium heat. Stand pork chops in pan, stuffing side up, spaced evenly. Pour soup mixture around chops; bring to a boil. Reduce the heat; simmer, covered, 35-40 minutes or until pork is no longer pink and a thermometer inserted in stuffing reads 165°.
4. Remove from the heat; let stand for 5 minutes. Transfer chops to a serving dish. Spoon sauce over top. If desired, sprinkle with chives or parsley.

1 stuffed pork chop with 3 Tbsp. sauce: 532 cal., 30g fat (11g sat. fat), 116mg chol., 973mg sod., 22g carb. (5g sugars, 2g fiber), 40g pro.

GARLIC CHICKEN WITH MAPLE-CHIPOTLE GLAZE

This herby one-dish garlic chicken dinner is an updated version of an old standby recipe. The smoky flavors pair well with the savory chicken and the hint of sweetness from the maple syrup.
—Taste of Home *Test Kitchen*

Prep: 35 min. • **Bake:** 45 min.
Makes: 4 servings

- **4 chicken leg quarters**
- **1¼ tsp. kosher salt, divided**
- **½ tsp. coarsely ground pepper**
- **1 cup all-purpose flour**
- **½ tsp. dried rosemary, crushed**
- **½ tsp. dried thyme**
- **½ tsp. rubbed sage**
- **½ tsp. dried marjoram**
- **¼ tsp. dried parsley flakes**
- **1 large egg, lightly beaten**
- **½ cup 2% milk**
- **1 Tbsp. lemon juice**
- **½ cup plus 1 Tbsp. canola oil, divided**
- **½ lb. red potatoes, halved**
- **1 medium onion, halved and sliced**
- **20 garlic cloves, peeled**

GLAZE

- **⅓ cup maple syrup**
- **2 tsp. finely chopped chipotle peppers in adobo sauce**
- **1 tsp. Dijon mustard**
- **¾ tsp. kosher salt**
- **½ tsp. chili powder**

1. With a sharp knife, cut leg quarters at the joints. Sprinkle chicken with ¾ tsp. salt and pepper.
2. In a large bowl, combine the flour and herbs. In a shallow bowl, combine egg, milk and lemon juice. Add chicken pieces, 1 at a time, to flour mixture. Toss to coat. Dip chicken in egg mixture; coat again with flour mixture.
3. In a 12-in. cast-iron or other ovenproof skillet, heat ½ cup oil. Fry the chicken, a few pieces at a time, until golden brown, 5-6 minutes. Remove chicken and keep warm; drain drippings.
4. In the same skillet, cook the potatoes in the remaining oil until slightly tender, 8-10 minutes. Add onion and remaining salt; cook until the onion is tender, 5-6 minutes longer. Stir in garlic; top with chicken.
5. Bake, uncovered, at 375° until a thermometer reads 170°-175° and potatoes are tender, 45-50 minutes.
6. In a small bowl, combine the glaze ingredients. Brush over chicken just before serving.

1 chicken quarter with about ½ cup potato mixture: 834 cal., 55g fat (8g sat. fat), 142mg chol., 1112mg sod., 49g carb. (20g sugars, 3g fiber), 36g pro.

SPINACH & SHRIMP FRA DIAVOLO

This quick dish is spicy, garlicky, saucy and loaded with delicious shrimp. Plus, with the addition of spinach, you're also getting a serving of veggies. When you need a lovely low-fat weeknight meal that is easy to pull together, this is it. You can substitute arugula or kale for the spinach if you'd like.
—Julie Peterson, Crofton, MD

Takes: 30 min. • **Makes:** 4 servings

- 2 **Tbsp. olive oil**
- 1 **medium onion, chopped**
- 5 **garlic cloves, minced**
- ½ **to 1 tsp. crushed red pepper flakes**
- 1 **cup dry white wine**
- 1 **can (14½ oz.) diced tomatoes, undrained**
- 1 **can (8 oz.) tomato sauce**
- 3 **Tbsp. minced fresh basil or 1 Tbsp. dried basil**
- 1 **tsp. dried oregano**
- ¼ **tsp. salt**
- ¼ **tsp. pepper**
- 1 **lb. uncooked shrimp (26-30 per lb.), peeled and deveined**
- 3 **cups finely chopped fresh spinach**
- **Grated Parmesan cheese, optional**

1. In a large skillet, heat oil over medium-high heat. Add onion; cook and stir until tender, 5-7 minutes.
2. Add garlic and pepper flakes; cook 1 minute longer. Stir in wine. Bring to a boil; cook until liquid is reduced by half. Stir in the tomatoes, tomato sauce and seasonings. Cook and stir until sauce is slightly thickened, about 10 minutes.
3. Add shrimp and spinach; cook and stir until the shrimp turn pink and the spinach is wilted, 3-5 minutes. If desired, sprinkle with cheese.
1½ cups: 235 cal., 9g fat (1g sat. fat), 138mg chol., 727mg sod., 14g carb. (6g sugars, 4g fiber), 22g pro. **Diabetic exchanges:** 3 lean meat, 2 vegetable, 1½ fat.

ADD A STARCH

Serve this saucy dish with pasta, rice or quinoa or with Italian bread for dipping.

TUNA NOODLE CASSEROLE

Families are sure to crave the creamy texture and comforting taste of this traditional tuna casserole that goes together in a jiffy. I serve it with a green salad and warm rolls for a nutritious supper.
—Ruby Wells, Cynthiana, KY

Prep: 20 min. • **Bake:** 30 min.
Makes: 4 servings

- 1 **can (10¾ oz.) reduced-fat reduced-sodium condensed cream of celery soup, undiluted**
- ½ **cup fat-free milk**
- 2 **cups yolk-free noodles, cooked**
- 1 **cup frozen peas, thawed**
- 1 **can (5 oz.) light water-packed tuna, drained and flaked**
- 1 **jar (2 oz.) diced pimientos, drained**
- 2 **Tbsp. dry bread crumbs**
- 1 **Tbsp. butter, melted**

1. In a large bowl, combine soup and milk until smooth. Add the noodles, peas, tuna and pimientos; mix well.
2. Pour into a 1½-qt. baking dish coated with cooking spray. Bake, uncovered, at 400° for 25 minutes. Toss bread crumbs and butter; sprinkle over the top. Bake 5 minutes longer or until golden brown.
1 cup: 238 cal., 5g fat (2g sat. fat), 27mg chol., 475mg sod., 32g carb. (6g sugars, 4g fiber), 15g pro. **Diabetic exchanges:** 2 starch, 2 lean meat, ½ fat.

SLOW-COOKED SHORT RIBS WITH SALT-SKIN POTATOES

I love short ribs, and they are best prepared low and slow in a flavorful sauce. I also adore salt potatoes, so I combined the two with an Italian twist. My family was wowed!

—Devon Delaney, Westport, CT

Prep: 40 min. • **Cook:** 6 hours
Makes: 8 servings

- **6 thick slices pancetta or thick-sliced bacon, chopped**
- **6 lbs. bone-in beef short ribs**
- **1 tsp. plus 1 cup kosher salt, divided**
- **1 tsp. pepper**
- **1 Tbsp. olive oil**
- **3 medium carrots, chopped**
- **1 medium red onion, chopped**
- **1 cup beef broth**
- **1 cup dry red wine**
- **¼ cup honey**
- **¼ cup balsamic vinegar**
- **1 Tbsp. minced fresh thyme or 1 tsp. dried thyme**
- **2 tsp. minced fresh oregano or ¾ tsp. dried oregano**
- **2 garlic cloves, minced**
- **2 lbs. small red potatoes**
- **4 tsp. cornstarch**
- **3 Tbsp. cold water**

1. In a large skillet, cook the pancetta over medium heat until crisp, stirring occasionally. Remove with a slotted spoon; drain on paper towels.
2. Meanwhile, sprinkle ribs with 1 tsp. salt and pepper. In another large skillet, heat the oil over medium-high heat. In batches, brown ribs on all sides; transfer to a 4- or 5-qt. slow cooker.
3. To same skillet, add carrots and onion; cook and stir over medium heat until crisp-tender, 2-4 minutes. Add the broth, wine, honey and vinegar, stirring to loosen browned bits from pan. Transfer to slow cooker; add pancetta, herbs and garlic.
4. Cook, covered, on low 6-8 hours or until meat is tender. In the last hour of cooking, place potatoes in a 6-qt. stockpot and cover with water. Add remaining salt. Cover and bring to a boil over medium-high heat; stir to dissolve salt. Cook 15-30 minutes or until tender. Drain well.
5. Remove the ribs to a serving platter; keep warm. Strain cooking juices into a small saucepan; skim fat. Add vegetables and pancetta to platter. Bring juices to a boil. In a small bowl, mix cornstarch and water until smooth; stir into cooking juices. Return to a boil; cook and stir 1-2 minutes or until thickened. Serve with ribs and vegetables.

1 serving: 507 cal., 24g fat (9g sat. fat), 96mg chol., 859mg sod., 35g carb. (14g sugars, 3g fiber), 33g pro.

CITRUS-HERB ROAST CHICKEN

This dish is one of my all-time favorites. The tasty, juicy chicken combines with the aromas of spring in fresh herbs, lemon and onions to form the perfect one-pot meal. I make the gravy right in the pan.

—Megan Fordyce, Fairchance, PA

Prep: 25 min. • **Bake:** 2 hours + standing
Makes: 8 servings

- **6 garlic cloves**
- **1 roasting chicken (6 to 7 lbs.)**
- **3 lbs. baby red potatoes, halved**
- **6 medium carrots, halved lengthwise and cut into 1-in. pieces**
- **4 fresh thyme sprigs**
- **4 fresh dill sprigs**
- **2 fresh rosemary sprigs**
- **1 medium lemon**
- **1 small navel orange**
- **1 tsp. salt**
- **½ tsp. pepper**
- **3 cups chicken broth, warmed**
- **6 green onions, cut into 2-in. pieces**

1. Preheat oven to 350°. Peel and cut garlic into quarters. Place the chicken on a cutting board. Tuck wings under chicken. With a sharp paring knife, cut 24 small slits in the breasts, drumsticks and thighs. Insert garlic in slits. Tie the drumsticks together.
2. Place potatoes and carrots in a shallow roasting pan; top with herbs. Place the chicken, breast side up, over vegetables and herbs. Cut lemon and orange in half; gently squeeze juices over chicken and vegetables. Place squeezed fruits inside chicken cavity. Sprinkle chicken with salt and pepper. Pour broth around chicken.
3. Roast until a thermometer inserted in thickest part of thigh reads 170°-175°, 2-2½ hours, sprinkling green onions over the vegetables during the last 20 minutes. (Cover loosely with foil if chicken browns too quickly.)
4. Remove chicken from oven; tent with foil. Let stand 15 minutes before carving. Discard herbs. If desired, skim fat and thicken pan drippings for gravy. Serve gravy with chicken and vegetables.

7 oz. cooked chicken with 1¼ cups vegetables: 561 cal., 24g fat (7g sat. fat), 136mg chol., 826mg sod., 39g carb. (5g sugars, 5g fiber), 47g pro.

CASSOULET FOR TODAY

Cassoulet is traditionally cooked for hours, but this version of the rustic French classic offers the same homey taste in less time. It's easy on the wallet, too.

—Virginia Anthony, Jacksonville, FL

Prep: 45 min. • **Bake:** 50 min.
Makes: 6 servings

- **6 boneless skinless chicken thighs (about 1½ lbs.)**
- **¼ tsp. salt**
- **¼ tsp. coarsely ground pepper**
- **3 tsp. olive oil, divided**
- **1 large onion, chopped**
- **1 garlic clove, minced**
- **½ cup white wine or chicken broth**
- **1 can (14½ oz.) diced tomatoes, drained**
- **1 bay leaf**
- **1 tsp. minced fresh rosemary or ¼ tsp. dried rosemary, crushed**
- **1 tsp. minced fresh thyme or ¼ tsp. dried thyme**
- **2 cans (15 oz. each) cannellini beans, rinsed and drained**
- **¼ lb. smoked turkey kielbasa, chopped**
- **3 bacon strips, cooked and crumbled**

TOPPING

- **½ cup soft whole wheat bread crumbs**
- **¼ cup minced fresh parsley**
- **1 garlic clove, minced**

1. Preheat the oven to 325°. Sprinkle the chicken with salt and pepper. In a broiler-safe Dutch oven, heat 2 tsp. oil over medium heat; brown chicken on both sides. Remove from pan.
2. In same pan, saute onion in remaining 1 tsp. oil over medium heat until crisp-tender. Add garlic; cook 1 minute. Add wine; bring to a boil, stirring to loosen browned bits from pan. Add tomatoes, herbs and chicken; return to a boil.
3. Transfer to oven; bake, covered, 30 minutes. Stir in beans and kielbasa; bake, covered, until chicken is tender, 20-25 minutes.
4. Remove from oven; preheat broiler. Discard bay leaf; stir in bacon. Toss bread crumbs with parsley and garlic; sprinkle over the top. Place in oven so surface of cassoulet is 4-5 in. from heat; broil until crumbs are golden brown, 2-3 minutes.

1 serving: 394 cal., 14g fat (4g sat. fat), 91mg chol., 736mg sod., 29g carb. (4g sugars, 8g fiber), 33g pro. **Diabetic exchanges:** 4 lean meat, 2 starch, ½ fat.

HEALTH TIP

Adding pulses such as cannellini beans to a meat-based main dish bumps up the fiber and protein without adding saturated fat.

SKILLET PLUM CHICKEN TENDERS

If you love plums, this recipe is for you! I combine the fruit with chicken tenders for a quick and flavorful meal. Serve with brown rice or orzo pasta.

—Nancy Heishman, Las Vegas, NV

Prep: 20 min. • **Cook:** 15 min.
Makes: 4 servings

- **½ tsp. garlic salt**
- **½ tsp. lemon-pepper seasoning**
- **1½ lbs. chicken tenderloins**
- **1 Tbsp. extra virgin olive oil**
- **2 cups sliced fresh plums**
- **½ cup diced red onion**
- **⅓ cup apple jelly**
- **1 Tbsp. grated fresh gingerroot**
- **1 Tbsp. balsamic vinegar**
- **2 tsp. reduced-sodium soy sauce**
- **1 tsp. minced fresh thyme or ½ tsp. dried thyme**
- **1 Tbsp. cornstarch**
- **2 Tbsp. white wine**
- **1 Tbsp. sesame seeds, toasted**

1. Combine garlic salt and lemon pepper; sprinkle mixture over chicken. In a large nonstick skillet, heat oil over medium-high heat; brown chicken. Add plums and red onion; cook and stir 1-2 minutes.
2. Reduce heat. Stir in next 5 ingredients. Mix cornstarch and wine until smooth; gradually stir into pan. Cook, covered, until the chicken juices run clear and the plums are tender, about 10 minutes. Just before serving, sprinkle with the toasted sesame seeds.

1 serving: 343 cal., 6g fat (1g sat. fat), 83mg chol., 483mg sod., 33g carb. (26g sugars, 2g fiber), 41g pro.

BBQ CHICKEN & APPLE BREAD PUDDING

To me, bread pudding is the epitome of comfort food and is simply too good to reserve only for dessert. This sweet-and-savory twist on the classic is a delicious new way to enjoy an old favorite.

—Shauna Havey, Roy, UT

Prep: 45 min. + cooling • **Bake:** 35 min.
Makes: 8 servings

- **1 pkg. (8½ oz.) cornbread/muffin mix**
- **6 Tbsp. butter, divided**
- **1 large sweet onion, thinly sliced**
- **⅔ cup barbecue sauce, divided**
- **2 cups diced cooked chicken**
- **2 large eggs, beaten**
- **1 cup half-and-half cream**
- **1 tsp. salt**
- **½ tsp. pepper**
- **1¼ cups shredded Monterey Jack cheese**
- **1 small green apple, peeled and diced**
- **Minced chives**

1. Prepare cornbread according to package directions and bake using a greased and floured 8-in. square baking pan. Cool. Reduce oven setting to 375°.
2. Meanwhile, in a small skillet, heat 2 Tbsp. butter over medium heat. Add the onion; cook and stir until softened. Reduce heat to medium-low; cook until deep golden brown and caramelized, 30-40 minutes. Remove from heat and set aside.
3. Pour ¼ cup barbecue sauce over chicken; toss to coat. Cube cornbread.
4. Microwave remaining butter, covered, on high until melted, about 30 seconds. Whisk in eggs, cream, salt and pepper. Add caramelized onions. Pour the egg mixture over the cornbread cubes. Add chicken, cheese and apple. Toss gently to combine.
5. Pour mixture into a greased 8-in. square or 1½-qt. baking dish; bake until bubbly and top is golden brown, about 35 minutes. Drizzle remaining barbecue sauce over bread pudding. Sprinkle with chives.

1 serving: 465 cal., 25g fat (13g sat. fat), 156mg chol., 1028mg sod., 37g carb. (19g sugars, 3g fiber), 21g pro.

❄ LOUISIANA JAMBALAYA

My husband helped add a little spice to my life. He grew up on Cajun cooking, while I ate mostly meat-and-potato meals.
—Sandra Pichon, Slidell, LA

Prep: 10 min. • **Cook:** 30 min.
Makes: 12 servings

- **¼ cup canola oil**
- **½ lb. smoked sausage, halved and sliced**
- **2 cups cubed fully cooked ham**
- **2 celery ribs, chopped**
- **1 large onion, chopped**
- **1 medium green pepper, chopped**
- **5 green onions, thinly sliced**
- **2 garlic cloves, minced**
- **1 can (14½ oz.) diced tomatoes, undrained**
- **1 tsp. dried thyme**
- **1 tsp. salt**
- **½ tsp. pepper**
- **¼ tsp. cayenne pepper**
- **2 cans (14½ oz. each) chicken broth**
- **1 cup uncooked long grain rice**
- **⅓ cup water**
- **4½ tsp. Worcestershire sauce**
- **2 lbs. peeled and deveined cooked shrimp (31-40 per lb.)**

1. In a Dutch oven, heat oil over medium-high heat. Add sausage and ham; saute until lightly browned. Remove and keep warm. In drippings, saute the celery, onion, green pepper and green onions until tender. Add garlic; cook and stir 1 minute longer. Stir in the tomatoes, thyme, salt, pepper and cayenne; cook 5 minutes longer.
2. Stir in the broth, rice, water and Worcestershire sauce. Bring to a boil. Reduce heat; simmer, covered, until rice is tender, about 20 minutes. Stir in the sausage mixture and shrimp; heat through.

Freeze option: Prepare as directed, omitting rice and shrimp. Freeze the shrimp and cooled jambalaya in separate freezer containers. To use, partially thaw jambalaya in refrigerator overnight. Place jambalaya in a 6-qt. stockpot; heat through. Add rice; cook, covered, about 10 minutes. Add the frozen shrimp; continue cooking until the shrimp are heated through and rice is tender, 5-7 minutes.

1 cup: 295 cal., 12g fat (3g sat. fat), 143mg chol., 1183mg sod., 20g carb. (3g sugars, 1g fiber), 25g pro.

BEEF & TATER BAKE

Your entire family will enjoy this delicious and heartwarming all-in-one dinner. Plus, it offers easy cleanup!
—Mike Tchou, Pepper Pike, OH

Prep: 10 min. • **Bake:** 35 min.
Makes: 8 servings

- **4 cups frozen Tater Tots**
- **1 lb. ground beef**
- **¼ tsp. garlic powder**
- **⅛ tsp. pepper**
- **1 can (10¾ oz.) condensed cream of broccoli soup, undiluted**
- **⅓ cup 2% milk**
- **1 pkg. (16 oz.) frozen chopped broccoli, thawed**
- **1 can (2.8 oz.) french-fried onions, divided**
- **1 cup shredded Colby-Monterey Jack cheese, divided**
- **1 medium tomato, chopped**

1. Preheat oven to 400°. Spread Tater Tots evenly in an ungreased 13x9-in. baking dish. Bake, uncovered, 10 minutes.
2. Meanwhile, in a large skillet, cook and crumble beef over medium heat until no longer pink, 5-7 minutes; drain. Stir in the seasonings, soup, milk, broccoli, ¾ cup onions, ½ cup cheese and tomato; heat through. Pour over potatoes.
3. Bake, covered, 20 minutes. Sprinkle with the remaining onions and cheese. Bake, uncovered, until cheese is melted, 5-10 minutes.

1 piece: 400 cal., 24g fat (9g sat. fat), 50mg chol., 805mg sod., 29g carb. (3g sugars, 4g fiber), 17g pro.

Corn, Beef & Tater Bake: Substitute a package of frozen corn for the broccoli and 1 can cream of celery soup for the cream of broccoli soup.

Perfect Pot Roasts

In a survey to name the perfect comfort food, pot roast would top of a lot of lists—and everyone would have their own way of making it! Simmered on the stovetop, cooked in the oven or prepared in a slow cooker, it's a crowd pleaser in every variation!

LONE STAR POT ROAST

Pot roast becomes especially scrumptious with the addition of chopped green chiles and taco seasoning.

—Helen Carpenter, Albuquerque, NM

Prep: 20 min. • **Cook:** 2 hours
Makes: 8 servings

- **1 boneless beef chuck roast (3 to 3½ lbs.)**
- **2 Tbsp. canola oil**
- **1 can (14½ oz.) diced tomatoes, undrained**
- **1 can (4 oz.) chopped green chiles**
- **2 Tbsp. taco seasoning**
- **2 tsp. beef bouillon granules**
- **1 tsp. sugar**
- **¼ cup cold water**
- **3 Tbsp. all-purpose flour**

1. In a Dutch oven, brown the roast in oil. Combine the tomatoes, chiles, taco seasoning, bouillon and sugar; pour over the roast. Cover and simmer 2-2½ hours or until meat is tender.
2. Remove roast to a platter and keep warm. For gravy, pour 2 cups pan juices into a saucepan. Combine cold water and flour; stir into pan juices over high heat until thickened and bubbly, about 3 minutes. Serve with roast.

Freeze option: Place sliced pot roast in freezer containers; top with gravy. Cool and freeze. To use, partially thaw in refrigerator overnight. Microwave, covered, on high in a microwave-safe dish until heated through, gently stirring; add a little water if necessary.

1 serving: 352 cal., 20g fat (7g sat. fat), 111mg chol., 594mg sod., 8g carb. (2g sugars, 1g fiber), 34g pro.

SATURDAY AFTERNOON OVEN POT ROAST

This pot roast will be a welcome sight on your weekend dinner table and will leave your house smelling heavenly. If you find that the cooking liquid evaporates too quickly, you can add more broth.

—Colleen Delawder, Herndon, VA

Prep: 40 min. • **Bake:** 3 hours
Makes: 8 servings

- **1 boneless beef chuck roast (2½ lbs.)**
- **1 tsp. salt**
- **½ tsp. pepper**
- **1 Tbsp. olive oil**
- **1 Tbsp. butter**
- **4 cups sliced sweet onion**
- **1 can (6 oz.) tomato paste**
- **4 garlic cloves, minced**
- **1 tsp. dried thyme**
- **½ tsp. celery seed**
- **½ cup dry red wine**
- **1 carton (32 oz.) reduced-sodium beef broth**
- **6 medium carrots, cut into 1½ in. pieces**
- **½ lb. medium fresh mushrooms, quartered**

1. Preheat oven to 325°. Sprinkle roast with salt and pepper. In a Dutch oven, heat oil and butter over medium-high heat; brown roast on all sides. Remove from pot.
2. Add onion to same pot; cook and stir over medium heat 8-10 minutes or until tender. Add tomato paste, garlic, thyme and celery seed; cook and stir 1 minute longer. Add the wine, stirring to loosen browned bits from pot; stir in broth.
3. Return roast to pot. Arrange carrots and mushrooms around roast; bring to a boil. Bake, covered, until the meat is fork-tender, 2½-3 hours. If desired, skim fat and thicken cooking juices for gravy.

4 oz. cooked beef with ½ cup vegetables and ¼ cup gravy: 339 cal., 17g fat (6g sat. fat), 98mg chol., 621mg sod., 14g carb. (7g sugars, 2g fiber), 32g pro.

BALSAMIC BRAISED POT ROAST

Pot roast can be an easy, elegant way to serve a relatively inexpensive cut of meat, so I have spent years perfecting this recipe. Believe it or not, there is an art to perfect pot roast, and every time I make this dish, parents and kids alike gobble it up.
—Kelly Anderson, Glendale, CA

Prep: 40 min. • **Bake:** 2½ hours
Makes: 8 servings

- **1 boneless beef chuck roast (3 to 4 lbs.)**
- **1 tsp. salt**
- **½ tsp. pepper**
- **2 Tbsp. olive oil**
- **3 celery ribs with leaves, cut into 2-in. pieces**
- **2 medium carrots, cut into 1-in. pieces**
- **1 medium onion, cut into wedges**
- **3 medium turnips, peeled and quartered**
- **1 large sweet potato, peeled and cubed**
- **3 garlic cloves, minced**
- **1 cup dry red wine or beef broth**
- **1 can (14½ oz.) beef broth**
- **½ cup balsamic vinegar**
- **1 small bunch fresh thyme sprigs**
- **4 fresh sage leaves**
- **2 bay leaves**
- **¼ cup cornstarch**
- **¼ cup cold water**

1. Preheat oven to 325°. Sprinkle roast with salt and pepper. In a Dutch oven, heat oil over medium heat. Brown roast on all sides. Remove from pot.
2. Add celery, carrots and onion to the pot; cook and stir 3-4 minutes or until fragrant. Add turnips, sweet potato and garlic; cook 1 minute longer.
3. Add wine, stirring to loosen browned bits from pot. Stir in broth, vinegar and herbs. Return roast to pot; bring to a boil. Bake, covered, 2½-3 hours or until meat is tender.
4. Remove the beef and vegetables; keep warm. Discard herbs from cooking juices; skim fat. In a small bowl, mix cornstarch and water until smooth; stir into cooking juices. Bring to a boil; cook and stir for 2 minutes or until thickened. Serve with pot roast and vegetables.

4 oz. cooked beef with 1 cup vegetables and ½ cup gravy: 405 cal., 20g fat (7g sat. fat), 111mg chol., 657mg sod., 19g carb. (9g sugars, 3g fiber), 35g pro.

GRAMPA'S GERMAN-STYLE POT ROAST

Grandpa was of German heritage and loved the Old-World recipes given to him by his mother. I made a few changes so I could prepare this dish in the slow cooker and give it a slightly updated flavor.
—Nancy Heishman, Las Vegas, NV

Prep: 20 min. • **Cook:** 6 hours + standing
Makes: 8 servings

- **4 thick-sliced bacon strips**
- **1 lb. baby Yukon Gold potatoes**
- **4 medium carrots, sliced**
- **1 can (14 oz.) sauerkraut, rinsed and well drained**
- **¾ cup chopped dill pickles**
- **1 tsp. smoked paprika**
- **1 tsp. ground allspice**
- **½ tsp. kosher salt**
- **½ tsp. pepper**
- **1 boneless beef chuck roast (3 lbs.)**
- **2 pkg. (14.4 oz. each) frozen pearl onions, thawed**
- **4 garlic cloves, minced**
- **½ cup stout beer or beef broth**
- **⅓ cup Dusseldorf mustard**
- **½ cup sour cream**
- **½ cup minced fresh parsley**

1. In a large skillet, cook bacon over medium heat until crisp. Remove to paper towels to drain.
2. Meanwhile, place potatoes, carrots, sauerkraut and pickles in a 7-qt. slow cooker. Mix paprika, allspice, salt and pepper; rub over roast. Brown roast in drippings over medium heat. Transfer to slow cooker. Add onions and garlic to drippings; cook and stir 1 minute. Stir in the beer and mustard; pour over meat. Crumble bacon; add to slow cooker.
3. Cook, covered, on low until meat and vegetables are tender, 6-8 hours. Remove roast; let stand 10 minutes before slicing. Strain cooking juices. Reserve vegetables and juices; skim fat. Return the reserved vegetables and cooking juices to slow cooker. Stir in sour cream; heat through. Serve with roast; sprinkle with parsley.

1 serving: 552 cal., 31g fat (12g sat. fat), 127mg chol., 926mg sod., 28g carb. (9g sugars, 6g fiber), 39g pro.

Meals in Minutes

Some busy weeknights, you need to get a meal on the table fast—but that doesn't mean you need to resort to fast food or frozen dinners. With minimal prep work and quick cooking times, the 28 recipes in this chapter are just what you need when you have to prioritize speed but refuse to sacrifice freshness and flavor.

BREADED PORK TENDERLOIN

Meat is a hard sell with my teenage daughter, unless I make it look like a restaurant dish. Drizzle ranch dressing or barbecue sauce on top, and this is a home run!

—Donna Carney, New Lexington, OH

Takes: 30 min. • **Makes:** 4 servings

- **1 pork tenderloin (1 lb.)**
- **⅓ cup all-purpose flour**
- **⅓ cup cornbread/muffin mix**
- **½ tsp. salt**
- **¼ tsp. pepper**
- **1 large egg, beaten**
- **4 Tbsp. canola oil**
- **Optional: Ranch or barbecue sauce**

1. Cut pork crosswise into ½-in. slices. In a shallow bowl, mix flour, cornbread mix, salt and pepper. Place egg in a separate shallow bowl. Dip pork in egg, then in flour mixture, patting to help coating adhere.
2. In a large skillet, heat 2 Tbsp. oil over medium heat. Add half of the pork; cook until a thermometer inserted in pork reads 145°, 3-4 minutes on each side. Drain on paper towels. Wipe skillet clean; repeat with remaining oil and pork. If desired, serve with sauce.

3 oz. cooked pork: 338 cal., 20g fat (3g sat. fat), 110mg chol., 327mg sod., 12g carb. (2g sugars, 1g fiber), 26g pro.

Country Chicken Breasts: Substitute 4 boneless skinless chicken breasts (4 oz. each) for the pork. Cook as directed until a thermometer reads 165°.

CHICKEN BISCUIT SKILLET

My mother always made this while we were growing up. Now I make it for my own husband and kids. I use the small biscuits because they brown up so nicely on top. I also add mushrooms to this recipe sometimes because my family loves 'em.

—Keri Boffeli, Monticello, IA

Takes: 30 min. • **Makes:** 6 servings

- **1 Tbsp. butter**
- **⅓ cup chopped onion**
- **¼ cup all-purpose flour**
- **1 can (10½ oz.) condensed chicken broth, undiluted**
- **¼ cup fat-free milk**
- **⅛ tsp. pepper**
- **2 cups shredded cooked chicken breast**
- **2 cups frozen peas and carrots (about 10 oz.), thawed**
- **1 tube (12 oz.) refrigerated buttermilk biscuits, quartered**

1. Preheat oven to 400°. Melt butter in a 10-in. cast-iron or other ovenproof skillet over medium-high heat. Add onion; cook and stir until tender, 2-3 minutes.
2. In a small bowl, mix flour, broth, milk and pepper until smooth; stir into pan. Bring to a boil, stirring constantly; cook and stir until thickened, 1-2 minutes. Add the shredded chicken and the peas and carrots; heat through.
3. Arrange biscuits over stew. Bake until biscuits are golden brown, 15-20 minutes.

1 serving: 320 cal., 11g fat (4g sat. fat), 42mg chol., 861mg sod., 36g carb. (4g sugars, 2g fiber), 22g pro.

KOREAN BEEF & RICE

A friend raved about Korean bulgogi—beef cooked in soy sauce and ginger—so I tried it. It's delicious! Dazzle the table with this tasty version of beef and rice.

—Elizabeth King, Duluth, MN

Takes: 15 min. • **Makes:** 4 servings

- **1 lb. lean ground beef (90% lean)**
- **3 garlic cloves, minced**
- **¼ cup packed brown sugar**
- **¼ cup reduced-sodium soy sauce**
- **2 tsp. sesame oil**
- **¼ tsp. ground ginger**
- **¼ tsp. crushed red pepper flakes**
- **¼ tsp. pepper**
- **2⅔ cups hot cooked brown rice**
- **3 green onions, thinly sliced**

1. In a large skillet, cook beef and garlic over medium heat 6-8 minutes or until beef is no longer pink, breaking up beef into crumbles. Meanwhile, in a small bowl, mix brown sugar, soy sauce, sesame oil and seasonings.
2. Stir sauce into beef; heat through. Serve with cooked rice. Sprinkle with green onions.

Freeze option: Freeze cooled meat mixture in freezer containers. To use, partially thaw in the refrigerator overnight. Heat through in a saucepan, stirring occasionally.

½ cup beef mixture with ⅔ cup rice: 413 cal., 13g fat (4g sat. fat), 71mg chol., 647mg sod., 46g carb. (14g sugars, 3g fiber), 27g pro. **Diabetic exchanges:** 3 starch, 3 lean meat, ½ fat.

GOING LEAN

Using lean ground beef instead of beef that's 80% lean saves 45 calories per 4-oz. serving of beef. Lean ground beef is also 29% lower in saturated fat.

SEARED SALMON WITH STRAWBERRY BASIL RELISH

Take a sweet new approach to salmon by topping it off with a relish of strawberries, basil and honey.

—Stacy Mullens, Gresham, OR

Takes: 20 min. • **Makes:** 6 servings

- **6 salmon fillets (4 oz. each)**
- **1 Tbsp. butter, melted**
- **¼ tsp. salt**
- **⅛ tsp. freshly ground pepper**

RELISH

- **1¼ cups finely chopped fresh strawberries**
- **1 Tbsp. minced fresh basil**
- **1 Tbsp. honey**
- **Dash freshly ground pepper**

1. Brush salmon fillets with melted butter; sprinkle with salt and pepper. Heat a large skillet over medium-high heat. Add fillets, skin side up, in batches if necessary; cook 2-3 minutes on each side or until fish just begins to flake easily with a fork.
2. In a small bowl, toss strawberries with basil, honey and pepper. Serve salmon with relish.

1 salmon fillet with 3 Tbsp. relish: 215 cal., 12g fat (3g sat. fat), 62mg chol., 169mg sod., 6g carb. (5g sugars, 1g fiber), 19g pro. **Diabetic exchanges:** 3 lean meat, ½ starch, ½ fat.

SAUSAGE-STUFFED BUTTERNUT SQUASH

Load butternut squash shells with an Italian turkey sausage and squash mixture for a quick and easy meal. Even better, it's surprisingly low in calories.

—Katia Slinger, West Jordan, UT

Takes: 30 min. • **Makes:** 4 servings

- **1 medium butternut squash (about 3 lbs.)**
- **1 lb. Italian turkey sausage links, casings removed**
- **1 medium onion, finely chopped**
- **4 garlic cloves, minced**
- **½ cup shredded Italian cheese blend**
- **Crushed red pepper flakes, optional**

1. Preheat broiler. Cut squash lengthwise in half; discard seeds. Place squash in a large microwave-safe dish, cut side down; add ½ in. of water. Microwave, covered, on high until soft, 20-25 minutes. Cool slightly.
2. Meanwhile, in a large nonstick skillet, cook and crumble sausage with onion over medium-high heat until no longer pink, 5-7 minutes. Add garlic; cook and stir 1 minute.
3. Leaving ½-in.-thick shells, scoop flesh from squash and stir it into the sausage mixture. Place squash shells on a baking sheet; fill with sausage mixture. Sprinkle with cheese.
4. Broil 4-5 in. from heat until cheese is melted, 1-2 minutes. If desired, sprinkle with pepper flakes. To serve, cut each half into 2 portions.

1 serving: 325 cal., 10g fat (4g sat. fat), 52mg chol., 587mg sod., 44g carb. (10g sugars, 12g fiber), 19g pro. **Diabetic exchanges:** 3 starch, 3 lean meat.

BUTTERNUT SQUASH BENEFITS

Butternut squash is an excellent source of vitamin A in the form of beta carotene. It's important for normal vision and a healthy immune system, and it helps the heart, lungs and kidneys function properly.

SHRIMP WITH WARM GERMAN-STYLE COLESLAW

We love anything that's tangy or bacony. With fennel and tarragon, this is a super savory dish. I use the medley from Minute Rice if I don't have time to make my own.
—Ann Sheehy, Lawrence, MA

Takes: 30 min. • **Makes:** 4 servings

- 6 **bacon strips**
- 2 **Tbsp. canola oil, divided**
- 3 **cups finely shredded green cabbage**
- ½ **cup finely shredded carrot (1 medium carrot)**
- 1 **cup finely shredded red cabbage, optional**
- ½ **cup finely shredded fennel bulb, optional**
- 6 **green onions, finely chopped**
- 3 **Tbsp. minced fresh parsley**
- 2 **Tbsp. minced fresh tarragon or 2 tsp. dried tarragon**
- ¼ **tsp. salt**
- ⅛ **tsp. pepper**
- ¼ **cup red wine vinegar**
- 1 **lb. uncooked shrimp (26-30 per lb.), peeled and deveined**
- 3 **cups hot cooked rice or multigrain medley**

1. In a large skillet, cook bacon strips over medium heat until crisp. Remove to paper towels to drain. Pour off the drippings, discarding all but 2 Tbsp. Crumble bacon.
2. In same skillet, heat 1 Tbsp. drippings with 1 Tbsp. oil over medium heat. Add green cabbage and carrot and, if desired, red cabbage and fennel; cook and stir until the vegetables are just tender, 1-2 minutes. Remove to a bowl. Stir in green onions, parsley, tarragon, salt and pepper; toss with vinegar. Keep warm.
3. Add remaining drippings and remaining 1 Tbsp. oil to skillet. Add shrimp; cook and stir over medium heat until shrimp turn pink, 2-3 minutes. Remove from heat.
4. To serve, spoon rice and coleslaw into soup bowls. Top with shrimp; sprinkle with crumbled bacon.

1 serving: 472 cal., 20g fat (5g sat. fat), 156mg chol., 546mg sod., 44g carb. (2g sugars, 3g fiber), 28g pro.

ZUCCHINI & SAUSAGE STOVETOP CASSEROLE

Gather zucchini from your garden or farm stand and start cooking. My family goes wild for this wholesome casserole. Sometimes we'll grate the zucchini instead of slicing it.
—LeAnn Gray, Taylorsville, UT

Takes: 30 min. • **Makes:** 6 servings

- 1 **lb. bulk pork sausage**
- 1 **Tbsp. canola oil**
- 3 **medium zucchini, thinly sliced**
- 1 **medium onion, chopped**
- 1 **can (14½ oz.) stewed tomatoes, cut up**
- 1 **pkg. (8.8 oz.) ready-to-serve long grain rice**
- 1 **tsp. prepared mustard**
- ½ **tsp. garlic salt**
- ¼ **tsp. pepper**
- 1 **cup shredded sharp cheddar cheese**

1. In a large skillet, cook sausage over medium heat for 5-7 minutes or until no longer pink, breaking into crumbles. Drain and remove sausage from pan.
2. In same pan, heat oil over medium heat. Add zucchini and onion; cook and stir 5-7 minutes or until tender. Stir in sausage, tomatoes, rice, mustard, garlic salt and pepper. Bring to a boil. Reduce heat; simmer, covered, 5 minutes to allow flavors to blend.
3. Remove from heat; sprinkle with cheese. Let stand, covered, 5 minutes or until the cheese is melted.

1⅓ cups: 394 cal., 26g fat (9g sat. fat), 60mg chol., 803mg sod., 24g carb. (6g sugars, 2g fiber), 16g pro.

APPLE-GLAZED CHICKEN THIGHS

My "pickatarian" child is choosy but willing to eat this chicken glazed with apple juice and thyme. I like to dish it up with mashed potatoes and green beans.
—Kerry Picard, Spokane, WA

Takes: 25 min. • **Makes:** 6 servings

- **6 boneless skinless chicken thighs (1½ lbs.)**
- **¾ tsp. seasoned salt**
- **¼ tsp. pepper**
- **1 Tbsp. canola oil**
- **1 cup unsweetened apple juice**
- **1 tsp. minced fresh thyme or ¼ tsp. dried thyme**

1. Sprinkle chicken with seasoned salt and pepper. In a large skillet, heat oil over medium-high heat. Brown chicken on both sides. Remove from pan.
2. Add juice and thyme to skillet. Bring to a boil, stirring to loosen browned bits from pan; cook until the liquid is reduced by half. Return chicken to pan; cook, covered, over medium heat 3-4 minutes longer or until a thermometer inserted in chicken reads 170°.

1 chicken thigh with about 1 Tbsp. glaze: 204 cal., 11g fat (2g sat. fat), 76mg chol., 255mg sod., 5g carb. (4g sugars, 0 fiber), 21g pro. **Diabetic exchanges:** 3 lean meat, ½ fat.

SPICY SHEPHERD'S PIE

Taco seasoning adds zip to this hearty main dish. It's easy to top with instant mashed potatoes, which I stir up while browning the beef.
—Mary Malchow, Neenah, WI

Takes: 30 min. • **Makes:** 6 servings

- **3 cups mashed potato flakes**
- **1 lb. ground beef**
- **1 medium onion, chopped**
- **1 can (14½ oz.) diced tomatoes, undrained**
- **1 can (11 oz.) Mexicorn, drained**
- **1 can (2¼ oz.) sliced ripe olives, drained**
- **1 envelope taco seasoning**
- **1½ tsp. chili powder**
- **½ tsp. salt**
- **⅛ tsp. garlic powder**
- **1 cup shredded cheddar cheese, divided**

1. Preheat oven to 350°. Prepare mashed potatoes according to package directions. Meanwhile, in a large skillet, cook beef and onion over medium heat until meat is no longer pink; drain. Add the tomatoes, corn, olives, taco seasoning, chili powder, salt and garlic powder. Bring to a boil; cook and stir for 1-2 minutes.
2. Transfer to a greased 2½-qt. baking dish. Top with ¾ cup cheese. Spread mashed potatoes over the top; sprinkle with the remaining ¼ cup cheese. Bake, uncovered, for 12-15 minutes or until the cheese is melted.

1 serving: 516 cal., 25g fat (13g sat. fat), 90mg chol., 1337mg sod., 49g carb. (10g sugars, 5g fiber), 24g pro.

EASY STUFFED POBLANOS

My partner adores these saucy stuffed peppers—and I love how quickly they come together. Top with low-fat sour cream and your favorite salsa.

—Jean Erhardt, Portland, OR

Takes: 25 min. • **Makes:** 4 servings

- **½ lb. Italian turkey sausage links, casings removed**
- **½ lb. lean ground beef (90% lean)**
- **1 pkg. (8.8 oz.) ready-to-serve Spanish rice**
- **4 large poblano peppers**
- **1 cup enchilada sauce**
- **½ cup shredded Mexican cheese blend**
- **Minced fresh cilantro, optional**

1. Preheat broiler. In a large skillet, cook turkey and beef over medium heat until no longer pink, 5-7 minutes, breaking into crumbles; drain.
2. Prepare rice according to package directions. Add rice to the meat mixture.
3. Cut peppers lengthwise in half; remove the seeds. Place on a foil-lined 15x10x1-in. baking pan, cut side down. Broil 4 in. from heat until skins blister, about 5 minutes. With tongs, turn peppers.
4. Fill with the turkey mixture; top with enchilada sauce and sprinkle with cheese. Broil until cheese is melted, 1-2 minutes longer. If desired, top with cilantro.

2 stuffed pepper halves: 312 cal., 13g fat (4g sat. fat), 63mg chol., 1039mg sod., 27g carb. (5g sugars, 2g fiber), 22g pro.

QUICK SUBSTITUTIONS

Prepared Spanish rice adds so much flavor with so little effort! If you have leftover Spanish rice—or make your own—use about 2 cups cooked rice for the filling. Bell peppers would also work in this recipe.

SMOKY SPANISH CHICKEN

After enjoying a similar dish at a Spanish tapas restaurant, my husband and I were eager to make our own version of this saucy chicken at home. When I want to make it extra healthy, I remove the skin from the chicken after browning.

—Ryan Haley, San Diego, CA

Takes: 30 min. • **Makes:** 4 servings

- **3 tsp. smoked paprika**
- **½ tsp. salt**
- **¼ tsp. pepper**
- **1 Tbsp. water**
- **4 bone-in chicken thighs**
- **1½ cups baby portobello mushrooms, quartered**
- **1 cup chopped green onions, divided**
- **1 can (14½ oz.) fire-roasted diced tomatoes, undrained**

1. Mix the paprika, salt, pepper and water into a paste; rub over chicken.
2. Place a large skillet over medium heat. Add chicken, skin side down. Cook until browned, 4-5 minutes per side; remove from pan. Remove all but 1 Tbsp. of the drippings from pan.
3. In the drippings, saute mushrooms and ½ cup green onions over medium heat until tender, 1-2 minutes. Stir in tomatoes. Add chicken; bring to a boil. Reduce heat; simmer, covered, until a thermometer inserted in chicken reads 170°, 10-12 minutes. Top with remaining green onions.

1 serving: 272 cal., 15g fat (4g sat. fat), 81mg chol., 646mg sod., 10g carb. (4g sugars, 2g fiber), 25g pro.

ABOUT PAPRIKA

Smoked paprika is made from peppers that are dried over wood fires, giving it a rich, smoky flavor. Make the most of the flavorful sauce and serve this with a starchy side like couscous or rice.

SMOKED SAUSAGE & VEGGIE SHEET-PAN SUPPER

This recipe is tasty and quick, and can easily be doubled for last-minute dinner guests. Cook it in the oven or on the grill, and add the veggies of your choice.

—Judy Batson, Tampa, FL

Takes: 30 min. • **Makes:** 4 servings

- **1 pkg. (13½ oz.) smoked sausage, cut into ½-in. slices**
- **8 fresh Brussels sprouts, thinly sliced**
- **1 large sweet onion, halved and sliced**
- **1 medium yellow summer squash, halved and sliced**
- **1 medium zucchini, halved and sliced**
- **1 medium sweet yellow pepper, chopped**
- **1 medium green pepper, chopped**
- **1 medium tomato, chopped**
- **¾ cup sliced fresh mushrooms**
- **½ cup Greek vinaigrette**

Preheat oven to 400°. Place the first 9 ingredients into a greased 15x10x1-in. baking pan. Drizzle with vinaigrette; toss to coat. Bake, uncovered, 15 minutes. Remove pan from oven; preheat broiler. Broil sausage mixture 3-4 in. from heat until vegetables are lightly browned, 3-4 minutes.

2 cups: 491 cal., 37g fat (13g sat. fat), 64mg chol., 1430mg sod., 22g carb. (13g sugars, 5g fiber), 18g pro.

CLASSIC CHICKEN & WAFFLES

A down-home diner special gets weeknight-easy with the help of rotisserie chicken. Want 'em even faster? Make the waffles ahead of time and freeze until dinnertime.

—Lauren Reiff, East Earl, PA

Takes: 30 min. • **Makes:** 6 servings

- **3 Tbsp. butter**
- **3 Tbsp. all-purpose flour**
- **½ tsp. salt**
- **¼ tsp. pepper**
- **½ cup chicken broth**
- **1¼ cups 2% milk**
- **2 cups coarsely shredded rotisserie chicken**

WAFFLES

- **2 cups all-purpose flour**
- **2 Tbsp. sugar**
- **4 tsp. baking powder**
- **½ tsp. salt**
- **2 large eggs**
- **1½ cups 2% milk**
- **5 Tbsp. butter, melted**
- **Sliced green onions, optional**

1. In a large saucepan, melt butter over medium heat. Stir in flour, salt and pepper until smooth; gradually whisk in broth and milk. Bring to a boil, stirring constantly; cook and stir until thickened, 1-2 minutes. Stir in chicken; heat through. Keep warm.
2. Preheat waffle maker. Whisk together flour, sugar, baking powder and salt. In another bowl, whisk together eggs, milk and melted butter; add to dry ingredients, stirring just until moistened.
3. Bake waffles according to the manufacturer's directions until golden brown. Top waffles with chicken mixture and, if desired, green onions.

2 waffles with ⅔ cup chicken mixture: 488 cal., 23g fat (13g sat. fat), 154mg chol., 981mg sod., 45g carb. (10g sugars, 1g fiber), 24g pro.

BLACKENED HALIBUT

Serve these spicy fillets with garlic mashed potatoes, hot crusty bread and a crisp salad to lure in your crew. This is what my family eats when we want to celebrate.

—Brenda Williams, Santa Maria, CA

Takes: 25 min. • **Makes:** 4 servings

- **2 Tbsp. garlic powder**
- **1 Tbsp. salt**
- **1 Tbsp. onion powder**
- **1 Tbsp. dried oregano**
- **1 Tbsp. dried thyme**
- **1 Tbsp. cayenne pepper**
- **1 Tbsp. pepper**
- **2½ tsp. paprika**
- **4 halibut fillets (4 oz. each)**
- **2 Tbsp. butter**

1. In a large shallow dish, combine the first 8 ingredients. Add fillets, 2 at a time, and turn to coat.
2. In a large cast-iron skillet, cook fillets in butter over medium heat until the fish flakes easily with a fork, 3-4 minutes on each side.

1 fillet: 189 cal., 8g fat (4g sat. fat), 51mg chol., 758mg sod., 3g carb. (1g sugars, 1g fiber), 24g pro. **Diabetic exchanges:** 3 lean meat, 1 fat.

BEEF & MUSHROOMS WITH SMASHED POTATOES

I was inspired to make this recipe after I couldn't stop thinking of a similar dish served in my elementary school cafeteria more than 50 years ago! I like that it's quick to make, and my husband and grandchildren absolutely love it.

—Ronna Farley, Rockville, MD

Takes: 30 min. • **Makes:** 4 servings

- **1½ lbs. red potatoes (about 6 medium), cut into 1½-in. pieces**
- **1 lb. ground beef**
- **½ lb. sliced fresh mushrooms**
- **1 medium onion, halved and sliced**
- **3 Tbsp. all-purpose flour**
- **¾ tsp. pepper, divided**
- **½ tsp. salt, divided**
- **1 can (14½ oz.) beef broth**
- **2 Tbsp. butter, softened**
- **½ cup half-and-half cream**
- **½ cup french-fried onions**

1. Place potatoes in a large saucepan; add water to cover. Bring to a boil. Reduce heat to medium; cook, uncovered, until tender, 10-15 minutes.
2. Meanwhile, in a large skillet, cook and crumble beef with mushrooms and onion over medium-high heat until no longer pink, 6-8 minutes; drain. Stir in flour, ½ tsp. pepper and ¼ tsp. salt until blended. Gradually stir in broth; bring to a boil. Reduce heat; simmer, uncovered, until thickened, about 5 minutes, stirring occasionally.
3. Drain potatoes; return to pan. Mash potatoes to desired consistency, adding butter, cream and the remaining salt and pepper. Spoon into bowls; top with beef mixture. Sprinkle with fried onions.

1 serving: 517 cal., 26g fat (12g sat. fat), 100mg chol., 896mg sod., 40g carb. (5g sugars, 4g fiber), 28g pro.

ASIAN SLAW WITH STEAK

Main-dish salads are so perfect for summer, especially this one with its Asian-inspired dressing. The colorful slaw and juicy steak combo is super quick and wonderful for breezy weeknight dinners.
—Roxanne Chan, Albany, CA

Takes: 30 min. • **Makes:** 4 servings

- **⅓ cup rice vinegar**
- **3 Tbsp. minced fresh mint**
- **3 Tbsp. sesame oil**
- **⅓ cup miso paste**
- **1 beef top sirloin steak (1 in. thick and 1 lb.)**
- **1 pkg. (12 oz.) broccoli coleslaw mix**
- **1 medium mango, peeled and diced**
- **1 cup frozen shelled edamame, thawed**
- **¼ cup sliced radishes**
- **¼ cup minced fresh cilantro**
- **1 green onion, sliced**
- **Grated lime zest, optional**

1. For dressing, place first 4 ingredients in a blender; cover and process until blended. Reserve ½ cup of the dressing for slaw. Brush the remaining dressing onto both sides of steak; let stand while preparing slaw.
2. Place coleslaw mix, mango, edamame, radishes, cilantro and green onion in a large bowl. Toss with reserved dressing.
3. Grill steak, covered, over medium heat until meat reaches desired doneness (for medium-rare, a thermometer should read 135°; medium, 140°), 5-7 minutes per side. Let stand 5 minutes before slicing. Serve with slaw. If desired, sprinkle with lime zest.

1 serving: 423 cal., 18g fat (3g sat. fat), 46mg chol., 1370mg sod., 32g carb. (24g sugars, 5g fiber), 34g pro.

PECAN-COCONUT CRUSTED TILAPIA

When I have guests with gluten restrictions, this tilapia coated in pecans and coconut makes everyone happy. It's gluten free and loaded with flavor.

—Caitlin Roth, Chicago, IL

Takes: 25 min. • **Makes:** 4 servings

- **2 large eggs**
- **½ cup unsweetened finely shredded coconut**
- **½ cup finely chopped pecans**
- **½ tsp. salt**
- **¼ tsp. crushed red pepper flakes**
- **4 tilapia fillets (6 oz. each)**
- **2 Tbsp. canola oil**

1. In a shallow bowl, whisk eggs. In a separate shallow bowl, combine coconut, pecans, salt and pepper flakes. Dip fillets in eggs, then in coconut mixture, patting to help coating adhere.
2. In a large skillet, heat oil over medium heat. In batches, add tilapia and cook until fish is lightly browned and just begins to flake easily with a fork, 2-3 minutes on each side.

1 fillet: 380 cal., 26g fat (8g sat. fat), 129mg chol., 377mg sod., 4g carb. (1g sugars, 3g fiber), 35g pro.

Parmesan-Crusted Tilapia: Omit coconut, pecans and pepper flakes. In a shallow bowl, combine ½ cup crushed Ritz crackers, ¼ cup grated Parmesan cheese and salt. Proceed as directed. (This variation is not gluten-free.)

LINGUINE WITH BROCCOLI RABE & PEPPERS

Broccoli rabe is one of my very favorite vegetables. Since the rabe cooks right along with the pasta, you can multitask. Before you know it, dinner is served.

—Gilda Lester, Millsboro, DE

Takes: 25 min. • **Makes:** 6 servings

- **1 lb. broccoli rabe**
- **1 pkg. (16 oz.) linguine**
- **3 Tbsp. olive oil**
- **2 anchovy fillets, finely chopped, optional**
- **3 garlic cloves, minced**
- **½ cup sliced roasted sweet red peppers**
- **½ cup pitted Greek olives, halved**
- **½ tsp. crushed red pepper flakes**
- **¼ tsp. pepper**
- **⅛ tsp. salt**
- **½ cup grated Romano cheese**

1. Cut ½ in. off ends of broccoli rabe; trim woody stems. Cut stems and leaves into 2-in. pieces. Cook linguine according to the package directions, adding broccoli rabe during the last 5 minutes of cooking. Drain, reserving ½ cup pasta water.
2. Meanwhile, in a large skillet, heat oil over medium-high heat. Add anchovies and garlic; cook and stir 1 minute. Stir in red peppers, olives, pepper flakes, pepper and salt.
3. Add the linguine and broccoli rabe to skillet; toss to combine, adding reserved pasta water as desired to moisten. Serve with cheese.

1¼ cups: 429 cal., 15g fat (4g sat. fat), 2mg chol., 487mg sod., 60g carb. (4g sugars, 5g fiber), 17g pro.

LEMON CHICKEN SKEWERS

This easy-to-assemble recipe, with tender chunks of chicken and garden-fresh veggies, is always a hit—whether served for dinner at home or offered on platters for parties.
—Margaret Allen, Abingdon, VA

Prep: 10 min. + marinade. • **Grill:** 15 min.
Makes: 6 servings

- **¼ cup olive oil**
- **3 Tbsp. lemon juice**
- **1 Tbsp. white wine vinegar**
- **2 garlic cloves, minced**
- **2 tsp. grated lemon zest**
- **1 tsp. salt**
- **½ tsp. sugar**
- **¼ tsp. dried oregano**
- **¼ tsp. pepper**
- **1½ lbs. boneless skinless chicken breasts, cut into 1½-in. pieces**
- **3 medium zucchini, halved lengthwise and cut into 1½-in. slices**
- **3 medium onions, cut into wedges**
- **12 cherry tomatoes**

1. In a large bowl, combine the first 9 ingredients; set aside ¼ cup for basting. Pour half into a large bowl. Add chicken; turn to coat. Pour the remaining marinade into another large bowl. Add the zucchini, onions and tomatoes; turn to coat. Cover and refrigerate chicken and vegetables for up to 4 hours or overnight.
2. Drain and discard the marinade. Alternately thread chicken and vegetables onto metal or soaked wooden skewers. Grill, covered, over medium heat for 6 minutes on each side or until chicken juices run clear, basting occasionally with the reserved marinade.

1 serving: 219 cal., 6g fat (1g sat. fat), 66mg chol., 278mg sod., 12g carb. (0 sugars, 3g fiber), 29g pro. **Diabetic exchanges:** 3 lean meat, 2 vegetable.

PEPPERED PORK WITH MUSHROOM SAUCE

Using preseasoned pork tenderloin gives us flavorful, quick and satisfying meals without a big mess or leftovers. I have used all flavors of pork tenderloin for this recipe. Making the sauce doesn't take much extra time and the results are well worth it.
—Jolene Roszel, Helena, MT

Takes: 30 min. • **Makes:** servings

- **2 Tbsp. olive oil, divided**
- **1 peppercorn pork tenderloin (1 lb.) or flavor of your choice, cut into ¾-in. slices**
- **½ cup sliced fresh mushrooms**
- **¼ cup chopped onion**
- **2 Tbsp. all-purpose flour**
- **1 cup reduced-sodium beef broth**

1. In a large skillet, heat 1 Tbsp. oil over medium heat. Brown pork on both sides. Remove from pan.
2. In same pan, heat remaining oil over medium-high heat. Add the mushrooms and chopped onion; cook and stir until tender, 4-5 minutes.
3. In a small bowl, mix flour and broth until smooth. Stir into the mushroom mixture. Bring to a boil; cook and stir until sauce is thickened. Return pork to pan. Cook until a thermometer inserted in pork reads 145°.

3 oz. cooked pork with ¼ cup sauce: 208 cal., 11g fat (2g sat. fat), 55mg chol., 785mg sod., 7g carb. (1g sugars, 0 fiber), 21g pro.

SHORTCUT, NOT SHORT ON FLAVOR

Premarinated pork tenderloin makes easy work of weeknight dinners. Flavors vary by grocery store, but this versatile sauce will complement most varieties.

ROSEMARY-THYME LAMB CHOPS

My father loves lamb, so I make this dish whenever he visits. It's the perfect main course for holidays or get-togethers.
—Kristina Mitchell, Clearwater, FL

Takes: 30 min. • **Makes:** 4 servings

- **8 lamb loin chops (3 oz. each)**
- **½ tsp. pepper**
- **¼ tsp. salt**
- **3 Tbsp. Dijon mustard**
- **1 Tbsp. minced fresh rosemary**
- **1 Tbsp. minced fresh thyme**
- **3 garlic cloves, minced**

1. Sprinkle lamb chops with pepper and salt. In a small bowl, mix mustard, rosemary, thyme and garlic.
2. Grill chops, covered, on an oiled rack over medium heat for 6 minutes. Turn; spread herb mixture over chops. Grill 6-8 minutes longer or until meat reaches desired doneness (for medium-rare, a thermometer should read 135°; medium, 140°; medium-well, 145°).

2 lamb chops: 231 cal., 9g fat (4g sat. fat), 97mg chol., 493mg sod., 3g carb. (0 sugars, 0 fiber), 32g pro. **Diabetic exchanges:** 4 lean meat.

SWEET POTATO & TURKEY COUSCOUS

After a big turkey dinner, we always have leftover turkey and sweet potatoes. I put them together in this quick, easy and nutritious main dish that satisfies with a simple green salad alongside. This recipe works with leftover chicken, too!
—Roxanne Chan, Albany, CA

Takes: 30 min. • **Makes:** 6 servings

- **1 lb. sweet potatoes (about 2 medium), peeled and cut into ¾-in. cubes**
- **1 Tbsp. canola oil**
- **1 pkg. (8.8 oz.) uncooked pearl (Israeli) couscous**
- **¼ cup chopped onion**
- **¼ cup chopped celery**
- **½ tsp. poultry seasoning**
- **½ tsp. salt**
- **½ tsp. pepper**
- **2 cans (14½ oz. each) chicken broth**
- **2 cups chopped cooked turkey**
- **¼ cup dried cranberries**
- **1 tsp. grated orange zest**
- **Chopped fresh parsley**

1. Place sweet potatoes in a saucepan; add water to cover. Bring to a boil. Reduce the heat; cook, uncovered, until tender, 8-10 minutes. Drain.
2. Meanwhile, in a large cast-iron or other heavy skillet, heat oil over medium-high heat; saute couscous, onion and celery until couscous is lightly browned. Stir in seasonings and broth; bring to a boil. Reduce heat; simmer, uncovered, until couscous is tender, about 10 minutes.
3. Stir in the turkey, cranberries, orange zest and potatoes. Cook, covered, over low heat until heated through. Sprinkle with parsley.

1 cup: 365 cal., 5g fat (1g sat. fat), 50mg chol., 848mg sod., 59g carb. (13g sugars, 3g fiber), 21g pro.

GREEK TORTELLINI SKILLET

Looking to please picky little palates? One of our staff testers loved this simple skillet entree so much, she made it at home for her 2-year-old daughter, who said "*Mmm!*" after every bite.

—Taste of Home *Test Kitchen*

Takes: 30 min. • **Makes:** 6 servings

- **1 pkg. (19 oz.) frozen cheese tortellini**
- **1 lb. ground beef**
- **1 medium zucchini, sliced**
- **1 small red onion, chopped**
- **3 cups marinara or spaghetti sauce**
- **½ cup water**
- **¼ tsp. pepper**
- **2 medium tomatoes, chopped**
- **½ cup cubed feta cheese**
- **½ cup pitted Greek olives, halved**
- **2 Tbsp. minced fresh basil, divided**

1. Cook tortellini according to package directions. Meanwhile, in a large skillet, cook beef, zucchini and red onion over medium heat until the meat is no longer pink; drain.
2. Drain tortellini; add to skillet. Stir in the marinara sauce, water and pepper. Bring to a boil. Reduce heat; simmer, uncovered, for 5 minutes. Add the tomatoes, cheese, olives and 1 Tbsp. basil. Sprinkle with remaining basil.

1½ cups: 543 cal., 20g fat (8g sat. fat), 89mg chol., 917mg sod., 58g carb. (13g sugars, 6g fiber), 32g pro.

BAKED CHICKEN WITH BACON-TOMATO RELISH

We eat a lot of chicken for dinner, so I'm always trying to do something a little different with it. My children love the crispness of this chicken and my husband and I love the flavorful relish—you can't go wrong with bacon!

—Elisabeth Larsen, Pleasant Grove, UT

Takes: 30 min. • **Makes:** 4 servings

- **1 cup panko bread crumbs**
- **2 Tbsp. plus 1 tsp. minced fresh thyme, divided**
- **½ tsp. salt, divided**
- **½ tsp. pepper, divided**
- **⅓ cup all-purpose flour**
- **1 large egg, beaten**
- **1 lb. chicken tenderloins**
- **4 bacon strips, cut into ½-in. pieces**
- **1½ cups grape tomatoes, halved**
- **1 Tbsp. red wine vinegar**
- **1 Tbsp. brown sugar**

1. Preheat oven to 425°. In a shallow bowl, mix bread crumbs, 2 Tbsp. thyme, and ¼ tsp. each salt and pepper. Place flour and egg in separate shallow bowls. Dip chicken in flour; shake off excess. Dip in egg, then in crumb mixture, patting to help coating adhere. Place chicken on a greased rack in a 15x10x1-in. baking pan. Bake until a thermometer reads 165°, about 15 minutes.
2. Meanwhile, in a large skillet, cook bacon over medium heat until crisp, stirring occasionally, about 5 minutes. Remove with a slotted spoon; drain on paper towels. Reserve 2 Tbsp. drippings in pan; discard remaining drippings.
3. Add tomatoes, vinegar, sugar and remaining salt and pepper to drippings; cook and stir until tomatoes are tender, 2-3 minutes. Stir in bacon and remaining thyme. Serve with chicken.

2 chicken tenders with ¼ cup relish: 326 cal., 13g fat (4g sat. fat), 95mg chol., 602mg sod., 19g carb. (6g sugars, 2g fiber), 34g pro.
Diabetic exchanges: 4 lean meat, 2 fat, 1 starch.

RACK OR NO RACK?

Baking on a rack will help the coating on the underside of the chicken stay crunchy, but it isn't a must if you don't have a rack that fits into the pan.

Get Ready for Taco Night!

This selection of great recipes turns any busy weeknight into fiesta night! Each takes a new spin on the Mexican classic by using different regional flavors and ingredients. There's even one that loses the shell entirely, for a deconstructed taco!

ZESTY CHICKEN SOFT TACOS

We've made these tacos with both corn and flour tortillas, but naan flatbread is our favorite. Set out toppings and let people make their own.

—Jessie Grearson, Falmouth, ME

Takes: 25 min. • **Makes:** 6 servings

- **1 cup reduced-fat sour cream**
- **2 Tbsp. Sriracha chili sauce**
- **2 Tbsp. lime juice**
- **1½ tsp. grated lime zest**
- **½ tsp. salt**
- **⅛ tsp. pepper**
- **6 naan flatbreads, warmed**
- **1 rotisserie chicken, skin removed, shredded**
- **Minced fresh cilantro, optional**

In a small bowl, mix the first 6 ingredients. Spread over flatbreads; top with chicken and, if desired, cilantro.

1 taco: 420 cal., 14g fat (5g sat. fat), 111mg chol., 942mg sod., 33g carb. (7g sugars, 1g fiber), 37g pro.

QUICK TACOS AL PASTOR

My husband and I tried pork and pineapple tacos at a truck stand in Hawaii. Something about them was so tasty, I decided to make my own version at home.

—Lori McLain, Denton, TX

Takes: 25 min. • **Makes:** 4 servings

- **1 pkg. (15 oz.) refrigerated pork roast au jus**
- **1 cup well-drained unsweetened pineapple chunks, divided**
- **1 Tbsp. canola oil**
- **½ cup enchilada sauce**
- **8 corn tortillas (6 in.), warmed**
- **½ cup finely chopped onion**
- **¼ cup chopped fresh cilantro**
- **Optional: Crumbled queso fresco, salsa verde and lime wedges**

1. Coarsely shred pork, reserving juices. In a small bowl, crush half the pineapple with a fork.
2. In a large nonstick skillet, heat oil over medium-high heat. Add whole pineapple chunks; cook until lightly browned, 2-3 minutes, turning occasionally. Remove from pan.
3. Add enchilada sauce and the crushed pineapple to same skillet; stir in the pork and reserved juices. Cook over medium-high heat until the liquid is evaporated, 4-6 minutes, stirring occasionally.
4. Serve in corn tortillas with pineapple chunks, onion and cilantro. If desired, top with queso fresco and salsa, and serve with lime wedges.

2 tacos: 317 cal., 11g fat (3g sat. fat), 57mg chol., 573mg sod., 36g carb. (12g sugars, 5g fiber), 24g pro. **Diabetic exchanges:** 3 lean meat, 2 starch, 1 fat.

TACOS ON A STICK

Kids like assembling these creative kabobs almost as much as they like devouring them. The sensational Southwestern flavor is a taco-night twist on beef shish kabobs.
—Dixie Terry, Goreville, IL

Prep: 15 min. + marinating • **Grill:** 15 min.
Makes: 6 servings

- **1 envelope taco seasoning**
- **1 cup tomato juice**
- **2 Tbsp. canola oil**
- **2 lbs. beef top sirloin steak, cut into 1-in. cubes**
- **1 medium green pepper, cut into chunks**
- **1 medium sweet red pepper, cut into chunks**
- **1 large onion, cut into wedges**
- **16 cherry tomatoes**
- **Optional: Salsa con queso or sour cream**

1. In a large shallow dish, combine the taco seasoning, tomato juice and oil; mix well. Remove ½ cup for basting; refrigerate. Add beef and turn to coat. Cover; refrigerate for at least 5 hours.
2. Drain and discard marinade from beef. On metal or soaked wooden skewers, alternately thread beef, peppers, onion and tomatoes. Grill, uncovered, over medium heat for 3 minutes on each side. Baste with reserved marinade. Continue turning and basting until meat reaches desired doneness, 8-10 minutes. If desired, serve with salsa con queso or sour cream.

1 serving: 277 cal., 10g fat (3g sat. fat), 61mg chol., 665mg sod., 12g carb. (4g sugars, 2g fiber), 34g pro. **Diabetic exchanges:** 4 lean meat, 2 vegetable, 1 fat.

PO'BOY TACOS

I intended to make tostadas, but I misread a couple of ingredients and had to use what I had on hand. I put my own twist on a classic po'boy recipe and ended up with something even better.
—Cynthia Nelson, Saskatoon , SK

Takes: 30 min. • **Makes:** 4 servings

- **¼ cup mayonnaise**
- **2 Tbsp. seafood cocktail sauce**
- **½ tsp. Buffalo wing sauce**
- **½ medium ripe avocado, peeled**
- **1 Tbsp. lime juice**
- **½ cup all-purpose flour**
- **½ cup cornmeal**
- **2 Tbsp. Creole seasoning**
- **1 lb. uncooked shrimp (26-30 per lb.), peeled and deveined**
- **2 Tbsp. canola oil**
- **8 flour tortillas (6 in.)**
- **1 medium tomato, chopped**
- **2 Tbsp. minced fresh cilantro**

1. Combine mayonnaise, cocktail sauce and wing sauce; set aside. In another bowl, mash avocado with lime juice until combined; set aside.
2. In a shallow bowl, mix flour, cornmeal and Creole seasoning. Add shrimp, a few pieces at a time, and turn to coat; shake off excess. In a large skillet, heat oil over medium-high heat. Add shrimp; cook and stir until shrimp turn pink, 4-6 minutes.
3. Spread avocado mixture over tortillas. Top with shrimp, mayonnaise mixture, tomato and cilantro.

2 tacos: 551 cal., 29g fat (5g sat. fat), 139mg chol., 977mg sod., 47g carb. (3g sugars, 5g fiber), 25g pro.

Cooking for Two

Empty nest? Just starting out? Discover the joy of small-batch cooking! These smart, handy recipes are ideal for a tiny household and won't leave you dealing with a week's worth of leftovers. From entrees to three-ingredient sorbet, you'll find super meal ideas that all serve two. We even have cake!

LEMON PUDDING CAKE

My husband, Lloyd, loves this cake because it tastes like lemon meringue pie. The cake is no-fuss and makes just enough for the two of us.

—Dawn Fagerstrom, Warren, MN

Prep: 15 min. • **Bake:** 40 min.
Makes: 2 servings

- **1 large egg, separated, room temperature**
- **½ cup sugar**
- **⅓ cup whole milk**
- **2 Tbsp. all-purpose flour**
- **2 Tbsp. lemon juice**
- **1 tsp. grated lemon zest**
- **⅛ tsp. salt**
- **Optional: Confectioners' sugar, lemon slices and whipped cream**

1. Preheat oven to 325°. In a bowl, beat egg yolk. Add sugar, milk, flour, lemon juice, zest and salt; beat until smooth. Beat egg white until stiff peaks form; gently fold into lemon mixture. Pour into 2 ungreased 6-oz. custard cups (cups will be very full).
2. Place the cups in an 8-in. square baking pan. Pour boiling water into the pan to a depth of 1 in. Bake until a knife inserted in the center comes out clean and top is golden, 40-45 minutes. If desired, top with confectioners' sugar, lemon slices and whipped cream.

1 serving: 288 cal., 4g fat (2g sat. fat), 112mg chol., 200mg sod., 60g carb. (51g sugars, 0 fiber), 5g pro.

FOUR-CHEESE STUFFED SHELLS

More cheese, please! You'll get your fill from saucy jumbo pasta shells loaded with four different kinds—ricotta, Asiago, mozzarella and cottage cheese. Do the prep work, then freeze according to the recipe directions to have a ready-to-bake meal.

—Taste of Home *Test Kitchen*

Prep: 20 min. • **Bake:** 25 min.
Makes: 2 servings

- **6 uncooked jumbo pasta shells**
- **½ cup shredded part-skim mozzarella cheese, divided**
- **¼ cup shredded Asiago cheese**
- **¼ cup ricotta cheese**
- **¼ cup 4% cottage cheese**
- **1 Tbsp. minced chives**
- **1 pkg. (10 oz.) frozen chopped spinach, thawed and squeezed dry**
- **1 cup meatless spaghetti sauce**

1. Preheat oven to 350°. Cook pasta according to package directions. Meanwhile, in a small bowl, combine ¼ cup mozzarella cheese, Asiago cheese, ricotta cheese, cottage cheese, chives and ½ cup spinach (save the remaining spinach for another use).
2. Spread ½ cup spaghetti sauce into a shallow 1½-qt. baking dish coated with cooking spray. Drain pasta; stuff with cheese mixture. Arrange in prepared dish. Top with the remaining spaghetti sauce and mozzarella.
3. Bake, covered, until heated through, 25-30 minutes.

Freeze option: Cover and freeze unbaked casserole. To use, partially thaw in refrigerator overnight. Remove from the refrigerator 30 minutes before baking. Preheat oven to 350°. Bake as directed, increasing the time as necessary to heat through and for a thermometer inserted in the center of 2 or 3 shells to read 165°.

3 stuffed shells: 376 cal., 14g fat (9g sat. fat), 49mg chol., 959mg sod., 39g carb. (13g sugars, 4g fiber), 25g pro.

GROUND BEEF WELLINGTON

Trying new recipes is one of my favorite hobbies. It's also the most gratifying. What could beat the smiles and compliments of the ones you love?
—Julie Frankamp, Nicollet, MN

Prep: 30 min. • **Bake:** 25 min.
Makes: 2 servings

- ½ **cup chopped fresh mushrooms**
- 1 **Tbsp. butter**
- 2 **tsp. all-purpose flour**
- ¼ **tsp. pepper, divided**
- ½ **cup half-and-half cream**
- 1 **large egg yolk**
- 2 **Tbsp. finely chopped onion**
- ¼ **tsp. salt**
- ½ **lb. ground beef**
- 1 **tube (4 oz.) refrigerated crescent rolls**
- **Large egg, lightly beaten, optional**
- 1 **tsp. dried parsley flakes**

1. In a saucepan, saute mushrooms in butter until softened. Stir in flour and ⅛ tsp. pepper until blended. Gradually add the cream. Bring to a boil; cook and stir until thickened, about 2 minutes. Remove from the heat and set aside.
2. In a bowl, combine egg yolk, onion, 2 Tbsp. mushroom sauce, salt and remaining ⅛ tsp. pepper. Crumble beef over mixture and mix well. Shape into 2 loaves. Separate crescent dough into 2 rectangles on a baking sheet. Seal perforations. Place a meat loaf on each rectangle. Bring dough edges together and pinch to seal. If desired, brush with egg wash. Bake at 350° until golden brown and a thermometer inserted into meat loaf reads 160°, 24-28 minutes.
3. Meanwhile, warm the remaining sauce over low heat; stir in parsley. Serve sauce with Wellingtons.
1 serving: 578 cal., 37g fat (16g sat. fat), 207mg chol., 909mg sod., 28g carb. (7g sugars, 1g fiber), 28g pro.

CREAMY BUTTERSCOTCH PUDDING FOR 2

One day when I had a craving for something homemade, I tried from-scratch pudding. It's much better than the store-bought kind!
—EMR, tasteofhome.com

Prep: 10 min. • **Cook:** 10 min. + chilling
Makes: 2 servings

- **¼ cup packed brown sugar**
- **1 Tbsp. plus 1 tsp. cornstarch**
- **Dash salt**
- **1 cup fat-free milk**
- **1 large egg yolk, lightly beaten**
- **1½ tsp. butter**
- **¾ tsp. vanilla extract**
- **2 Pirouette cookies, optional**

1. In a small saucepan, combine the brown sugar, cornstarch and salt. Add milk and egg yolk; stir until smooth. Cook and stir over medium heat until mixture comes to a boil. Cook and stir until thickened, 1-2 minutes longer.
2. Remove from the heat; stir in butter and vanilla. Cool to room temperature, stirring several times. Pour into 2 individual dessert dishes. Cover and refrigerate until chilled, 1-2 hours. If desired, serve with Pirouette cookies.

½ cup: 217 cal., 5g fat (2g sat. fat), 111mg chol., 157mg sod., 38g carb. (33g sugars, 0 fiber), 5g pro.

CHIPOTLE-ORANGE CHICKEN

Big on flavor and easy on the cook's time, this slow-cooker chicken recipe is appealing. The sweet-hot sauce gets its heat from the chipotle pepper. I serve this dish with a side of rice to use up every delectable drop of the sauce.
—Susan Hein, Burlington, WI

Prep: 15 min. • **Cook:** 3 hours
Makes: 2 servings

- **2 boneless skinless chicken breast halves (6 oz. each)**
- **⅛ tsp. salt**
- **Dash pepper**
- **¼ cup chicken broth**
- **3 Tbsp. orange marmalade**
- **1½ tsp. canola oil**
- **1½ tsp. balsamic vinegar**
- **1½ tsp. minced chipotle pepper in adobo sauce**
- **1½ tsp. honey**
- **½ tsp. chili powder**
- **⅛ tsp. garlic powder**
- **2 tsp. cornstarch**
- **1 Tbsp. cold water**

1. Sprinkle chicken with salt and pepper. Transfer to a 1½-qt. slow cooker. In a small bowl, combine the chicken broth, marmalade, oil, vinegar, chipotle pepper, honey, chili powder and garlic powder; pour over chicken. Cover; cook on low for 3-4 hours or until a thermometer reads 165°.
2. Remove chicken to a serving platter and keep warm. Place cooking juices in a small saucepan; bring to a boil. Combine the cornstarch and water until smooth. Gradually stir into the pan. Bring to a boil; cook and stir 2 minutes or until thickened. Serve with chicken.

Freeze option: Cool chicken mixture. Freeze in freezer containers. To use, partially thaw in refrigerator overnight. Heat through slowly in a covered skillet until a thermometer inserted in chicken reads 165°, stirring occasionally; add broth or water if necessary.

1 chicken breast half: 324 cal., 8g fat (1g sat. fat), 95mg chol., 414mg sod., 29g carb. (24g sugars, 1g fiber), 35g pro.

CHICKEN PAELLA

Turmeric lends a pretty golden color to this Spanish-style entree. Haven't tried arborio rice? You'll love its creamy texture.
—Taste of Home *Test Kitchen*

Prep: 10 min. • **Cook:** 45 min.
Makes: 2 servings

- **2 boneless skinless chicken thighs (about ½ lb.), cut into 2-in. pieces**
- **½ cup cubed fully cooked ham**
- **⅓ cup chopped onion**
- **⅓ cup julienned sweet red pepper**
- **1 Tbsp. olive oil, divided**
- **½ cup uncooked arborio rice**
- **½ tsp. ground turmeric**
- **½ tsp. ground cumin**
- **½ tsp. minced garlic**
- **⅛ tsp. salt**
- **1 cup plus 2 Tbsp. chicken broth**
- **¾ cup frozen peas, thawed**

1. In a large skillet, saute the chicken, ham, onion and red pepper in 2 tsp. oil until chicken is browned on all sides. Remove with a slotted spoon.
2. In the same skillet, saute rice in the remaining 1 tsp. oil until lightly browned. Stir in the turmeric, cumin, garlic and salt. Return meat and vegetables to pan; toss lightly. Add broth; bring to a boil. Reduce heat to medium; cover and simmer until rice is tender, 30-35 minutes. Stir in peas.

1½ cups: 516 cal., 17g fat (4g sat. fat), 99mg chol., 1242mg sod., 52g carb. (5g sugars, 4g fiber), 36g pro.

STRAWBERRY PRETZEL DESSERT

I love the sweet-salty flavor of this pretty layered dessert. Sliced strawberries and gelatin top a smooth cream cheese filling and crispy pretzel crust. I think it's best when eaten within a day of being made.
—Wendy Weaver, Leetonia, OH

Prep: 15 min. + chilling • **Makes:** 2 servings

- **⅓ cup crushed pretzels**
- **2 Tbsp. butter, softened**
- **2 oz. cream cheese, softened**
- **¼ cup sugar**
- **¾ cup whipped topping**
- **2 Tbsp. plus 1½ tsp. strawberry gelatin**
- **½ cup boiling water**
- **1 cup sliced fresh strawberries**
- **Optional: Whipped topping and pretzel twists**

1. Preheat oven to 375°. In a large bowl, combine pretzels and butter. Press onto the bottom of 2 greased 10-oz. custard cups. Bake until set, 6-8 minutes. Cool on a wire rack.
2. In a small bowl, combine cream cheese and sugar until smooth. Fold in whipped topping. Spoon over crust. Refrigerate for 30 minutes.
3. Meanwhile, in a small bowl, dissolve the gelatin in boiling water. Cover and refrigerate for 20 minutes or until slightly thickened. Fold in strawberries. Carefully spoon over filling. Cover and refrigerate for at least 3 hours. If desired, top with whipped topping and pretzel twist.

1 serving: 516 cal., 27g fat (18g sat. fat), 62mg chol., 458mg sod., 64g carb. (47g sugars, 2g fiber), 6g pro.

CREAMY TWICE-BAKED POTATOES

With a yummy cream cheese filling, these rich, delicious potatoes are sure winners. They look fancy but aren't tricky to make.
—Linda Wheeler, Harrisburg, PA

Prep: 1¼ hours • **Bake:** 20 min.
Makes: 2 servings

- **2 medium baking potatoes**
- **2 Tbsp. butter, softened**
- **1 Tbsp. 2% milk**
- **¼ tsp. salt**
- **3 oz. cream cheese, cubed**
- **2 Tbsp. sour cream**
- **Paprika**
- **Optional: Minced fresh parsley and chopped green onions**

1. Preheat oven to 350°. Pierce potatoes and bake on a baking sheet until tender, about 1 hour. When cool enough to handle, cut a thin slice from top of each potato and discard. Scoop out pulp, leaving a thin shell.
2. In a small bowl, mash the pulp with butter, milk and salt. Stir in cream cheese and sour cream. Spoon into potato shells. Sprinkle with paprika.
3. Place on a baking sheet. Bake potatoes, uncovered, until heated through and the tops are golden brown, 20-25 minutes. If desired, sprinkle with parsley and onions.

1 serving: 452 cal., 29g fat (18g sat. fat), 88mg chol., 561mg sod., 40g carb. (5g sugars, 3g fiber), 8g pro.

CURRY COCONUT CHICKEN

My husband and I love this yummy dish! It's a breeze to prepare in the slow cooker, and it tastes just like a meal you'd have at your favorite Indian or Thai restaurant.
—Andi Kauffman, Beavercreek, OR

Prep: 20 min. • **Cook:** 4 hours
Makes: 2 servings

- **1 medium potato, peeled and cubed**
- **¼ cup chopped onion**
- **2 boneless skinless chicken breast halves (4 oz. each)**
- **½ cup light coconut milk**
- **2 tsp. curry powder**
- **1 garlic clove, minced**
- **½ tsp. reduced-sodium chicken bouillon granules**
- **⅛ tsp. salt**
- **⅛ tsp. pepper**
- **1 cup hot cooked rice**
- **1 green onion, thinly sliced**
- **Optional: Raisins, shredded coconut and chopped unsalted peanuts**

1. Place potatoes and onion in a 1½- or 2-qt. slow cooker. In a large skillet coated with cooking spray, brown chicken on both sides.
2. Transfer to slow cooker. In a small bowl, combine the coconut milk, curry, garlic, bouillon, salt and pepper; pour over chicken. Cover and cook on low 4-5 hours, until meat is tender.
3. Serve chicken and sauce with rice; sprinkle with green onions. If desired, garnish with raisins, coconut and peanuts.

1 serving: 353 cal., 7g fat (4g sat. fat), 63mg chol., 266mg sod., 42g carb. (3g sugars, 3g fiber), 27g pro.

VEGGIE-STUFFED TOMATOES

This recipe is my wife's favorite, and she loves when I cook it for her. These tomatoes make a great side dish, but they're also substantial enough to enjoy as a main course.

—Scott Szekretar, Islip, NY

Prep: 20 min. • **Bake:** 20 min.
Makes: 2 servings

2 medium tomatoes
½ small carrot
½ celery rib, sliced
½ small onion, peeled
1 small garlic clove, peeled
¼ tsp. dried oregano
2 tsp. olive oil
1 Tbsp. white wine or vegetable broth
⅓ cup dry bread crumbs
2 Tbsp. grated Parmesan cheese
3 to 4 fresh basil leaves, thinly sliced

1. Cut a thin slice off the top of each tomato. Leaving a ½-in. shell, scoop out and reserve pulp. Invert tomatoes onto paper towels to drain.
2. Meanwhile, in a food processor, cover and process carrot, celery, onion, garlic and reserved pulp until finely chopped. In large skillet, saute vegetable mixture and oregano in oil until tender. Add wine or broth; simmer, uncovered, until liquid is reduced by half, about 2 minutes. Remove from heat; cool slightly. Stir in the bread crumbs, Parmesan cheese and basil.
3. Stuff tomatoes; replace tops. Place in a shallow baking dish coated with cooking spray. Bake, uncovered, at 350° until heated through, 15-20 minutes.

1 tomato: 182 cal., 7g fat (2g sat. fat), 4mg chol., 234mg sod., 23g carb. (7g sugars, 4g fiber), 6g pro. **Diabetic exchanges:** 2 vegetable, 1½ fat, 1 starch.

PEAR PANDOWDY

I pulled out this recipe one night when my husband was craving something sweet, and it was a big hit with both of us. It's a superb last-minute dessert that practically melts in your mouth.

—Jennifer Class, Snohomish, WA

Prep: 20 min. • **Bake:** 20 min.
Makes: 2 servings

2 medium firm pears, peeled and sliced
2 Tbsp. brown sugar
4½ tsp. butter
1½ tsp. lemon juice
⅛ tsp. ground cinnamon
⅛ tsp. ground nutmeg

TOPPING

½ cup all-purpose flour
2 Tbsp. plus ½ tsp. sugar, divided
½ tsp. baking powder
⅛ tsp. salt
¼ cup cold butter, cubed
2 Tbsp. water
Vanilla ice cream, optional

1. In a small saucepan, combine the first 6 ingredients. Cook and stir over medium heat until pears are tender, 5 minutes. Pour into a greased 3-cup baking dish.
2. In a small bowl, combine the flour, 2 Tbsp. sugar, baking powder and salt; cut in butter until crumbly. Stir in water. Sprinkle over pear mixture. Sprinkle with remaining sugar.
3. Bake, uncovered, at 375° until a toothpick inserted into topping comes out clean and topping is lightly browned, 20-25 minutes. If desired, serve warm with ice cream.

½ cup: 594 cal., 32g fat (20g sat. fat), 84mg chol., 572mg sod., 76g carb. (45g sugars, 5g fiber), 4g pro.

EYE OF THE BEHOLDER

The origin of "pandowdy" is unknown, but one theory is that the deep-dish treat gets its name from its rather plain and dowdy appearance. Brown sugar or molasses (which was far cheaper than refined white sugar used to be) is the traditional sweetener in this thrifty centuries-old dessert.

PAN-SEARED COD

Cod has a soft, buttery appeal that goes great with cilantro, onions and crunchy pine nuts. This is the easiest, tastiest cod preparation I've found.

—Lucy Lu Wang, Seattle, WA

Takes: 25 min. • **Makes:** 2 servings

- **2 cod fillets (6 oz. each)**
- **½ tsp. salt**
- **¼ tsp. pepper**
- **3 Tbsp. olive oil, divided**
- **½ large sweet onion, thinly sliced**
- **½ cup dry white wine**
- **¼ cup coarsely chopped fresh cilantro**
- **1 Tbsp. pine nuts or sliced almonds**

1. Pat cod dry with paper towels; sprinkle with salt and pepper. In a large nonstick skillet, heat 2 Tbsp. oil over medium-high heat. Brown fillets lightly on both sides; remove from pan.
2. In same skillet, heat remaining oil over medium heat. Add onion; cook and stir until softened, 4-5 minutes. Stir in wine; cook until onion is lightly browned, stirring occasionally, 3-4 minutes longer. Return cod to pan. Reduce heat to low; cook, covered, until fish just begins to flake easily with a fork, 2-3 minutes.
3. Remove cod from pan. Stir cilantro and pine nuts into onion; serve with fish.

1 fillet with ¼ cup onion mixture: 378 cal., 24g fat (3g sat. fat), 65mg chol., 691mg sod., 8g carb. (5g sugars, 1g fiber), 28g pro.

SWEET ONIONS

Sweet onions are easy to recognize by their shape. They are shorter from pole to pole and bigger around than regular cooking onions. Many carry the names from the place they're grown, such as Vidalia (from Vidalia, Georgia), Walla Walla (from Washington) and Hawaii's Maui onion.

SIMPLE HERBED SCALLOPS

Living in Kansas as we do, fresh seafood can be hard to come by. Luckily, frozen scallops are always easy to find. This dish offers wonderful coastal flavor.
—Sarah Befort, Hays, KS

Takes: 30 min. • **Makes:** 2 servings

- **½ to ¾ lb. sea scallops**
- **3 Tbsp. butter, divided**
- **¾ tsp. lemon juice**
- **1 tsp. minced fresh parsley or ¼ tsp. dried parsley**
- **1½ tsp. minced fresh chives or ½ tsp. dried chives**
- **¼ tsp. minced fresh tarragon or ⅛ tsp. dried tarragon**
- **⅛ tsp. garlic salt**
- **Dash pepper**
- **2 Tbsp. dry bread crumbs**

1. Preheat oven to 350°. Place scallops in a greased 1-qt. baking dish. Mix 2 Tbsp. melted butter, lemon juice, herbs, garlic salt and pepper; drizzle over scallops.
2. Mix bread crumbs with remaining melted butter; sprinkle over top. Bake, uncovered, until scallops are firm and opaque, 20-25 minutes.

1 serving: 260 cal., 18g fat (11g sat. fat), 73mg chol., 754mg sod., 9g carb. (1g sugars, 1g fiber), 15g pro.

DARK CHOCOLATE PECAN CAKE

Made in a little loaf pan, this chocolate cake has a nutty praline layer and two layers of fluffy whipped cream. It's the only cake my husband really likes.
—Laura Draper, Garfield, WA

Prep: 30 min. • **Bake:** 25 min. + cooling
Makes: 2 servings

- **1 Tbsp. butter**
- **3 Tbsp. brown sugar**
- **1½ tsp. heavy whipping cream**
- **3 Tbsp. chopped pecans**

BATTER

- **2 Tbsp. shortening**
- **¼ cup sugar**
- **2 Tbsp. beaten egg**
- **⅛ tsp. vanilla extract**
- **6 Tbsp. cake flour**
- **2 Tbsp. baking cocoa**
- **¼ tsp. baking soda**
- **⅛ tsp. baking powder**
- **⅛ tsp. salt**
- **3 Tbsp. water**

TOPPING

- **¼ cup heavy whipping cream**
- **2 tsp. confectioners' sugar**
- **⅛ tsp. vanilla extract**
- **Optional: Chocolate curls and chopped pecans**

1. Line a 5¾x3x2-in. loaf pan with parchment; coat with cooking spray. In a small saucepan, melt butter; stir in brown sugar and cream. Cook and stir over low heat until sugar dissolves. Pour into prepared pan. Top with pecans. Cover and refrigerate.
2. In a small bowl, cream shortening and sugar until light and fluffy. Beat in egg and vanilla. Combine the flour, cocoa, baking soda, baking powder and salt; add to creamed mixture alternately with water. Beat just until combined.
3. Pour over pecans. Bake at 325° until a toothpick comes out clean, 25-30 minutes. Cool completely in pan.
4. In a small bowl, beat cream until it begins to thicken. Add confectioners' sugar and vanilla; beat until stiff peaks form. Remove cake from pan; split into two horizontal layers. Place bottom cake layer, nut side up, on a serving plate. Spread with half of the topping. Top with remaining layer and topping. If desired, garnish with chocolate curls and chopped pecans.

½ cake: 669 cal., 40g fat (15g sat. fat), 126mg chol., 428mg sod., 73g carb. (49g sugars, 3g fiber), 7g pro.

SEASONED TILAPIA FILLETS

If you need a healthy, keep-it-simple solution to dinner tonight, you just found it. This restaurant-quality dish relies on everyday spices to deliver big flavor.

—Dana Alexander, Lebanon, MO

Takes: 25 min. • **Makes:** 2 servings

- **2 tilapia fillets (6 oz. each)**
- **1 Tbsp. butter, melted**
- **1 tsp. Montreal steak seasoning**
- **½ tsp. dried parsley flakes**
- **¼ tsp. paprika**
- **¼ tsp. dried thyme**
- **⅛ tsp. onion powder**
- **⅛ tsp. salt**
- **⅛ tsp. pepper**
- **Dash garlic powder**

1. Preheat oven to 425°. Place tilapia in a greased 11x7-in. baking dish; drizzle with butter. In a small bowl, mix the remaining ingredients; sprinkle over fillets.
2. Bake, covered, 10 minutes. Uncover; bake until fish just begins to flake easily with a fork, 5-8 minutes.

1 fillet: 193 cal., 7g fat (4g sat. fat), 98mg chol., 589mg sod., 1g carb. (0 sugars, 0 fiber), 32g pro. **Diabetic exchanges:** 5 lean meat, 1½ fat.

RASPBERRY SORBET FOR TWO

You won't believe that you made this refreshing, fruity sorbet yourself! It's healthy freezer fare that will satisfy even your sweetest tooth.

—Taste of Home *Test Kitchen*

Prep: 5 min. + freezing • **Makes:** 2 servings

- **4½ tsp. lemon juice**
- **1¼ cups fresh or frozen unsweetened raspberries**
- **¾ cup confectioners' sugar**

In a food processor, combine all the ingredients; cover and process until smooth. Pour into 2 dessert dishes. Cover and freeze for 1 hour or until edges begin to firm. Stir and return to freezer. Freeze 1½ hours longer or until firm. Remove from the freezer 15 minutes before serving. If desired, garnish with raspberries.

½ cup: 216 cal., 0 fat (0 sat. fat), 0 chol., 1mg sod., 55g carb. (46g sugars, 5g fiber), 1g pro.

GOAT CHEESE & SPINACH STUFFED CHICKEN

This spinach-stuffed chicken breast recipe is special to me because it has so much flavor and not many calories. I love Italian food, but most of the time it is too heavy for me. This is a healthy twist on an Italian dish!

—Nicole Stevens, Charleston, SC

Prep: 30 min. • **Bake:** 20 min.
Makes: 2 servings

- **1½ cups fresh spinach, chopped**
- **⅓ cup julienned soft sun-dried tomatoes (not packed in oil), chopped**
- **¼ cup crumbled goat cheese**
- **2 garlic cloves, minced**
- **½ tsp. pepper, divided**
- **¼ tsp. salt, divided**
- **2 boneless skinless chicken breasts (6 oz. each)**
- **1 Tbsp. olive oil, divided**
- **½ lb. fresh asparagus, trimmed**
- **Aged balsamic vinegar or balsamic glaze, optional**

1. Preheat oven to 400°. In small bowl, combine the chopped spinach, sun-dried tomatoes, goat cheese, garlic, ¼ tsp. pepper and ⅛ tsp. salt.
2. Cut a pocket horizontally in the thickest part of each chicken breast. Fill with spinach mixture and secure with toothpicks.
3. In an 8-in. cast-iron or ovenproof skillet, heat 1½ tsp. oil over medium heat. Brown chicken on each side. Place in oven; bake 10 minutes.
4. Toss asparagus with remaining 1½ tsp. oil, ¼ tsp. pepper, and ⅛ tsp. salt; add to skillet. Bake until a thermometer inserted in chicken reads 165° and asparagus is tender, 10-15 minutes longer. If desired, drizzle with vinegar. Discard toothpicks before serving.

Note: This recipe was tested with soft sun-dried tomatoes that do not need to be softened in hot water.

1 stuffed chicken breast: 347 cal., 14g fat (4g sat. fat), 111mg chol., 532mg sod., 13g carb. (6g sugars, 5g fiber), 39g pro. **Diabetic exchanges:** 7 lean meat, 1 vegetable, 1 fat.

ITALIAN CHICKEN SKILLET SUPPER

Romano cheese, sliced vegetables and pine nuts jazz up this saucy chicken dinner. It's easy, and we love it!
—Barbara Lento, Houston, PA

Takes: 30 min. • **Makes:** 2 servings

- **2 boneless skinless chicken breast halves (4 oz. each)**
- **¼ tsp. garlic salt**
- **¼ tsp. pepper**
- **2 tsp. reduced-fat butter**
- **1 tsp. olive oil**
- **¼ lb. small fresh mushrooms, sliced**
- **½ medium onion, chopped**
- **¼ cup chopped sweet red pepper**
- **1 Tbsp. pine nuts**
- **2 cups fresh baby spinach**
- **1 Tbsp. all-purpose flour**
- **½ cup reduced-sodium chicken broth**
- **1½ tsp. spicy brown mustard**
- **2 tsp. shredded Romano cheese**
- **Optional: Penne pasta and fresh basil**

1. Flatten chicken slightly; sprinkle with garlic salt and pepper. In a large nonstick skillet, cook the chicken in butter and oil over medium heat until no longer pink, 3-4 minutes on each side. Remove and keep warm.
2. In the same skillet, saute the sliced mushrooms, onion, red pepper and pine nuts until vegetables are tender. Add the spinach; cook and stir until wilted, 2-3 minutes. Stir in flour. Gradually stir in chicken broth and mustard. Bring to a boil. Reduce heat; cook and stir until thickened, 2 minutes.
3. Return chicken to pan; heat through. Sprinkle with cheese. If desired, served with pasta and top with basil.

1 chicken breast half with ½ cup vegetable mixture: 248 cal., 10g fat (3g sat. fat), 70mg chol., 548mg sod., 12g carb. (4g sugars, 3g fiber), 29g pro. **Diabetic exchanges:** 3 lean meat, 2 vegetable, 1½ fat.

CHOCOLATE PEAR & CHERRY SALAD

It's fun to come up with new ways to use the ingredients we love. I developed a chocolate vinaigrette knowing how well it would play with stone fruit, the peppery bite of arugula, and the deep acidic sweetness of balsamic. There are tons of other options that can go with this vinaigrette, so feel free to play!
—Ryan Christie, Pacheco, CA

Prep: 25 min. + chilling • **Bake:** 15 min. • **Makes:** 2 servings

- **¾ cup cut French green beans (haricots verts)**
- **3 Tbsp. olive oil, divided**
- **⅛ tsp. salt**
- **⅛ tsp. pepper**
- **¼ cup balsamic vinegar**
- **1 oz. dark chocolate candy bar, chopped**
- **1 Tbsp. red wine vinegar**
- **4 cups fresh arugula**
- **1 medium pear, peeled and cut into ½-in. cubes**
- **½ cup frozen pitted sweet cherries, thawed and halved**
- **¼ cup dried cranberries**
- **3 Tbsp. coarsely chopped pecans**
- **1 Tbsp. minced dried apricots**
- **2 tsp. thinly sliced fresh mint leaves**

1. Heat oven to 350°. In an 8-in. square baking dish, toss beans with 1 Tbsp. olive oil, salt and pepper. Roast until tender, 12-15 minutes. Remove from oven. Toss with balsamic vinegar; refrigerate, covered, 1½-2 hours.
2. Meanwhile, in a microwave, melt chocolate; stir until smooth. Pulse the melted chocolate, red wine vinegar and the remaining 2 Tbsp. olive oil in a blender until smooth.
3. Divide arugula evenly between 2 salad bowls. Drizzle with chocolate mixture. Top with pears, cherries, cranberries and beans; sprinkle with pecans, apricots and mint leaves.

1 serving: 511 cal., 33g fat (6g sat. fat), 2mg chol., 166mg sod., 62g carb. (47g sugars, 8g fiber), 4g pro.

BAKED VIDALIA ONIONS

Served alongside any of a variety of fish and meats, this tender onion dish is a nice change of pace. It's a fun and flavorful side.
—Norma Durham, Rogersville, TN

Prep: 5 min. • **Bake:** 50 min.
Makes: 2 servings

- **2 small Vidalia or sweet onions**
- **4 tsp. butter**
- **¼ tsp. salt**
- **Dash pepper**
- **Garlic salt to taste, optional**

Preheat oven to 350°. Quarter onions halfway through and open slightly. Place each on a 18x12-in. piece of heavy-duty foil. Place 2 tsp. butter in the center of each onion; sprinkle with salt, pepper and, if desired, garlic salt. Fold foil to seal tightly. Bake until the onions are tender, 50-60 minutes. Open foil carefully to allow steam to escape.

1 onion: 148 cal., 8g fat (5g sat. fat), 20mg chol., 376mg sod., 19g carb. (12g sugars, 2g fiber), 2g pro.

MARINATED BROCCOLI

This festive side dish couldn't be easier to throw together. But because it's so pretty, it's perfect for special occasions.
—Edna Hoffman, Hebron, IN

Prep: 15 min. + chilling • **Makes:** 2 servings

- **4 tsp. olive oil**
- **1 Tbsp. water**
- **1 Tbsp. white wine vinegar**
- **1½ tsp. lemon juice**
- **1 tsp. honey**
- **1 garlic clove, minced**
- **¼ tsp. salt**
- **Dash cayenne pepper**
- **2 cups fresh broccoli florets**
- **2 Tbsp. chopped sweet red pepper**

In a jar with a tight-fitting lid, combine the first 8 ingredients; shake well. In a small bowl, combine broccoli and red pepper; add dressing and toss to coat. Cover and refrigerate for at least 1 hour. Serve with a slotted spoon.

1 cup: 119 cal., 9g fat (1g sat. fat), 0 chol., 315mg sod., 9g carb. (5g sugars, 2g fiber), 2g pro. **Diabetic exchanges:** 1½ fat, 1 vegetable.

Cool Salads to Share

Say yes to healthy veggies and lean protein when you reach for a zesty main-dish salad. Mediterranean, classic American, tropical and Asian flavors await your consideration here. These quick, easy dinners keep both you and the kitchen nice and cool.

GARDEN CHICKPEA SALAD

Looking for something different on a hot summer's day? This refreshing salad makes a terrific cold entree.

—Sally Sibthorpe, Shelby Township, MI

Takes: 25 min. • **Makes:** 2 servings

- ½ **tsp. cumin seeds**
- ¼ **cup chopped tomato**
- ¼ **cup lemon juice**
- ¼ **cup olive oil**
- 1 **garlic clove, minced**
- ¼ **tsp. salt**
- ¼ **tsp. cayenne pepper**

SALAD

- ¾ **cup canned garbanzo beans or chickpeas, rinsed and drained**
- 1 **medium carrot, julienned**
- 1 **small zucchini, julienned**
- 2 **green onions, thinly sliced**
- ½ **cup coarsely chopped fresh parsley**
- ¼ **cup thinly sliced radishes**
- ¼ **cup crumbled feta cheese**
- 3 **Tbsp. chopped walnuts**
- 3 **cups spring mix salad greens**

1. For dressing, in a dry small skillet, toast cumin seeds over medium heat until aromatic, stirring frequently. Transfer to a small bowl. Stir in tomato, lemon juice, oil, garlic, salt and cayenne pepper.
2. In a bowl, combine the chickpeas, carrot, zucchini, green onions, parsley, radishes, cheese and walnuts. Stir in ⅓ cup dressing.
3. To serve, divide greens between 2 plates; top with chickpea mixture. Drizzle with the remaining dressing.

1 serving: 492 cal., 38g fat (6g sat. fat), 8mg chol., 619mg sod., 30g carb. (7g sugars, 9g fiber), 12g pro.

SHRIMP COBB SALAD

This is a healthy salad that combines the best of both worlds. I often use a grill pan, but you can simply saute the shrimp, too. Use any greens you like—it's a versatile salad.

—Nicholas Monfre, Hudson, FL

Takes: 30 min. • **Makes:** 2 servings

- ½ **lb. uncooked shrimp (31-40 per lb.), peeled and deveined**
- 2 **Tbsp. olive oil**
- 1 **tsp. lemon juice**
- ½ **tsp. salt**
- ¼ **tsp. white pepper**

DRESSING

- ¼ **cup mayonnaise**
- 2 **Tbsp. crumbled Gorgonzola cheese**
- 1 **Tbsp. water**
- ½ **tsp. dried parsley flakes**
- ¼ **tsp. white wine vinegar**

SALAD

- 4 **cups spring mix salad greens**
- 1 **medium ripe avocado, peeled and cut into wedges**
- 4 **pieces bacon strips, cooked and chopped**
- 2 **hard-cooked large eggs, sliced**
- 1 **medium tomato, sliced**
- ¼ **cup slices red onion**

1. Toss shrimp with oil, lemon juice, salt and pepper; refrigerate, covered, 15 minutes. Mix dressing ingredients, mashing cheese with a fork. Place the greens on a platter; arrange remaining ingredients over top.
2. Grill shrimp, covered, over medium heat until pink, 2-3 minutes per side. Place over salad. Serve with dressing.

1 serving: 726 cal., 59g fat (12g sat. fat), 349mg chol., 1392mg sod., 16g carb. (3g sugars, 8g fiber), 36g pro.

SHRIMP & SCALLOPS TROPICAL SALAD

A fruity dressing makes seafood salad shine. Served on a bed of greens, the scrumptious combination of grilled seafood, veggies and macadamia nuts is the perfect way to celebrate a special summer occasion.
—Jackie Pressinger, Stuart, FL

Prep: 35 min. • **Cook:** 5 min.
Makes: 2 servings

- **2 Tbsp. diced peeled mango**
- **1 Tbsp. diced fresh pineapple**
- **1½ tsp. mango chutney**
- **1½ tsp. olive oil**
- **1 tsp. rice vinegar**
- **¾ tsp. lime juice**
- **Dash salt**
- **Dash crushed red pepper flakes**
- **3 cups torn Bibb or Boston lettuce**
- **1 cup chopped peeled cucumber**
- **½ medium ripe avocado, peeled and sliced**
- **2 Tbsp. coarsely chopped macadamia nuts, toasted**
- **1 Tbsp. finely chopped red onion**
- **1 Tbsp. minced fresh cilantro**
- **2 Tbsp. canola oil**
- **1½ tsp. Caribbean jerk seasoning**
- **6 uncooked large shrimp, peeled and deveined**
- **6 sea scallops, halved**

1. Place first 8 ingredients in a blender. Cover and process until blended; set aside. Divide the lettuce, cucumber, avocado, nuts, red onion and cilantro between 2 serving plates.
2. In a small bowl, combine oil and jerk seasoning. Thread shrimp and scallops onto 2 metal or soaked wooden skewers; brush with oil mixture.
3. Grill skewers, covered, over medium heat until shrimp turn pink and scallops are firm and opaque, 2-3 minutes on each side. Place on salads; drizzle with dressing.

1 salad: 413 cal., 32g fat (4g sat. fat), 96mg chol., 523mg sod., 16g carb. (6g sugars, 5g fiber), 19g pro.

Contest Winner

CRISPY ASIAN CHICKEN SALAD

Asian flavor, crunchy almonds and crispy chicken make this salad special.
—Beth Dauenhauer, Pueblo, CO

Takes: 30 min. • **Makes:** 2 servings

- **2 boneless skinless chicken breast halves (4 oz. each)**
- **2 tsp. hoisin sauce**
- **1 tsp. sesame oil**
- **½ cup panko bread crumbs**
- **4 tsp. sesame seeds**
- **2 tsp. canola oil**
- **4 cups spring mix salad greens**
- **1 small green pepper, julienned**
- **1 small sweet red pepper, julienned**
- **1 medium carrot, julienned**
- **½ cup sliced fresh mushrooms**
- **2 Tbsp. thinly sliced onion**
- **2 Tbsp. sliced almonds, toasted**
- **¼ cup reduced-fat sesame ginger salad dressing**

1. Flatten chicken breasts to ½-in. thickness. Combine hoisin sauce and sesame oil; brush over chicken. In a shallow bowl, combine the panko and sesame seeds; dip chicken in mixture.
2. In a large nonstick, cook the chicken in oil until no longer pink, 5-6 minutes on each side.
3. Meanwhile, divide salad greens between 2 plates. Top with peppers, carrot, mushrooms and onion. Slice chicken; place on top. Sprinkle with almonds and drizzle with dressing.

1 salad: 386 cal., 17g fat (2g sat. fat), 63mg chol., 620mg sod., 29g carb. (11g sugars, 6g fiber), 30g pro. **Diabetic exchanges:** 3 lean meat, 2 vegetable, 2 fat, 1 starch.

Slow Cooker & Instant Pot™

Whether you want to cook your meal fast or slow, have it ready in an instant or let it simmer for hours, this chapter is for you! The most popular and effective kitchen gadgets are all about making your kitchen time fit into your schedule. Plus, a special section highlights the newest kid on the block, the air fryer!

BACON LIMA BEANS

An unusual twist on traditional baked beans, this sweet and spicy version is easy to make in the slow cooker and is a surefire crowd pleaser—in winter or summer!
—Bette Banjack, Norristown, PA

Prep: 15 min. + soaking • **Cook:** 6 hours
Makes: 8 servings

- **1 lb. dried lima beans**
- **½ lb. bacon strips, cooked and crumbled**
- **1 can (10¾ oz.) condensed tomato soup, undiluted**
- **1⅓ cups water**
- **1 cup packed brown sugar**
- **1 garlic clove, minced**
- **1 tsp. salt**
- **1 tsp. paprika**
- **½ tsp. ground mustard**

Rinse and sort beans; soak according to package directions. Drain and rinse beans, discarding liquid. In a 3-qt. slow cooker, combine the beans and the remaining ingredients. Cook, covered, on low until beans are tender, 6-8 hours.

¾ cup: 375 cal., 5g fat (1g sat. fat), 10mg chol., 635mg sod., 69g carb. (35g sugars, 12g fiber), 16g pro.

PRESSURE-COOKER COLA BBQ CHICKEN

This recipe is really simple, and the sauce is filled with sweet smoky deliciousness. It is not a thick sauce, but you can easily put a little more on the top of each sandwich if you'd like. The meat is juicy and tender, and I enjoy adding a few tasty toppings to my sandwiches: sliced dill pickles and slices of pepper jack cheese. This recipe is for a pressure cooker, but it also can be made in the slow cooker—just cook on low for 8 hours.
—Ashley Lecker, Green Bay, WI

Prep: 10 min. • **Cook:** 10 min.
Makes: 14 servings

- **1 bottle (18 oz.) barbecue sauce**
- **1 cup cola**
- **2 Tbsp. cider vinegar**
- **1 tsp. garlic powder**
- **1 tsp. onion powder**
- **1 tsp. salt**
- **½ tsp. pepper**
- **2½ lbs. boneless skinless chicken breasts**
- **14 hamburger buns, split**
- **14 slices pepper jack cheese**
- **1 cup sliced sweet pickles**

1. Place the first 7 ingredients in a 6-qt. electric pressure cooker; add chicken. Lock lid; close pressure-release valve. Adjust to pressure-cook on high for 7 minutes. Quick-release pressure. A thermometer inserted in chicken should read at least 165°.
2. Remove chicken; cool slightly. Reserve 2 cups cooking juices; discard remaining juices. Shred the chicken with 2 forks. Combine with reserved juices. Serve on buns with cheese and pickles.

Freeze option: Freeze cooled meat mixture in freezer containers. To use, partially thaw in refrigerator overnight. Heat through in a saucepan, stirring occasionally; add a little water if necessary.

1 sandwich: 367 cal., 10g fat (5g sat. fat), 66mg chol., 971mg sod., 41g carb. (18g sugars, 1g fiber), 26g pro.

EASY CHICKEN TAMALE PIE

All you need are some simple ingredients from the pantry to put this slow-cooker meal together. I love the fact that I can go fishing while it cooks!

—Peter Halferty, Corpus Christi, TX

Prep: 20 min. • **Cook:** 7 hours
Makes: 8 servings

- **1 lb. ground chicken**
- **1 tsp. ground cumin**
- **1 tsp. chili powder**
- **½ tsp. salt**
- **¼ tsp. pepper**
- **1 can (15 oz.) black beans, rinsed and drained**
- **1 can (14½ oz.) diced tomatoes, undrained**
- **1 can (11 oz.) whole kernel corn, drained**
- **1 can (10 oz.) enchilada sauce**
- **2 green onions, chopped**
- **¼ cup minced fresh cilantro**
- **1 pkg. (8½ oz.) cornbread/muffin mix**
- **2 large eggs, lightly beaten**
- **1 cup shredded Mexican cheese blend**
- **Optional: Sour cream, salsa and minced fresh cilantro**

1. In a large skillet, cook the chicken over medium heat until no longer pink, 6-8 minutes, breaking it into crumbles. Stir in seasonings.
2. Transfer to a 4-qt. slow cooker. Stir in beans, tomatoes, corn, enchilada sauce, green onions and cilantro. Cook, covered, on low until heated through, 6-8 hours.
3. In a small bowl, combine muffin mix and eggs; spoon over chicken mixture. Cook, covered, on low until a toothpick inserted in cornbread layer comes out clean, 1-1½ hours longer.
4. Sprinkle with the cheese; let stand, covered, 5 minutes. If desired, serve with toppings.

1 serving: 359 cal., 14g fat (5g sat. fat), 110mg chol., 1021mg sod., 40g carb. (11g sugars, 5g fiber), 20g pro.

"EVERYTHING" STUFFING

My family goes crazy for this stuffing that I make in the slow cooker. It freezes well so we can enjoy it long after Thanksgiving.

—Bette Votral, Bethlehem, PA

Prep: 30 min. • **Cook:** 3 hours
Makes: 9 servings

- **½ lb. bulk Italian sausage**
- **4 cups seasoned stuffing cubes**
- **1½ cups crushed cornbread stuffing**
- **½ cup chopped toasted chestnuts or pecans**
- **½ cup minced fresh parsley**
- **1 Tbsp. minced fresh sage or 1 tsp. rubbed sage**
- **⅛ tsp. salt**
- **⅛ tsp. pepper**
- **1¾ cups sliced baby portobello mushrooms**
- **1 pkg. (5 oz.) sliced fresh shiitake mushrooms**
- **1 large onion, chopped**
- **1 medium apple, peeled and chopped**
- **1 celery rib, chopped**
- **3 Tbsp. butter**
- **1 can (14½ oz.) chicken broth**

1. In a large skillet, cook the sausage over medium heat until no longer pink, breaking it into crumbles; drain. Transfer to a large bowl. Stir in stuffing cubes, cornbread stuffing, chestnuts, parsley, sage, salt and pepper.
2. In the same skillet, saute mushrooms, onion, apple and celery in butter until tender. Stir into stuffing mixture. Add enough broth to reach desired moistness. Transfer to a 4-qt. slow cooker. Cover and cook on low for 3 hours, stirring once.

¾ cup: 267 cal., 13g fat (4g sat. fat), 21mg chol., 796mg sod., 30g carb. (5g sugars, 3g fiber), 8g pro.

CORNBREAD STUFFING?

We used a bagged cornbread stuffing from Pepperidge Farm in this recipe. If you can't find cornbread stuffing in your area, you can crumble up cornbread instead. If you're watching your sodium intake, omit the salt and use low-sodium chicken broth.

PRESSURE-COOKER CHEESY EGG CASSEROLE

This egg casserole is delicious, plus it's loaded with healthy veggies. It is easy to prepare and an excellent make-ahead option, too. It makes a fabulous breakfast, brunch or light lunch.
—Joan Hallford, North Richland Hills, TX

Prep: 10 min. • **Cook:** 40 min. + standing.
Makes: 6 servings

- **2 tsp. olive oil**
- **1½ cups sliced fresh mushrooms**
- **1 small onion, finely chopped**
- **½ cup finely chopped sweet red pepper**
- **1 can (10 oz.) diced tomatoes and green chiles, drained well**
- **¼ cup vegetable broth**
- **1 cup chopped fresh kale or baby spinach**
- **8 large eggs**
- **½ cup 2% milk**
- **½ tsp. salt**
- **½ tsp. pepper**
- **½ cup shredded sharp cheddar cheese**
- **½ cup shredded pepper jack cheese**
- **Optional: Sour cream, salsa, thinly sliced green onions and hot pepper sauce**

1. Select saute setting on a 6-qt. electric pressure cooker. Adjust for medium heat; add oil. When the oil is hot, cook and stir mushrooms, onion and sweet red pepper until crisp-tender, 3-5 minutes. Add the tomatoes and broth, stirring to loosen browned bits from pan. Press cancel. Add kale; stir until wilted.
2. In a large bowl, whisk the eggs, milk, salt and pepper. Stir in cheeses and kale mixture. Pour into a greased 4-cup baking dish; cover with foil.
3. Wipe pressure cooker clean. Place trivet insert and 1 cup water in pressure cooker. Fold an 18x12-in. piece of foil lengthwise into thirds, making a sling. Use the sling to lower the baking dish onto the trivet. Lock lid; close pressure-release valve. Adjust to pressure-cook on high for 40 minutes. Quick-release the pressure.
4. Using the foil sling, carefully remove baking dish. Let stand 10 minutes. Serve warm with optional toppings as desired.
⅔ cup: 223 cal., 15g fat (6g sat. fat), 269mg chol., 562mg sod., 8g carb. (4g sugars, 1g fiber), 15g pro.

PRESSURE-COOKER CINNAMON APPLESAUCE

Homemade applesauce is a breeze in an electric pressure cooker. A few minutes of prep and a short cook time put this treat on the table very quickly!
—Ally Billhorn, Wilton, IA

Prep: 20 min. • **Cook:** 5 min. + releasing
Makes: 8 cups

- **5 lbs. apples (about 15 medium), peeled and chopped**
- **1 cup water**
- **⅓ cup sugar**
- **2 tsp. ground cinnamon**
- **½ tsp. ground nutmeg**
- **⅛ tsp. salt**

1. Combine all ingredients in a 6-qt. electric pressure cooker. Lock the lid; close pressure-release valve. Adjust to pressure-cook on high for 5 minutes. Let pressure release naturally.
2. Mash apples with a potato masher or use an immersion blender until blended. Serve warm or store in airtight container in the refrigerator.
⅔ cup: 101 cal., 0 fat (0 sat. fat), 0 chol., 25mg sod., 26g carb. (22g sugars, 3g fiber), 0 pro.

PRESSURE-COOKER HERBED TURKEY BREASTS

Tender turkey breast is enhanced with an array of flavorful herbs in this juicy, comforting dish.

—Laurie Mace, Los Osos, CA

Prep: 25 min. + marinating
Cook: 20 min. + releasing
Makes: 12 servings

- **1 can (14½ oz.) chicken broth**
- **½ cup lemon juice**
- **¼ cup packed brown sugar**
- **¼ cup fresh sage**
- **¼ cup fresh thyme leaves**
- **¼ cup lime juice**
- **¼ cup cider vinegar**
- **¼ cup olive oil**
- **1 envelope onion soup mix**
- **2 Tbsp. Dijon mustard**
- **1 Tbsp. minced fresh marjoram**
- **1½ tsp. paprika**
- **1 tsp. garlic powder**
- **1 tsp. pepper**
- **½ tsp. salt**
- **2 boneless skinless turkey breast halves (2 lbs. each)**
- **Optional: Additional fresh thyme and marjoram and lemon wedges**

1. In a blender, process the first 15 ingredients until blended. Place turkey in a bowl or shallow dish; pour marinade over turkey and turn to coat. Refrigerate, covered, 8 hours or overnight, turning occasionally.
2. Transfer turkey and marinade to a 6-qt. electric pressure cooker. Lock lid; close pressure-release valve. Adjust to pressure-cook on high for 20 minutes.
3. Let the pressure release naturally for 10 minutes; quick-release any remaining pressure. A thermometer inserted in the turkey breasts should read at least 165°.
4. Remove turkey from pressure cooker; tent with foil. Let stand 10 minutes before slicing. If desired, top with additional fresh thyme and marjoram and serve with lemon wedges.

5 oz. cooked turkey: 219 cal., 5g fat (1g sat. fat), 87mg chol., 484mg sod., 5g carb. (3g sugars, 0 fiber), 36g pro.
Diabetic exchanges: 5 lean meat.

PRESSURE-COOKER LIGHT DEVILED EGGS

Our updated version of a classic appetizer uses only half the egg yolks of traditional deviled eggs and calls for soft bread crumbs to help firm up the filling. Light ingredients lower the fat grams even more.
—Taste of Home *Test Kitchen*

Prep: 20 min. • **Cook:** 5 min. + releasing
Makes: 16 pieces

- **8 large eggs**
- **¼ cup fat-free mayonnaise**
- **¼ cup reduced-fat sour cream**
- **2 Tbsp. soft bread crumbs**
- **1 Tbsp. prepared mustard**
- **¼ tsp. salt**
- **Dash white pepper**
- **4 pimiento-stuffed olives, sliced**
- **Paprika, optional**

1. Place trivet insert and 1 cup water in a 6-qt. electric pressure cooker. Set eggs on trivet. Lock lid; close pressure-release valve. Adjust to pressure-cook on high for 5 minutes. Let pressure release naturally for 5 minutes; quick-release any remaining pressure. Immediately place eggs in a bowl of ice water to cool. Remove shells.
2. Cut eggs lengthwise in half. Remove yolks; refrigerate 8 yolk halves for another use. Set whites aside. In a small bowl, mash remaining yolks. Stir in mayonnaise, sour cream, bread crumbs, mustard, salt and pepper. Stuff or pipe into egg whites. Garnish with olives. If desired, sprinkle with paprika.

1 stuffed egg half: 32 cal., 2g fat (1g sat. fat), 46mg chol., 132mg sod., 1g carb. (1g sugars, 0 fiber), 3g pro.

JALAPENO MAC & CHEESE

Many years ago after I had knee surgery, a friend brought me a big casserole of mac and cheese along with the recipe. I have fiddled with the recipe over the years, most recently adding jalapenos at the request of my son. What an awesome spicy twist!
—Teresa Gustafson, Elkton, MD

Prep: 25 min. • **Cook:** 3 hours
Makes: 15 servings

- **1 pkg. (16 oz.) uncooked elbow macaroni**
- **6 Tbsp. butter, divided**
- **4 jalapeno peppers, seeded and finely chopped**
- **3 cups shredded cheddar cheese**
- **2 cups shredded Colby-Monterey Jack cheese**
- **2 cups whole milk**
- **1 can (10¾ oz.) condensed cream of onion soup, undiluted**
- **1 can (10¾ oz.) condensed cheddar cheese soup, undiluted**
- **½ cup mayonnaise**
- **¼ tsp. pepper**
- **1 cup crushed Ritz crackers (about 25 crackers)**

1. Cook macaroni according to package directions for al dente; drain. Transfer to a greased 5-qt. slow cooker.
2. Melt 2 Tbsp. butter in a large skillet over medium-high heat. Add jalapenos; cook and stir until crisp-tender, about 5 minutes. Add to slow cooker. Stir in the cheeses, milk, soups, mayonnaise and pepper.
3. Cook, covered, on low for 3 hours or until the cheese is melted and the mixture is heated through. Melt the remaining butter; stir in crackers. Sprinkle over macaroni mixture.

¾ cup: 428 cal., 27g fat (13g sat. fat), 53mg chol., 654mg sod., 33g carb. (5g sugars, 2g fiber), 14g pro.

PRESSURE-COOKER EGGS IN PURGATORY

Tomatoes and red pepper flakes add spicy zing to these saucy eggs. Serve them with toasted bread or sauteed polenta rounds for an unforgettable morning meal.

—Nick Iverson, Denver, CO

Prep: 30 min. • **Cook:** 5 min.
Makes: 4 servings

- **2 cans (14½ oz. each) fire-roasted diced tomatoes, undrained**
- **1 medium onion, chopped**
- **½ cup water**
- **2 Tbsp. canola oil**
- **2 garlic cloves, minced**
- **2 tsp. smoked paprika**
- **½ tsp. sugar**
- **½ tsp. crushed red pepper flakes**
- **¼ cup tomato paste**
- **4 large eggs**
- **¼ cup shredded Manchego or Monterey Jack cheese**
- **2 Tbsp. minced fresh parsley**
- **1 tube (18 oz.) polenta, sliced and warmed, optional**

1. Place the first 8 ingredients in a 6-qt. electric pressure cooker. Lock lid; close the pressure-release valve. Adjust to pressure-cook on high for 4 minutes. Quick-release pressure. Press cancel.
2. Select saute setting and adjust for low heat. Add tomato paste; simmer, uncovered, until mixture is slightly thickened, about 10 minutes, stirring occasionally.
3. With the back of a spoon, make 4 wells in the sauce. Break an egg into each well; sprinkle with cheese. Cover (do not lock lid). Simmer until the egg whites are completely set and yolks begin to thicken but are not hard, 8-10 minutes. Sprinkle with parsley. If desired, serve with polenta.

1 serving: 255 cal., 14g fat (4g sat. fat), 193mg chol., 676mg sod., 20g carb. (9g sugars, 3g fiber), 11g pro. **Diabetic exchanges:** 1½ fat, 1 starch, 1 medium-fat meat.

PRESSURE-COOKER RAISIN NUT OATMEAL

There's no better feeling than starting off the day with a terrific breakfast. I love that the oats, fruit and spices in this homey meal cook together on their own.

—Valerie Sauber, Adelanto, CA

Prep: 10 min. + standing
Cook: 5 min. + releasing
Makes: 6 servings

- **3 cups vanilla almond milk**
- **¾ cup steel-cut oats**
- **¾ cup raisins**
- **3 Tbsp. brown sugar**
- **4½ tsp. butter**
- **¾ tsp. ground cinnamon**
- **½ tsp. salt**
- **1 large apple, peeled and chopped**
- **¼ cup chopped pecans**

1. In a 6-qt. electric pressure cooker, combine the first 7 ingredients. Lock lid; close pressure-release valve. Adjust to pressure-cook on high for 5 minutes. Let pressure release naturally. Press cancel.
2. Stir in the apple. Let stand 10 minutes before serving (oatmeal will thicken upon standing). Spoon oatmeal into bowls; sprinkle with pecans.

¾ cup: 272 cal., 9g fat (2g sat. fat), 8mg chol., 298mg sod., 47g carb. (29g sugars, 4g fiber), 4g pro.

PRESSURE-COOKER BEEF & VEGGIE SLOPPY JOES

Because I'm always looking for ways to serve my family healthy and delicious food, I started experimenting with my go-to veggies and ground beef. I came up with this favorite that my kids actually request!
—Megan Niebuhr, Yakima, WA

Prep: 35 min. • **Cook:** 5 min.
Makes: 10 servings

- **2 lbs. lean ground beef (90% lean)**
- **4 medium carrots, shredded**
- **1 medium yellow summer squash, shredded**
- **1 medium zucchini, shredded**
- **1 medium sweet red pepper, finely chopped**
- **2 medium tomatoes, seeded and chopped**
- **1 small red onion, finely chopped**
- **½ cup ketchup**
- **¼ cup water**
- **3 Tbsp. minced fresh basil or 3 tsp. dried basil**
- **2 Tbsp. cider vinegar**
- **2 garlic cloves, minced**
- **½ tsp. salt**
- **½ tsp. pepper**
- **3 Tbsp. molasses**
- **10 whole wheat hamburger buns, split**

1. Select saute or browning setting on a 6-qt. electric pressure cooker; adjust for medium heat. Cook the beef until meat is no longer pink, about 8-10 minutes, breaking into crumbles; drain. Return to pressure cooker. Press cancel. Add the carrots, summer squash, zucchini, red pepper, tomatoes, onion, ketchup, water, basil, vinegar, garlic, salt and pepper (do not stir).
2. Lock the lid; close pressure-release valve. Adjust to pressure-cook on high for 5 minutes. Quick-release pressure. Stir in molasses. Using a slotted spoon, serve beef mixture on buns.

Freeze option: Freeze cooled meat mixture and juices in freezer containers. To use, partially thaw in refrigerator overnight. Heat through in a saucepan, stirring occasionally; add a little water if necessary.

1 sandwich: 316 cal., 10g fat (3g sat. fat), 57mg chol., 566mg sod., 36g carb. (15g sugars, 5g fiber), 22g pro. **Diabetic exchanges:** 3 lean meat, 2½ starch.

PRESSURE-COOKER SUMMER SQUASH

We love squash, but I got bored with fixing plain old squash and cheese. I decided to jazz it up a bit by adding seasoned croutons and bacon. This was a huge hit with the family.
—Joan Hallford, North Richland Hills, TX

Takes: 25 min. • **Makes:** 8 servings

- **1 lb. medium yellow summer squash**
- **1 lb. medium zucchini**
- **2 medium tomatoes, chopped**
- **1 cup vegetable broth**
- **¼ cup thinly sliced green onions**
- **½ tsp. salt**
- **¼ tsp. pepper**
- **1½ cups Caesar salad croutons, coarsely crushed**
- **½ cup shredded cheddar cheese**
- **4 bacon strips, cooked and crumbled**

Cut squash and zucchini into ¼-in.-thick slices; place in a 6-qt. electric pressure cooker. Add next 5 ingredients. Lock lid; close pressure-release valve. Adjust to pressure-cook on high for 1 minute. Quick-release pressure. Remove veggies with a slotted spoon. To serve, top with croutons, cheese and bacon.

¾ cup: 111 cal., 6g fat (2g sat. fat), 12mg chol., 442mg sod., 10g carb. (4g sugars, 2g fiber), 6g pro. **Diabetic exchanges:** 1 vegetable, 1 fat.

PRESSURE-COOKER LENTIL & SAUSAGE SOUP

I prefer this soup made with red wine because I think the wine makes the flavors richer, but it will still be delicious if you opt for broth.
—Ashley Lecker, Green Bay, WI

Prep: 30 min. • **Cook:** 15 min. + releasing
Makes: 2¼ qt.

- **1 Tbsp. olive oil**
- **¾ lb. bulk Italian sausage**
- **1 small onion, chopped**
- **1 celery rib, chopped**
- **1 medium carrot, chopped**
- **1 carton (32 oz.) beef broth**
- **1 can (14½ oz.) diced tomatoes, undrained**
- **1 cup dried lentils, rinsed**
- **1 cup chopped fresh spinach**
- **1 cup dry red wine or additional beef broth**
- **1 garlic clove, minced**
- **½ tsp. salt**
- **½ tsp. pepper**
- **Grated Parmesan cheese, optional**

1. Select saute or browning setting on a 6-qt. electric pressure cooker. Adjust for medium heat; add oil. When the oil is hot, add the sausage, onion, celery and carrot. Cook until the sausage is no longer pink and the vegetables are tender, 6-8 minutes, breaking up sausage into crumbles; drain. Press cancel. Return all to pressure cooker.
2. Add broth, tomatoes, lentils, spinach, wine, garlic, salt and pepper. Lock the lid; close pressure-release valve. Adjust to pressure cook on high for 15 minutes. Let pressure release naturally for 10 minutes; quick-release any remaining pressure. If desired, serve with cheese.

Freeze option: Freeze cooled soup in freezer containers. To use, partially thaw in refrigerator overnight. Heat through in a saucepan, stirring occasionally; add a little water if necessary.

1 cup: 229 cal., 12g fat (3g sat. fat), 26mg chol., 977mg sod., 18g carb. (3g sugars, 4g fiber), 12g pro.

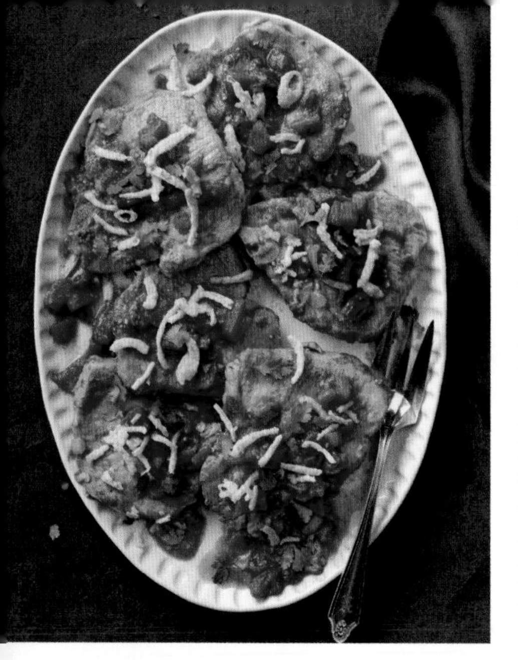

SLOW-COOKER CHIPOTLE PORK CHOPS

I love the tender texture of pork chops made in the slow cooker! The flavor of this sauce is similar to barbecue, but with a little kick. The crispy onions on top add an extra, delectable crunch.

—Elisabeth Larsen, Pleasant Grove, UT

Prep: 15 min. • **Cook:** 4 hours
Makes: 8 servings

- **8 bone-in pork loin chops (7 oz. each)**
- **1 small onion, finely chopped**
- **⅓ cup chopped chipotle peppers in adobo sauce**
- **¼ cup packed brown sugar**
- **2 Tbsp. red wine vinegar**
- **2 garlic cloves, minced**
- **½ tsp. salt**
- **¼ tsp. pepper**
- **1 can (15 oz.) tomato sauce**
- **1 can (14½ oz.) fire-roasted diced tomatoes, undrained**

TOPPINGS

- **1 can (6 oz.) french-fried onions**
- **¼ cup minced fresh cilantro**

Place all ingredients except toppings in a 5-qt. slow cooker. Cook, covered, on low until a thermometer inserted in pork reads at least 145°, 4-5 hours. Top with french-fried onions and cilantro just before serving.

1 pork chop: 408 cal., 20g fat (6g sat. fat), 86mg chol., 844mg sod., 24g carb. (10g sugars, 2g fiber), 32g pro.

PRESSURE-COOKER SMOKED SAUSAGE & WHITE BEANS

My husband grew up in the South, where sausage and beans were on the menu weekly. I quickly became a fan. The pressure cooker eliminates the lengthy process of soaking the beans overnight and then slow-cooking them. Serve the dish over rice, and use crusty bread to soak up the broth. I used gourmet smoked sausage flavored with Gouda and pear for this dish, but you can use any smoked sausage you like.

—Debbie Glasscock, Conway, AR

Prep: 20 min. • **Cook:** 25 min.
Makes: 8 servings

- **10 cups water**
- **1 lb. dried great northern beans**
- **1 lb. smoked sausage, sliced**
- **1 smoked ham hock (about ½ lb.)**
- **1 large onion, chopped**
- **5 garlic cloves, minced**
- **1 tsp. kosher salt**
- **1 tsp. sugar**
- **1 tsp. each dried parsley flakes, oregano and basil**
- **¼ tsp. pepper**
- **Hot cooked rice**
- **Minced fresh parsley**
- **Sriracha chili sauce, optional**

1. Place water, beans, sausage, ham hock, onion, garlic, salt, sugar and seasonings in a 6-qt. electric pressure cooker. Lock lid; close pressure-release valve. Adjust to pressure cook on high for 22 minutes.
2. Quick-release pressure. Press cancel. Remove ham hock. Serve bean mixture with rice, parsley and desired amount of cooking liquid. Serve with chili sauce as desired.

1¼ cups bean mixture: 382 cal., 16g fat (7g sat. fat), 38mg chol., 909mg sod., 40g carb. (4g sugars, 12g fiber), 21g pro.

SLOW-COOKER CHEDDAR BACON BEER DIP

My tangy, smoky dip won the top prize for our office party recipe contest. Other beers can work, but steer clear of dark varieties.
—Ashley Lecker, Green Bay, WI

Prep: 15 min. • **Cook:** 3 hours
Makes: 4½ cups

- **18 oz. cream cheese, softened**
- **¼ cup sour cream**
- **1½ Tbsp. Dijon mustard**
- **1 tsp. garlic powder**
- **1 cup amber beer or nonalcoholic beer**
- **2 cups shredded cheddar cheese**
- **1 lb. bacon strips, cooked and crumbled, divided**
- **¼ cup heavy whipping cream**
- **1 green onion, thinly sliced**
- **Soft pretzel bites**

1. In a greased 3-qt. slow cooker, combine the cream cheese, sour cream, mustard and garlic powder until smooth. Stir in beer, cheese and all but 2 Tbsp. bacon. Cook, covered, on low, stirring occasionally, until heated through, 3-4 hours.
2. In the last 30 minutes, stir in heavy cream. Top with onion and remaining bacon. Serve with soft pretzel bites.

¼ cup: 213 cal., 19g fat (10g sat. fat), 60mg chol., 378mg sod., 2g carb. (1g sugars, 0 fiber), 8g pro.

LIGHTEN IT UP!

To make a lighter version of this recipe, use reduced-fat cream cheese, light sour cream, reduced-fat shredded cheese, and half-and-half. Then serve with fresh celery and carrot sticks instead of soft pretzels.

SLOW-COOKER BREAKFAST BURRITOS

Prep these tasty, hearty burritos the night before for a quick breakfast in the morning, or let them cook while you are away on a weekend afternoon for an easy supper.
—Anna Miller, Churdan, IA

Prep: 25 min. • **Cook:** 3¾ hours + standing
Makes: 12 servings

- **1 pkg. (12 oz.) uncooked breakfast sausage links**
- **1 pkg. (28 oz.) frozen O'Brien potatoes, thawed**
- **2 cups shredded sharp cheddar cheese**
- **12 large eggs**
- **½ cup 2% milk**
- **¼ tsp. seasoned salt**
- **⅛ tsp. pepper**
- **12 flour tortillas (8 in.)**
- **Optional: Salsa, sliced jalapenos, chopped tomatoes, sliced green onions and cubed avocado**

1. Remove sausage from casings. In a large skillet, cook sausage over medium heat until no longer pink, 8-10 minutes, breaking into crumbles; drain.
2. In a greased 4- or 5-qt. slow cooker, layer potatoes, sausage and cheese. In a large bowl, whisk eggs, milk, seasoned salt and pepper until blended; pour over top.
3. Cook, covered, on low 3¾-4¼ hours or until eggs are set and a thermometer reads 160°. Uncover and let stand for 10 minutes. Serve wrapped in tortillas with the toppings of your choice.

1 burrito: 382 cal., 21g fat (9g sat. fat), 221mg chol., 711mg sod., 29g carb. (2g sugars, 3g fiber), 18g pro.

START THE NIGHT BEFORE

To get a head start on these burritos, do all the prep work in Steps 1 & 2 the night before and then place the loaded slow-cooker insert in the fridge. In the morning, let it sit out at room temperature for about 20 minutes before turning on the slow cooker—temperature shock may crack a ceramic insert!

PRESSURE-COOKER COUNTRY CAPTAIN CHICKEN

Whether or not it was brought to the region by a British sailor, as popular legend has it, this recipe has been around Georgia since the 1800s. Traditionally served over rice, it's also delicious with noodles or mashed potatoes.
—Suzanne Banfield, Basking Ridge, NJ

Prep: 25 min. • **Cook:** 10 min.
Makes: 8 servings

- **1 large onion, chopped**
- **1 medium sweet red pepper, chopped**
- **2 garlic cloves, minced**
- **3 lbs. boneless skinless chicken thighs**
- **½ cup chicken broth**
- **1 Tbsp. brown sugar**
- **1 Tbsp. curry powder**
- **1 tsp. ground ginger**
- **1 tsp. ground cinnamon**
- **1 tsp. dried thyme**
- **1 can (14½ oz.) diced tomatoes, undrained**
- **½ cup golden raisins or raisins**
- **Hot cooked rice**
- **Chopped fresh parsley, optional**

1. Place onion, red pepper and garlic in a 6-qt. electric pressure cooker; top with chicken. In a small bowl, whisk the broth, brown sugar and seasonings; pour over chicken. Top with tomatoes and raisins. Lock the lid; close pressure-release valve. Adjust to pressure-cook on high for 6 minutes.
2. Quick-release the pressure. A thermometer inserted in the chicken should read at least 170°. Thicken the cooking juices if desired. Serve with rice and, if desired, parsley.

Freeze option: Place the chicken and vegetables in freezer containers; top with cooking juices. Cool and freeze. To use, partially thaw in refrigerator overnight. Heat through in a covered saucepan, stirring occasionally; add a little broth if necessary.

1 serving: 298 cal., 13g fat (3g sat. fat), 114mg chol., 159mg sod., 13g carb. (9g sugars, 2g fiber), 32g pro. **Diabetic exchanges:** 4 lean meat, 1 vegetable, ½ starch.

BLACK & BLUE COBBLER

It never occurred to me that I could bake a cobbler in my slow cooker until I saw some recipes and decided to try to make my favorite fruity dessert. It took a bit of experimenting, but the tasty results are "berry" well worth it.
—Martha Creveling, Orlando, FL

Prep: 15 min. • **Cook:** 2 hours + standing
Makes: 6 servings

- **1 cup all-purpose flour**
- **1½ cups sugar, divided**
- **1 tsp. baking powder**
- **¼ tsp. salt**
- **¼ tsp. ground cinnamon**
- **¼ tsp. ground nutmeg**
- **2 large eggs, lightly beaten**
- **2 Tbsp. whole milk**
- **2 Tbsp. canola oil**
- **2 cups fresh or frozen blackberries**
- **2 cups fresh or frozen blueberries**
- **¾ cup water**
- **1 tsp. grated orange zest**
- **Optional: Whipped cream or vanilla ice cream**

1. In a large bowl, combine flour, ¾ cup sugar, the baking powder, salt, cinnamon and nutmeg. Combine eggs, milk and oil; stir into dry ingredients just until moistened. Spread batter evenly onto the bottom of a greased 5-qt. slow cooker.
2. In a large saucepan, combine the berries, water, orange zest and remaining sugar; bring to a boil. Remove from the heat; immediately pour over batter. Cover and cook on high for 2-2½ hours or until a toothpick inserted into batter comes out clean.
3. Turn cooker off. Uncover and let stand for 30 minutes before serving. Serve with whipped cream or ice cream if desired.

1 serving: 391 cal., 7g fat (1g sat. fat), 72mg chol., 190mg sod., 80g carb. (58g sugars, 4g fiber), 5g pro.

SLOW-COOKER MEMPHIS-STYLE RIBS

After my dad and I had dinner at the legendary Rendezvous Restaurant in Memphis, I was inspired to create a slow-cooked version of tasty dry-rub Memphis ribs. Smoked paprika in the rub mimics the flavor that the ribs would get from being grilled over hot coals.

—Matthew Hass, Ellison Bay, WI

Prep: 15 min. • **Cook:** 5 hours
Makes: 6 servings

- **½ cup white vinegar**
- **½ cup water**
- **2 racks pork baby back ribs (about 5 lbs.)**
- **3 Tbsp. smoked paprika**
- **2 Tbsp. brown sugar**
- **2 tsp. salt**
- **2 tsp. coarsely ground pepper**
- **1 tsp. garlic powder**
- **1 tsp. onion powder**
- **1 tsp. ground cumin**
- **1 tsp. ground mustard**
- **1 tsp. dried thyme**
- **1 tsp. dried oregano**
- **1 tsp. celery salt**
- **¾ tsp. cayenne pepper**

1. Combine vinegar and water; brush over ribs. Pour the remaining vinegar mixture into a 6-qt. slow cooker.
2. Mix together remaining ingredients. Sprinkle ribs with half the seasoning blend; reserve the other half. Cut ribs into serving-sized pieces; transfer to the slow cooker.
3. Cook, covered, on low until tender, 5-6 hours. Remove ribs; skim fat from cooking juices. Using a clean brush, brush ribs generously with skimmed cooking juices; sprinkle with reserved seasoning mixture. Serve ribs with the remaining juices.

1 serving: 509 cal., 35g fat (13g sat. fat), 136mg chol., 1137mg sod., 8g carb. (5g sugars, 2g fiber), 38g pro.

PRESSURE-COOKER SPAGHETTI SQUASH WITH TOMATOES

This squash is perfect as a side dish, or top it with canned tuna to serve it as an entree. I use my own home-canned tomatoes for the best flavor. The dish is easy, tasty and light!

—Carol Chase, Sioux City, IA

Prep: 15 min. • **Cook:** 10 min.
Makes: 10 servings

- **1 medium spaghetti squash, halved lengthwise, seeds removed**
- **1 can (14 oz.) diced tomatoes, drained**
- **¼ cup sliced green olives with pimientos**
- **1 tsp. dried oregano**
- **½ tsp. salt**
- **½ tsp. pepper**
- **½ cup shredded cheddar cheese**
- **¼ cup minced fresh basil**

1. Place trivet insert and 1 cup water in a 6-qt. electric pressure cooker. Set squash on the trivet, overlapping as needed to fit. Lock lid; close pressure-release valve. Adjust to pressure-cook on high for 7 minutes. Quick-release pressure. Press cancel.
2. Remove the squash and trivet from pressure cooker; drain cooking liquid from pressure cooker. Using a fork, separate squash into strands resembling spaghetti, discarding the skin. Return the squash to pressure cooker. Stir in the tomatoes, olives, oregano, salt and pepper. Select saute setting and adjust for low heat. Cook and stir until heated through, about 3 minutes. Top with the cheese and basil.

¾ cup: 92 cal., 3g fat (1g sat. fat), 6mg chol., 296mg sod., 15g carb. (1g sugars, 4g fiber), 3g pro. **Diabetic exchanges:** 1 starch, ½ fat.

SOUTHERN BARBECUE SPAGHETTI SAUCE

I revamped our favorite sloppy joe recipe into this thick spaghetti sauce that simmers in the slow cooker. The flavor is jazzy enough to be interesting to adults, yet mild enough for the kids to enjoy.

—Rhonda Melanson, Sarnia, ON

Prep: 20 min. • **Cook:** 4 hours
Makes: 12 servings

- **1 lb. lean ground turkey**
- **2 medium onions, chopped**
- **1½ cups sliced fresh mushrooms**
- **1 medium green pepper, chopped**
- **2 garlic cloves, minced**
- **1 can (14½ oz.) diced tomatoes, undrained**
- **1 can (12 oz.) tomato paste**
- **1 can (8 oz.) tomato sauce**
- **1 cup ketchup**
- **½ cup beef broth**
- **2 Tbsp. Worcestershire sauce**
- **2 Tbsp. brown sugar**
- **1 Tbsp. ground cumin**
- **2 tsp. chili powder**
- **12 cups hot cooked spaghetti**

1. In a large nonstick skillet, cook the turkey, onions, mushrooms and green pepper over medium heat until meat is no longer pink, breaking it into crumbles. Add garlic; cook 1 minute longer. Drain.
2. Transfer to a 3-qt. slow cooker. Stir in the tomatoes, tomato paste, tomato sauce, ketchup, broth, Worcestershire sauce, brown sugar, cumin and chili powder. Cover and cook on low for 4-5 hours or until the vegetables are tender. Serve with spaghetti.

⅔ cup sauce: 336 cal., 4g fat (1g sat. fat), 26mg chol., 516mg sod., 57g carb. (14g sugars, 5g fiber), 18g pro.

Amazing Air-Fryer Dishes

The new favorite gadget in home kitchens is the air fryer—delivering crispiness and flavor without frying in oil. These recipes show just what you can make while cutting back on the fat!

AIR-FRYER SWEET POTATO FRIES

I can never get enough of these sweet potato fries! Even though my grocery store sells them in the frozen foods section, I still love to pull sweet potatoes out of my garden and chop them up fresh!

—Amber Massey, Argyle, TX

Takes: 20 min. • **Makes:** 4 servings

- **2 large sweet potatoes, cut into thin strips**
- **2 Tbsp. canola oil**
- **1 tsp. garlic powder**
- **1 tsp. paprika**
- **1 tsp. kosher salt**
- **¼ tsp. cayenne pepper**

Preheat air fryer to 400°. Combine all ingredients; toss to coat. Place on greased tray in air-fryer basket. Cook until lightly browned, 10-12 minutes, stirring once. Serve immediately.

1 serving: 243 cal., 7g fat (1g sat. fat), 0 chol., 498mg sod., 43g carb. (17g sugars, 5g fiber), 3g pro.

PRETZEL-CRUSTED CATFISH

I love the flavor of this air-fryer catfish recipe. I'm not a big fish lover, so any concoction that has me loving fish is a keeper in my book! It is wonderful served with a nice buttery herb rice pilaf and corn muffins with butter and honey!

—Kelly Williams, Forked River, NJ

Prep: 15 min. • **Cook:** 10 min./batch
Makes: 4 servings

- **4 catfish fillets (6 oz. each)**
- **½ tsp. salt**
- **½ tsp. pepper**
- **2 large eggs**
- **⅓ cup Dijon mustard**
- **2 Tbsp. 2% milk**
- **½ cup all-purpose flour**
- **4 cups honey mustard miniature pretzels, coarsely crushed**
- **Cooking spray**
- **Lemon slices, optional**

1. Preheat air fryer to 325°. Sprinkle catfish with salt and pepper. Whisk eggs, mustard and milk in a shallow bowl. Place the flour and pretzels in separate shallow bowls. Coat fillets with flour, then dip in egg mixture and coat with pretzels.
2. In batches, place fillets in a single layer on greased tray in air-fryer basket; spritz with cooking spray. Cook until the fish flakes easily with a fork, 10-12 minutes. If desired, serve with lemon slices.

1 fillet: 466 cal., 14g fat (3g sat. fat), 164mg chol., 1580mg sod., 45g carb. (2g sugars, 2g fiber), 33g pro.

APPLE FRITTERS WITH BROWN BUTTER GLAZE

An air fryer makes these easy apple fritters healthier than old-fashioned fritters, yet they are still just as delicious. They are a fast and simple dessert that includes a positively scrumptious brown butter glaze!
—Alyssa Lang, North Scituate, RI

Prep: 10 min. • **Cook:** 8 min./batch
Makes: 15 servings

- **Cooking spray**
- **1½ cups all-purpose flour**
- **¼ cup sugar**
- **2 tsp. baking powder**
- **1½ tsp. ground cinnamon**
- **½ tsp. salt**
- **⅔ cup 2% milk**
- **2 large eggs, room temperature**
- **1 Tbsp. lemon juice**
- **1½ tsp. vanilla extract, divided**
- **2 medium Honeycrisp apples, peeled and chopped**
- **¼ cup butter**
- **1 cup confectioners' sugar**
- **1 Tbsp. 2% milk**

1. Line air-fryer basket with parchment (cut to fit); spritz with cooking spray. Preheat air fryer to 410°. In a large bowl, combine the flour, sugar, baking powder, cinnamon and salt. Add milk, eggs, lemon juice and 1 tsp. vanilla extract; stir just until moistened. Fold in apples.
2. In batches, drop dough by ¼ cupfuls 2-in. apart onto air-fryer basket. Spritz with cooking spray. Cook until golden brown, 5-6 minutes. Turn; continue to air-fry until golden brown, 1-2 minutes.
3. Melt the butter in small saucepan over medium-high heat. Carefully cook until butter starts to brown and foam, 5 minutes. Remove from the heat; cool slightly. Add confectioners' sugar, 1 Tbsp. milk and remaining ½ tsp. vanilla extract to browned butter; whisk until smooth. Drizzle over fritters before serving.

1 fritter: 145 cal., 4g fat (2g sat. fat), 34mg chol., 183mg sod., 24g carb. (14g sugars, 1g fiber), 3g pro. **Diabetic exchanges:** 1 fat.

AIR-FRYER CHICKEN TENDERS

I added all of the components of a loaded baked potato—cheddar, potato, bacon, sour cream and chives—to my latest quick and easy dish. Every kid will love these!
—Cyndy Gerken, Naples, FL

Prep: 25 min. • **Cook:** 15 min./batch
Makes: 4 servings

- **½ cup panko bread crumbs**
- **½ cup potato sticks, crushed**
- **½ cup crushed cheese crackers**
- **¼ cup grated Parmesan cheese**
- **2 bacon strips, cooked and crumbled**
- **2 tsp. minced fresh chives**
- **¼ cup butter, melted**
- **1 Tbsp. sour cream**
- **1 lb. chicken tenderloins**
- **Additional sour cream and chives**

1. Preheat air fryer to 400°. In a shallow bowl, combine the first 6 ingredients. In another shallow bowl, whisk butter and sour cream. Dip chicken in butter mixture, then in crumb mixture, patting to help coating adhere.
2. In batches, arrange chicken in a single layer on greased tray in air-fryer basket; spritz with cooking spray. Cook until coating is golden brown and chicken is no longer pink, 7-8 minutes on each side. Serve with additional sour cream and chives.

1 serving: 256 cal., 14g fat (7g sat. fat), 84mg chol., 267mg sod., 6g carb. (0 sugars, 0 fiber), 29g pro.

Cookies, Bars & Candies

These sweet treats are delightful for bake sales, lunch boxes, holiday platters and afternoon treats—and yes, those late-night munchies, too! Take your pick of delectable cookies, brownies, bars and confections to deliver sweet solutions when full desserts are just too much.

LAVENDER LEMON BARS

Hints of lavender and lemon zest in the crust make these treats a favorite.

—Judith Hilinski, Cuyahoga Falls, OH

Prep: 20 min. • **Bake:** 25 min. • **Makes:** 2 dozen

- **¾ cup butter, softened**
- **½ cup confectioners' sugar**
- **2 cups all-purpose flour**
- **½ cup ground almonds**
- **2 tsp. dried lavender flowers**
- **2 tsp. grated lemon zest**

TOPPING

- **1¾ cups sugar**
- **⅓ cup all-purpose flour**
- **½ tsp. baking soda**
- **4 large eggs, room temperature**
- **⅓ cup lemon juice**
- **Confectioners' sugar**

1. Preheat oven to 350°. In a small bowl, cream butter and confectioners' sugar. Add the flour, almonds, lavender and lemon zest; beat until crumbly. Pat into an ungreased 13x9-in. baking dish. Bake for 15 minutes or until the edges are golden brown.
2. Meanwhile, in another bowl, combine sugar, flour, baking soda, eggs and lemon juice; beat until frothy. Pour over the hot crust. Return to oven and bake until light golden brown, 20-25 minutes. Cool on a wire rack. Dust with confectioners' sugar. Refrigerate leftovers.

1 bar: 185 cal., 8g fat (4g sat. fat), 51mg chol., 95mg sod., 27g carb. (17g sugars, 1g fiber), 3g pro.

ZUCCHINI BROWNIES

A fast-to-fix peanut butter and chocolate frosting tops these cakelike brownies that are a sweet way to use up your garden bounty.

—Allyson Wilkins, Amherst, NH

Prep: 20 min. • **Bake:** 35 min.
Makes: 1½ dozen

- **1 cup butter, softened**
- **1½ cups sugar**
- **2 large eggs, room temperature**
- **½ cup plain yogurt**
- **1 tsp. vanilla extract**
- **2½ cups all-purpose flour**
- **¼ cup baking cocoa**
- **1 tsp. baking soda**
- **½ tsp. salt**
- **2 cups shredded zucchini**

FROSTING

- **⅔ cup semisweet chocolate chips**
- **½ cup creamy peanut butter**

1. Preheat oven to 350°. In a large bowl, cream butter and sugar until light and fluffy, 5-7 minutes. Add eggs, 1 at a time, beating well after each addition. Beat in yogurt and vanilla. In another bowl, combine flour, cocoa, baking soda and salt; gradually add to creamed mixture. Stir in zucchini.
2. Pour into a greased 13x9-in. baking pan. Bake until a toothpick inserted in the center comes out clean, 35-40 minutes.
3. For frosting, in a small saucepan, combine chocolate chips and peanut butter. Cook and stir over low heat until smooth. Spread over warm brownies. Cool on a wire rack. Cut into bars.

1 brownie: 307 cal., 17g fat (8g sat. fat), 52mg chol., 283mg sod., 37g carb. (21g sugars, 2g fiber), 5g pro.

GINGERBREAD OATMEAL COOKIES

Cookie butter and ground ginger add a new layer of flavor. The recipe makes about 18 cookies, and they go fast! You may want to make a double batch.

—Carole Resnick, Cleveland, OH

Prep: 10 min. + chilling
Bake: 15 min./batch + cooling
Makes: about 1½ dozen

- **¾ cup all-purpose flour**
- **½ tsp. baking soda**
- **½ tsp. salt**
- **½ tsp. ground ginger**
- **¼ tsp. baking powder**
- **1 cup Biscoff creamy cookie spread, room temperature**
- **½ cup unsalted butter**
- **½ cup sugar**
- **½ cup packed brown sugar**
- **1 large egg, room temperature**
- **1 tsp. vanilla extract**
- **1 cup quick-cooking oats**

1. Whisk together the first 5 ingredients. In another bowl, cream cookie spread, butter and sugars until light and fluffy, 5-7 minutes. Beat in the egg and vanilla. Gradually beat in the flour mixture; stir in oats. Refrigerate for at least 3 hours.
2. Preheat oven to 350°. Bring the dough to room temperature. Using a medium cookie scoop, drop mounds of dough on baking sheets lined with parchment or baking mats. Bake until lightly browned, 15-18 minutes, rotating the pans halfway through baking time. Cool the cookies on pans 5 minutes. Remove to wire racks to cool completely.

Note: Look for Biscoff creamy cookie spread near the peanut butter.

1 cookie: 210 cal., 11g fat (4g sat. fat), 24mg chol., 113mg sod., 26g carb. (17g sugars, 1g fiber), 2g pro.

COFFEE SHOP FUDGE

This smooth, creamy fudge has an irresistible crunch from pecans. Coffee and cinnamon blend nicely to provide subtle flavor.
—Beth Osborne Skinner, Bristol, TN

Prep: 15 min. + chilling • **Makes:** 2 lbs.

- **1 cup chopped pecans**
- **3 cups semisweet chocolate chips**
- **1 can (14 oz.) sweetened condensed milk**
- **2 Tbsp. strong brewed coffee, room temperature**
- **1 tsp. ground cinnamon**
- **⅛ tsp. salt**
- **1 tsp. vanilla extract**

1. Line an 8-in. square pan with foil and butter the foil; set aside. Place the pecans in a microwave-safe pie plate. Microwave, uncovered, on high for 3 minutes, stirring after each minute; set aside.
2. In 2-qt. microwave-safe bowl, combine chocolate chips, milk, coffee, cinnamon and salt. Microwave, uncovered, on high for 1 minute. Stir until smooth. Stir in the vanilla and pecans. Immediately spread into the prepared pan.
3. Cover and refrigerate until firm, about 2 hours. Remove from the pan; cut into 1-in. squares. Cover and store at room temperature (70°-80°).

1 piece: 77 cal., 4g fat (2g sat. fat), 3mg chol., 16mg sod., 10g carb. (9g sugars, 1g fiber), 1g pro.

LOVE STRONG COFFEE?

For a stronger coffee flavor, you can add more brewed coffee or experiment with adding espresso granules or coffee extract.

CHEWY SALTED PEANUT BARS

My family has been making this recipe for generations. Whenever we get together, someone offers to bring the crunchy bars.
—Ann Marie Heinz, Sturgeon Bay, WI

Prep: 10 min. • **Bake:** 20 min. + cooling
Makes: 2 dozen

- **1½ cups all-purpose flour**
- **¾ cup packed brown sugar**
- **½ cup cold butter, cubed**
- **2 cups lightly salted dry roasted peanuts**
- **1 cup butterscotch chips**
- **½ cup light corn syrup**
- **2 Tbsp. butter**

1. Preheat oven to 350°. Line a 13x9-in. baking pan with foil, letting ends extend up sides; grease foil. In a small bowl, mix flour and brown sugar; cut in butter until crumbly. Press into the prepared pan. Bake until lightly browned, 8-10 minutes. Sprinkle peanuts over crust.
2. In a small saucepan, melt butterscotch chips, corn syrup and butter over medium heat; stir until smooth. Drizzle over the peanuts. Bake until bubbly, 6-8 minutes longer. Cool completely in pan on a wire rack. Lifting with foil, remove from pan. Cut into bars.

1 bar: 239 cal., 13g fat (7g sat. fat), 13mg chol., 145mg sod., 27g carb. (9g sugars, 1g fiber), 4g pro.

CHOCOLATE LACE COOKIES

My mother and I make these elegant sandwich cookies filled with melted chocolate chips. Baking together is a fabulous way to spend an afternoon.
—Stacey B., Stillwater, OK

Prep: 35 min. • **Bake:** 5 min./batch + chilling
Makes: about 3 dozen

- **½ cup packed brown sugar**
- **⅓ cup butter, cubed**
- **1 Tbsp. 2% milk**
- **½ cup ground pecans**
- **3 Tbsp. all-purpose flour**
- **1 tsp. vanilla extract**
- **1⅔ cups semisweet chocolate chips**

1. Preheat oven to 350°. In a saucepan, combine the brown sugar, butter and milk. Cook and stir over medium heat 3-4 minutes or until slightly thickened. Stir in pecans, flour and vanilla.
2. Drop by ½ teaspoonfuls 3 in. apart onto foil-lined baking sheets. Bake 5-7 minutes or until golden brown and lacy. Cool completely before carefully removing from foil.
3. In a microwave, melt the chocolate chips; stir until smooth. Spread 1 tsp. on bottoms of half the cookies; cover with remaining cookies. Refrigerate 10 minutes or until set. Store between pieces of waxed paper in an airtight container.

1 sandwich cookie: 71 cal., 5g fat (2g sat. fat), 4mg chol., 14mg sod., 8g carb. (7g sugars, 1g fiber), 1g pro.

ORANGE PISTACHIO COOKIES

I had never tried pistachios until I visited a friend who served me these cookies. I was in love! I made the recipe my own, and now my family can't get enough of them!
—Lorraine Caland, Shuniah, ON

Prep: 20 min. + chilling • **Bake:** 10 min./batch
Makes: about 4½ dozen

- **¾ cup butter, softened**
- **1 cup sugar**
- **1 large egg, room temperature**
- **1 Tbsp. grated orange zest**
- **1 tsp. vanilla extract**
- **2 cups all-purpose flour**
- **¼ cup cornstarch**
- **½ cup pistachios, toasted and finely chopped**

ICING

- **2¼ cups confectioners' sugar**
- **¼ cup orange juice**
- **1 Tbsp. butter, melted**
- **Additional pistachios, toasted and finely chopped, optional**

1. In a large bowl, cream butter and sugar until light and fluffy, 5-7 minutes. Beat in egg, orange zest and vanilla. In another bowl, whisk the flour and cornstarch; gradually beat into the creamed mixture.
2. Divide the dough in half. Roughly shape each portion into a 7-in. roll along the long end of a 14x8-in. sheet of waxed paper. Tightly roll waxed paper over dough, using the waxed paper to mold the dough into a smooth roll. Place waxed paper-covered roll in an airtight container; freeze 30 minutes or until firm, or refrigerate overnight.
3. Preheat oven to 350°. Sprinkle the pistachios on a rimmed baking sheet. Unwrap and roll each roll of dough in pistachios. Cut dough crosswise into ¼-in. slices. Place slices ½ in. apart on parchment-lined baking sheets. Bake for 6-8 minutes or until bottoms are light brown. Cool slightly on pan. Remove from pans to wire racks to cool completely.
4. In small bowl, combine confectioners' sugar, orange juice and butter until smooth. Spread over cookies. If desired, sprinkle with additional pistachios. Let stand until set.

1 cookie: 83 cal., 3g fat (2g sat. fat), 10mg chol., 27mg sod., 13g carb. (9g sugars, 0 fiber), 1g pro.

SKILLET STOUT BROWNIES

These stout brownies are rich and fudgy. The skillet makes a beautiful presentation—just set it down in the center of the table and top with ice cream!

—Mandy Naglich, New York, NY

Prep: 30 min. • **Bake:** 25 min. + cooling
Makes: 12 servings

- **8 oz. semisweet chocolate, chopped**
- **1 cup butter, cubed**
- **1 cup milk stout beer**
- **1 large egg, room temperature**
- **2 large egg yolks, room temperature**
- **¾ cup sugar**
- **¼ cup packed brown sugar**
- **¾ cup all-purpose flour**
- **⅓ cup baking cocoa**
- **½ tsp. salt**
- **Vanilla ice cream, optional**

1. Preheat oven to 350°. Place chocolate in a large bowl. In a 10-in. cast-iron skillet or other ovenproof skillet, combine the butter and stout. Bring to a boil; reduce the heat. Simmer 10 minutes, stirring constantly. Pour over chocolate; stir with a whisk until smooth. Cool slightly.
2. In another large bowl, beat the egg, egg yolks and sugars until blended. Stir in chocolate mixture. In another bowl, mix the flour, baking cocoa and salt; gradually add to the chocolate mixture, mixing well.
3. Spread into skillet. Bake until set, 25-30 minutes. Cool completely in the skillet on a wire rack. If desired, serve with vanilla ice cream.

1 piece: 363 cal., 24g fat (14g sat. fat), 87mg chol., 229mg sod., 29g carb. (21g sugars, 1g fiber), 4g pro.

COFFEE-GLAZED MOLASSES COOKIES

I dreamed up these molasses cookies while sipping coffee and watching snow fall. The aroma from the baking cookies reaches all corners of the house.

—Faith Ford, Big Lake, MN

Prep: 40 min. • **Bake:** 10 min./batch + cooling
Makes: about 3 dozen

- **¾ cup butter, softened**
- **½ cup packed brown sugar**
- **½ cup plus ⅓ cup sugar**
- **⅓ cup molasses**
- **1 large egg, room temperature**
- **1 tsp. vanilla extract**
- **2¼ cups all-purpose flour**
- **2 tsp. baking soda**
- **1½ tsp. ground cinnamon**
- **1 tsp. ground ginger**
- **½ tsp. ground cloves**
- **¼ tsp. ground allspice**
- **½ tsp. salt**
- **1 cup confectioners' sugar**
- **⅓ cup heavy whipping cream**
- **1½ tsp. instant coffee granules**

1. Preheat oven to 350°. In a large bowl, cream butter, brown sugar and ½ cup granulated sugar until light and fluffy, 5-7 minutes. Beat in molasses, egg and vanilla. In another bowl, whisk flour, baking soda, spices and salt; gradually beat into creamed mixture.
2. Shape the dough into rounded tablespoonfuls; roll in remaining sugar. Place 2 in. apart on ungreased baking sheets. Bake 8-10 minutes or until edges begin to set. Cool on pans 5 minutes. Remove to wire racks to cool completely.
3. In a small bowl, mix confectioners' sugar, cream and coffee granules until blended; drizzle over cookies. Let stand until set.

Freeze option: Freeze shaped balls of dough on baking sheets until firm. Transfer to airtight containers; return to freezer. To use, roll balls in remaining sugar. Bake and decorate cookies as directed, increasing time by 1-2 minutes.

1 cookie: 106 cal., 4g fat (3g sat. fat), 15mg chol., 118mg sod., 17g carb. (11g sugars, 0 fiber), 1g pro.

❄ PUMPKIN COOKIES WITH BROWNED BUTTER FROSTING

The recipe for these pleasantly spiced pumpkin cookies won a champion ribbon at our local county fair. These are a family favorite, and everyone enjoys the soft, cakelike texture.

—Robin Nagel, Whitehall, MT

Prep: 25 min. • **Bake:** 10 min./batch + cooling
Makes: about 9 dozen

- **1½ cups butter, softened**
- **2 cups packed brown sugar**
- **1 cup canned pumpkin**
- **2 large eggs, room temperature**
- **½ cup crystallized ginger, finely chopped**
- **5 cups all-purpose flour**
- **2 tsp. baking soda**
- **2 tsp. ground cinnamon**
- **2 tsp. ground ginger**
- **½ tsp. salt**

FROSTING

- **⅔ cup butter, cubed**
- **4 cups confectioners' sugar**
- **1 tsp. vanilla extract**
- **4 to 5 Tbsp. 2% milk**

1. Preheat oven to 375°. In a large bowl, cream butter and brown sugar until light and fluffy, 5-7 minutes. Beat in pumpkin, eggs and crystallized ginger. In another bowl, whisk flour, baking soda, cinnamon, ginger and salt; gradually beat into the creamed mixture.
2. Drop the dough by tablespoonfuls 2 in. apart onto ungreased baking sheets. Bake for 6-8 minutes or until golden brown. Remove to wire racks to cool completely.
3. In a small heavy saucepan, melt butter over medium heat. Heat 5-7 minutes or until golden brown, stirring constantly. Transfer to a large bowl. Gradually beat in the confectioners' sugar, vanilla and enough milk to achieve desired spreading consistency. Spread over cookies.

Freeze option: Freeze unfrosted cookies in freezer containers. To use, thaw in covered containers and frost as directed.

1 cookie: 93 cal., 4g fat (2g sat. fat), 14mg chol., 64mg sod., 14g carb. (9g sugars, 0 fiber), 1g pro.

PEACH COBBLER COOKIES

My sister brought me fresh peaches one year, and we decided to make these fruity cookies. A fast and simple change from pie, they are a wonderfully creative way to use fresh peaches.

—Anna Miller, Churdan, IA

Prep: 30 min. • **Bake:** 15 min./batch
Makes: about 4½ dozen

- **1 cup butter, softened**
- **1 cup sugar**
- **⅓ cup packed brown sugar**
- **1 large egg, room temperature**
- **1 tsp. vanilla extract**
- **¼ tsp. almond extract**
- **3 cups all-purpose flour**
- **1½ tsp. ground cinnamon**
- **1 tsp. cream of tartar**
- **1 tsp. baking soda**
- **½ tsp. salt**
- **¼ tsp. ground nutmeg**
- **1 cup chopped peeled fresh peaches**

1. Preheat oven to 350°. In a large bowl, cream butter and sugars until light and fluffy, 5-7 minutes. Beat in the egg and extracts. In another bowl, whisk flour, cinnamon, cream of tartar, baking soda, salt and nutmeg; gradually beat into the creamed mixture. Stir in peaches.
2. Drop the dough by tablespoonfuls 2 in. apart onto parchment-lined baking sheets. Bake until set, 14-16 minutes. Cool on pans 2 minutes. Remove to wire racks to cool. Store in an airtight container.

1 cookie: 78 cal., 4g fat (2g sat. fat), 12mg chol., 74mg sod., 11g carb. (5g sugars, 0 fiber), 1g pro.

ANGEL FOOD CHRISTMAS CANDY

It was my dad who inspired me to first try making this candy. He remembered it from when he was a boy. The ultimate compliment was when he told me my version tasted even better! My husband is a driver with a parcel service, so he works long hours around the holidays—which gives me time to make treats!

—Shelly Matthys, New Richmond, WI

Prep: 20 min. • **Cook:** 25 min.
Makes: 1½ lbs. (12 servings)

- **1 cup sugar**
- **1 cup dark corn syrup**
- **1 Tbsp. white vinegar**
- **1 Tbsp. baking soda**
- **1 lb. milk chocolate candy coating, melted**

1. In a heavy saucepan, combine the sugar, corn syrup and vinegar. Cook over medium heat, stirring constantly, until the sugar dissolves. Cook without stirring until the temperature reaches 300° (hard-crack stage) on a candy thermometer. Do not overcook.
2. Remove from the heat and quickly stir in baking soda. Pour into a buttered 13x9-in. pan. Do not spread candy; the mixture will not fill the pan.
3. When the mixture is cool, break it into bite-sized pieces. Dip into melted chocolate; place on waxed paper until the chocolate is firm. Store candy in an airtight container.

2 oz.: 337 cal., 11g fat (10g sat. fat), 0 chol., 356mg sod., 63g carb. (61g sugars, 1g fiber), 1g pro.

GOOEY CHOCOLATE CARAMEL BARS

These rich, gooey bars are my most requested treats. They are popular at school functions, family barbecues and picnics. We like them alone or topped with a scoop of ice cream.
—Betty Hagerty, Philadelphia, PA

Prep: 25 min. • **Bake:** 20 min. + cooling
Makes: about 4½ dozen

- **2¼ cups all-purpose flour, divided**
- **2 cups quick-cooking oats**
- **1½ cups packed brown sugar**
- **1 tsp. baking soda**
- **½ tsp. salt**
- **1½ cups cold butter, cubed**
- **2 cups semisweet chocolate chips**
- **1 cup chopped pecans**
- **1 jar (12 oz.) caramel ice cream topping**

1. Preheat oven to 350°. In a large bowl, combine 2 cups flour, the oats, brown sugar, baking soda and salt. Cut in butter until crumbly. Set half aside for topping.
2. Press the remaining crumb mixture into a greased 13x9-in. baking pan. Bake for 15 minutes. Sprinkle with chocolate chips and pecans.
3. Whisk the caramel topping and the remaining flour until smooth; drizzle over the top. Sprinkle with the reserved crumb mixture. Bake for 18-20 minutes or until golden brown. Cool on a wire rack for 2 hours before cutting.

1 bar: 156 cal., 9g fat (5g sat. fat), 14mg chol., 110mg sod., 20g carb. (13g sugars, 1g fiber), 2g pro.

AMISH SUGAR COOKIES

These easy-to-make cookies simply melt in your mouth. I've passed the recipe around to many friends. After I gave the recipe to my sister, she entered the cookies in a local fair and won best of show!
—Sylvia Ford, Kennett, MO

Prep: 10 min. • **Bake:** 10 min./batch
Makes: about 5 dozen

- **1 cup butter, softened**
- **1 cup vegetable oil**
- **1 cup sugar**
- **1 cup confectioners' sugar**
- **2 large eggs, room temperature**
- **1 tsp. vanilla extract**
- **4½ cups all-purpose flour**
- **1 tsp. baking soda**
- **1 tsp. cream of tartar**

1. Preheat oven to 375°. In a large bowl, beat the butter, oil and sugars. Beat in eggs until well blended. Beat in vanilla. Combine flour, baking soda and cream of tartar; gradually add to creamed mixture.
2. Drop dough by small teaspoonfuls onto ungreased baking sheets. Bake until lightly browned, 8-10 minutes. Remove to wire racks to cool.

1 cookie: 117 cal., 7g fat (2g sat. fat), 14mg chol., 48mg sod., 13g carb. (5g sugars, 0 fiber), 1g pro.

PERFECT CHEMISTRY

Why cream of tartar? Baking soda needs an acidic ingredient to create the gas bubbles that make baked goods rise and lighten. Cream of tartar (aka tartaric acid) provides that in this recipe. Yea, chemistry! If you like your treats on the sweeter end of the spectrum, add a pinch of coarse sugar to the tops of these light and airy cookies.

MIXED NUT CLUSTERS

Serve these little candies with hot chocolate to keep everyone happy and warm. They also make standout gifts—box them up with each cluster in its own foil or paper candy cup.
—Ida Tuey, South Lyon, MI

Prep: 30 min. + chilling • **Makes:** 6 dozen

- **2 cups semisweet chocolate chips**
- **1 can (14 oz.) sweetened condensed milk**
- **1 Tbsp. honey**
- **1 Tbsp. vanilla extract**
- **1 cup each chopped walnuts, cashews, pecans and almonds**

1. In a large heavy saucepan, melt the chocolate chips, milk and honey over low heat; stir until blended. Remove from heat. Stir in vanilla; add nuts.
2. Drop by rounded tablespoonfuls onto waxed paper-lined baking sheets. Refrigerate until firm. Store in the refrigerator.

1 piece: 85 cal., 6g fat (2g sat. fat), 2mg chol., 20mg sod., 8g carb. (6g sugars, 1g fiber), 2g pro. **Diabetic exchanges:** 1 fat, ½ starch.

LEMONY COCONUT BARS

These chewy bars with a hint of citrus make a refreshing addition to cookie trays. Try lime juice and zest for a zingy twist.
—Nancy Zimmerman, Cape May Court House, NJ

Prep: 25 min. • **Bake:** 25 min. + cooling
Makes: 2 dozen

- **½ cup butter, softened**
- **½ cup packed light brown sugar**
- **1½ cups all-purpose flour**

FILLING

- **2 large eggs**
- **1 cup packed light brown sugar**
- **½ tsp. grated lemon zest**
- **½ tsp. vanilla extract**
- **¼ tsp. lemon extract**
- **2 Tbsp. all-purpose flour**
- **½ tsp. baking powder**
- **¼ tsp. salt**
- **1½ cups sweetened shredded coconut**
- **1 cup chopped pecans or walnuts**

GLAZE

- **1 cup confectioners' sugar**
- **1 Tbsp. butter, melted**
- **½ tsp. grated lemon zest**
- **3 Tbsp. lemon juice**

1. Preheat the oven to 350°. In a bowl, cream butter and sugar until light and fluffy, 5-7 minutes; gradually beat in the flour, mixing well.
2. Press onto the bottom of a greased 13x9-in. baking pan. Bake until edges are golden brown, 8-10 minutes. Cool on a wire rack.
3. For filling, in a large bowl, beat eggs, brown sugar, lemon zest and extracts until blended. In a small bowl, mix the flour, baking powder and salt; stir into egg mixture. Stir in coconut and pecans. Spread over crust.
4. Bake 17-20 minutes or until golden brown. Cool 10 minutes on a wire rack. Meanwhile, in a small bowl, mix the glaze ingredients until smooth; drizzle over warm filling. Cool completely. Cut into bars.

1 bar: 208 cal., 10g fat (5g sat. fat), 27mg chol., 96mg sod., 29g carb. (21g sugars, 1g fiber), 2g pro.

CHOCOLATE CHIP ZUCCHINI COOKIES

I love using zucchini in the summertime. This recipe reminds me of a zucchini bread my aunt makes, but I wanted to make cookies for a family get-together because they would be easier to grab and eat. These taste better if you make them the day before.
—Melissa Obernesser, Oriskany, NY

Prep: 15 min. • **Bake:** 12 min./batch + cooling
Makes: 4 dozen

- **½ cup unsalted butter, softened**
- **½ cup sugar**
- **⅓ cup packed brown sugar**
- **1 large egg, room temperature**
- **1½ tsp. vanilla extract**
- **1 cup all-purpose flour**
- **½ cup whole wheat flour**
- **1 tsp. ground cinnamon**
- **½ tsp. baking soda**
- **¼ tsp. salt**
- **1½ cups shredded zucchini**
- **1 cup quick-cooking oats**
- **1 cup semisweet chocolate chips**
- **¾ cup chopped pecans, toasted**

1. Preheat oven to 350°. In a large bowl, cream butter and sugars until light and fluffy, 5-7 minutes. Beat in the egg and vanilla. In another bowl, whisk the flours, cinnamon, baking soda and salt; gradually beat into the creamed mixture. Stir in remaining ingredients.
2. Drop dough by tablespoonfuls 2 in. apart onto greased baking sheets. Bake until edges start to brown, 12-14 minutes. Cool on pans 2 minutes. Remove to wire racks to cool. Store between pieces of waxed paper in an airtight container.

1 cookie: 79 cal., 4g fat (2g sat. fat), 9mg chol., 27mg sod., 10g carb. (6g sugars, 1g fiber), 1g pro.

KILNER
Milk Bottle

HOMEMADE HONEY GRAHAMS

The way my boys eat them, I would spend a fortune on honey graham crackers at the grocery store. So I decided to make a homemade version that is less processed—and less expensive. These are fantastic, although they *still* don't last long!

—Crystal Jo Bruns, Iliff, CO

Prep: 15 min. + chilling • **Bake:** 10 min./batch
Makes: 32 cookies

- **1 cup whole wheat flour**
- **¾ cup all-purpose flour**
- **½ cup toasted wheat germ**
- **2 Tbsp. dark brown sugar**
- **1 tsp. baking powder**
- **1 tsp. ground cinnamon**
- **½ tsp. salt**
- **½ tsp. baking soda**
- **6 Tbsp. cold butter, cubed**
- **¼ cup honey**
- **4 Tbsp. ice water**

1. Whisk together the first 8 ingredients; cut in butter until crumbly. In another bowl, whisk together honey and water; gradually add to dry ingredients, tossing with a fork until dough holds together when pressed.
2. Divide the dough in half. Shape each into a disk; cover and refrigerate until firm enough to roll, about 30 minutes.
3. Preheat the oven to 350°. On a lightly floured surface, roll each portion of the dough to an 8-in. square. Using a knife or fluted pastry wheel, cut each into sixteen 2-in. squares. If desired, prick holes with a fork. Place 1 in. apart on parchment-lined baking sheets.
4. Bake until the edges are light brown, 10-12 minutes. Remove to wire racks to cool. Store in an airtight container.

1 cookie: 60 cal., 2g fat (1g sat. fat), 6mg chol., 89mg sod., 9g carb. (3g sugars, 1g fiber), 1g pro. **Diabetic exchanges:** ½ starch, ½ fat.

SWEETER CLEAN-UP

When you need to measure honey for baking, first oil the measuring cup—use a little canola or vegetable oil or a quick spritz of cooking spray. The honey will come out easily, and you'll get the full measure without the messy process of scraping the cup.

DATE-NUT HONEY BARS

The flavor combination here reminds me of baklava—without the hours of work! These bars are perfect for holiday gifts, party platters and bake sales. They never fail to impress.

—Anna Wood, Cullowhee, NC

Prep: 45 min. • **Bake:** 25 min. + cooling
Makes: 2 dozen

- **¾ cup butter, softened**
- **⅓ cup sugar**
- **1¾ cups all-purpose flour**
- **½ cup old-fashioned oats**
- **¼ tsp. salt**

FILLING

- **½ cup honey**
- **½ cup apple jelly**
- **2 Tbsp. butter**
- **½ cup packed brown sugar**
- **2 large eggs, lightly beaten**
- **½ tsp. vanilla extract**
- **2 Tbsp. all-purpose flour**
- **½ tsp. baking powder**
- **¼ tsp. salt**
- **¼ tsp. ground cinnamon**
- **1¼ cups chopped walnuts**
- **1¼ cups chopped dates**

1. Preheat oven to 350°. In a large bowl, cream butter and sugar until light and fluffy, 5-7 minutes. In a small bowl, whisk the flour, oats and salt; gradually add to the creamed mixture, mixing well. Press onto the bottom and ½ in. up sides of an ungreased 13x9-in. baking pan. Bake until the edges begin to brown, 16-20 minutes. Cool on a wire rack.
2. For filling, in a large saucepan, combine honey, apple jelly and butter over medium heat; stir until jelly and butter are melted. Remove from heat; whisk in brown sugar, eggs and vanilla. In a small bowl, whisk the flour, baking powder, salt and cinnamon; whisk into honey mixture. Fold in walnuts and dates. Pour over crust; spread evenly. Bake until golden brown, 24-28 minutes. Cool completely in pan on a wire rack. Cut into bars.

1 bar: 235 cal., 11g fat (5g sat. fat), 33mg chol., 120mg sod., 33g carb. (22g sugars, 1g fiber), 3g pro.

LEMON THYME ICEBOX COOKIES

I found this recipe at my grandmother's house, and I made it as soon as I got home. It's a distinctive cookie that's almost savory because of the thyme, which pairs well with the lemon. It's a lovely melt-in-your-mouth butter cookie.

—Catherine Adams, Westwego, LA

Prep: 15 min. + chilling
Bake: 15 min./batch + cooling
Makes: about 2 dozen

- **½ cup butter, softened**
- **5 Tbsp. sugar**
- **1 Tbsp. minced fresh thyme**
- **1 to 2 tsp. grated lemon zest**
- **1 large egg yolk, room temperature**
- **1 cup all-purpose flour**
- **¼ tsp. baking powder**
- **¼ tsp. salt**

1. Cream butter, sugar, thyme and lemon zest until light and fluffy, 5-7 minutes. Beat in egg yolk. In another bowl, whisk flour, baking powder and salt; gradually beat into creamed mixture.
2. Roughly shape the dough into a 12-in. roll along the edge of a 12x12-in. sheet of waxed paper. Tightly roll waxed paper over dough, using the waxed paper to mold the dough into a smooth roll. Place the wrapped roll in an airtight container; refrigerate 1 hour or overnight.
3. Preheat oven to 350°. Unwrap and cut the dough crosswise into ½-in. slices. Place 2 in. apart on ungreased baking sheets. Bake until edges begin to brown, 12-15 minutes. Cool in pans 5 minutes. Remove to wire racks to finish cooling.

1 cookie: 65 cal., 4g fat (3g sat. fat), 18mg chol., 61mg sod., 7g carb. (3g sugars, 0 fiber), 1g pro.

PUMPKIN PIE BARS

These bars taste like a cross between pumpkin pie and pecan pie-
—Sue Draheim, Waterford, WI

Prep: 15 min. • **Bake:** 50 min. + chilling
Makes: 16 servings

- **1 can (29 oz.) pumpkin**
- **1 can (12 oz.) evaporated milk**
- **1½ cups sugar**
- **4 large eggs, room temperature**
- **2 tsp. ground cinnamon**
- **1 tsp. ground ginger**
- **½ tsp. ground nutmeg**
- **1 pkg. butter recipe golden cake mix (regular size)**
- **1 cup butter, melted**
- **1 cup chopped pecans**
- **Whipped topping, optional**

1. Preheat oven to 350°. In a large bowl, combine the first 7 ingredients; beat on medium speed until smooth. Pour into an ungreased 13x9-in. baking pan. Sprinkle with dry cake mix. Drizzle butter over top; sprinkle with pecans.
2. Bake for 50-60 minutes or until a toothpick inserted in the center comes out clean. Cool 1 hour on a wire rack.
3. Refrigerate 3 hours or overnight. Remove from refrigerator 15 minutes before serving. Cut into bars. If desired, serve with whipped topping.

1 bar: 419 cal., 22g fat (10g sat. fat), 91mg chol., 360mg sod., 53g carb. (38g sugars, 3g fiber), 5g pro.

PECAN PIE THUMBPRINTS

A good buttery dough and nutty filling take time to make, but the results are so worth it. After munching on a few, I think you'll agree.
—Peggy Key, Grant, AL

Prep: 30 min. + chilling
Bake: 10 min./batch + cooling
Makes: 4½ dozen

- **1 cup butter, softened**
- **½ cup sugar**
- **2 large eggs, separated**
- **½ cup dark corn syrup**
- **2½ cups all-purpose flour**

FILLING

- **¼ cup plus 2 Tbsp. confectioners' sugar**
- **3 Tbsp. butter**
- **2 Tbsp. dark corn syrup**
- **¼ cup plus 2 Tbsp. finely chopped pecans**

1. In a large bowl, cream butter and sugar until light and fluffy, 5-7 minutes. Beat in egg yolks and corn syrup. Gradually beat in flour. Refrigerate, covered, until firm enough to roll, 30 minutes.
2. For filling, in a small saucepan, combine the confectioners' sugar, butter and corn syrup. Bring to a boil over medium heat, stirring occasionally. Remove from heat; stir in the pecans. Remove from pan; refrigerate until cold, 30 minutes.
3. Preheat the oven to 375°. Shape the dough into 1-in. balls; place 2 in. apart on parchment-lined baking sheets. In a small bowl, whisk egg whites; brush over tops.
4. Bake 5 minutes. Remove from oven. Gently press an indentation in the center of each cookie with the end of a wooden spoon handle. Fill each with a scant ½ tsp. pecan mixture. Bake until the edges are light brown, 4-5 minutes longer. Cool on pans 5 minutes. Remove to wire racks to cool completely.

1 cookie: 86 cal., 5g fat (3g sat. fat), 18mg chol., 37mg sod., 10g carb. (4g sugars, 0 fiber), 1g pro.

GINGERBREAD MERINGUE BARS

For the best of both worlds, I combined my grandmother's gingerbread recipe with my aunt's special brown sugar meringue. The result? These lovable holiday-perfect bars.
—Eden Dranger, Los Angeles, CA

Prep: 20 min. • **Bake:** 30 min. + cooling
Makes: 2 dozen

- **¼ cup butter, softened**
- **1 cup molasses**
- **2 large egg yolks, room temperature**
- **1 large egg, room temperature**
- **¼ cup canned pumpkin**
- **1 tsp. vanilla extract**
- **1½ cups whole wheat flour**
- **2½ tsp. ground cinnamon**
- **2 tsp. ground ginger**
- **1 tsp. baking powder**
- **1 tsp. baking soda**
- **¾ tsp. ground allspice**
- **¼ tsp. salt**
- **1 cup miniature marshmallows**
- **½ cup chopped pecans**
- **½ cup semisweet chocolate chips**

MERINGUE

- **4 large egg whites, room temperature**
- **½ cup packed brown sugar**

1. In a large bowl, beat the butter and molasses until blended. Add egg yolks and egg, 1 at a time, beating well after each addition. Beat in pumpkin and vanilla.
2. In a small bowl, combine the flour, cinnamon, ginger, baking powder, baking soda, allspice and salt. Gradually add to molasses mixture. Pour into a greased 13x9-in. baking pan. Sprinkle with the marshmallows, pecans and chocolate chips. Bake at 350° for 20 minutes.
3. Meanwhile, in a small bowl, beat egg whites on medium speed until soft peaks form. Gradually beat in the brown sugar, 1 Tbsp. at a time, on high until stiff glossy peaks form and sugar is dissolved.
4. Remove the gingerbread from oven; spread with the meringue. Bake until the meringue is lightly browned, 9-11 minutes longer. Cool completely. Cut into bars.

1 bar: 135 cal., 4g fat (2g sat. fat), 31mg chol., 129mg sod., 24g carb. (15g sugars, 1g fiber), 2g pro. **Diabetic exchanges:** 1½ starch, 1 fat.

NANNY'S FRUITCAKE COOKIES

My grandmother always made a holiday fruitcake. I took her recipe and made it into a cookie that's perfect any time with a cup of tea.
—Amanda Digges, South Windsor, CT

Prep: 35 min. + chilling • **Bake:** 15 min./batch
Makes: about 4 dozen

- **1⅔ cups chopped pecans or walnuts**
- **1⅓ cups golden raisins**
- **1 cup pitted dried plums, chopped**
- **⅔ cup dried apricots, finely chopped**
- **½ cup dried cranberries**
- **¼ cup Triple Sec**
- **1 cup butter, softened**
- **½ cup sugar**
- **⅓ cup packed light brown sugar**
- **½ tsp. ground nutmeg**
- **1 large egg, room temperature**
- **2⅔ cups all-purpose flour**

1. Place the first 5 ingredients in a large bowl. Drizzle with Triple Sec and toss to combine. Let stand, covered, overnight.
2. In a large bowl, cream the butter, sugars and nutmeg until light and fluffy, 5-7 minutes. Beat in egg. Gradually beat in flour. Stir in fruit mixture.
3. Divide the dough in half; shape each into a 12x3x1-in. rectangular log. Cover; refrigerate overnight or until firm.
4. Preheat oven to 350°. Uncover and cut the dough crosswise into ½-in. slices. Place 2 in. apart on ungreased baking sheets. Bake until edges are light brown, 13-16 minutes. Remove from pans to wire racks to cool.

1 cookie: 131 cal., 7g fat (3g sat. fat), 14mg chol., 37mg sod., 17g carb. (9g sugars, 1g fiber), 2g pro.

Hooray for Whoopie Pies!

A cross between a cupcake and a cookie, a whoopie pie is a sentimental favorite in many parts of the country. Start with the traditional chocolate with snow-white cream filling, then try other flavors!

CHOCOLATE-RASPBERRY WHOOPIE PIES

I've saved this jam-filled whoopie pie recipe for years after cutting it out of a newspaper. It's one of my grandson's personal favorites.
—Nancy Foust, Stoneboro, PA

Prep: 40 min. • **Bake:** 10 min./batch + cooling
Makes: about 2½ dozen

- ½ **cup butter, softened**
- 1 **cup sugar**
- 1 **large egg, room temperature**
- 1 **tsp. vanilla extract**
- 2 **cups all-purpose flour**
- ½ **cup baking cocoa**
- 1½ **tsp. baking soda**
- ½ **tsp. baking powder**
- ½ **tsp. salt**
- 1 **cup 2% milk**

FILLING

- 1 **jar (7 oz.) marshmallow creme**
- ½ **cup shortening**
- ⅓ **cup seedless raspberry jam**
- 1 **tsp. vanilla extract**
- 2 **cups confectioners' sugar**

1. Preheat oven to 400°. In a large bowl, cream the butter and sugar until light and fluffy, 5-7 minutes. Beat in egg and vanilla. In another bowl, whisk the flour, cocoa, baking soda, baking powder and salt; add to creamed mixture alternately with milk, beating well after each addition.
2. Drop dough by tablespoonfuls 2 in. apart onto greased baking sheets. Bake until set, 6-8 minutes, and tops spring back when lightly touched. Remove from pans to wire racks to cool completely.
3. For the filling, in a large bowl, beat the marshmallow creme and shortening until blended. Beat in jam and vanilla. Gradually beat in confectioners' sugar until smooth. Spread on bottoms of half the cookies; cover with remaining cookies.

1 whoopie pie: 186 cal., 7g fat (3g sat. fat), 15mg chol., 148mg sod., 30g carb. (22g sugars, 0 fiber), 2g pro.

OLD-FASHIONED WHOOPIE PIES

Who can resist soft chocolate sandwich cookies filled with a layer of fluffy white frosting? Mom has made these for years. They're a treat that never lasts very long with me and my two brothers around.
—Maria Costello, Monroe, NC

Prep: 35 min. + chilling
Bake: 10 min./batch + cooling
Makes: 2 dozen

- ½ **cup baking cocoa**
- ½ **cup hot water**
- ½ **cup shortening**
- 1½ **cups sugar**
- 2 **large eggs, room temperature**
- 1 **tsp. vanilla extract**
- 2⅔ **cups all-purpose flour**
- 1 **tsp. baking powder**
- 1 **tsp. baking soda**
- ¼ **tsp. salt**
- ½ **cup buttermilk**

FILLING

- 3 **Tbsp. all-purpose flour**
- **Dash salt**
- 1 **cup 2% milk**
- ¾ **cup shortening**
- 1½ **cups confectioners' sugar**
- 2 **tsp. vanilla extract**

1. Preheat oven to 350°. In a small bowl, combine the cocoa and water. Cool for 5 minutes. In a large bowl, cream the shortening and sugar until light and fluffy, 5-7 minutes. Beat in the eggs, vanilla and cocoa mixture. Combine dry ingredients; gradually add to the creamed mixture alternately with the buttermilk, beating well after each addition
2. Drop by rounded tablespoonfuls 2 in. apart onto greased baking sheets. Bake until firm to the touch, 10-12 minutes. Remove to wire racks to cool.
3. For filling, in a small saucepan, combine flour and salt. Gradually whisk in milk until smooth; cook and stir over medium-high heat until thickened, 5-7 minutes. Remove from the heat. Cover and refrigerate until completely cool.
4. In a small bowl, cream the shortening, sugar and vanilla until light and fluffy, 5-7 minutes. Add milk mixture; beat until fluffy, 7 minutes. Spread filling on half the cookies; top with remaining cookies. Store in the refrigerator.

1 whoopie pie: 244 cal., 11g fat (3g sat. fat), 19mg chol., 116mg sod., 33g carb. (20g sugars, 1g fiber), 3g pro.

GO BANANAS WHOOPIE PIES

I love anything with peanut butter, so when I saw this recipe for soft banana cookies with a yummy peanut butter filling, I had to make them. Use a cookie scoop to keep them nicely rounded and all the same size.

—Jessie Sarrazin, Livingston, MT

Prep: 40 min. • **Bake:** 10 min./batch + cooling
Makes: 2 dozen

- ½ **cup butter, softened**
- ¾ **cup sugar**
- ¼ **cup packed brown sugar**
- 1 **large egg, room temperature**
- 1 **tsp. vanilla extract**
- ½ **cup mashed ripe banana**
- ½ **cup buttermilk**
- 2 **cups all-purpose flour**
- ½ **tsp. salt**
- ½ **tsp. baking powder**
- ½ **tsp. baking soda**

FILLING

- 1 **pkg. (8 oz.) cream cheese, softened**
- 1 **cup creamy peanut butter**
- 3 **Tbsp. butter, softened**
- 1 **cup confectioners' sugar**
- 1 **tsp. vanilla extract**
- **Additional confectioners' sugar**

1. Preheat oven to 350°. Cream the butter and sugars until light and fluffy, 5-7 minutes. Beat in the egg and vanilla. In a small bowl, combine banana and buttermilk. In another bowl, whisk flour, salt, baking powder and baking soda; gradually add to the creamed mixture alternately with the banana mixture.
2. Drop by tablespoonfuls 2 in. apart onto parchment-lined baking sheets. Bake until set, 8-10 minutes. Cool for 2 minutes before removing from pans to wire racks to cool completely.
3. For the filling, beat the cream cheese, peanut butter and butter until fluffy. Beat in confectioners' sugar and vanilla until smooth. Spread about 1 Tbsp. filling on the bottoms of half the cookies; cover with the remaining cookies. Dust with additional confectioners' sugar. Refrigerate.

1 whoopie pie: 244 cal., 14g fat (6g sat. fat), 31mg chol., 216mg sod., 26g carb. (16g sugars, 1g fiber), 5g pro.

CHOCOLATE CHIP RED VELVET WHOOPIE PIES

Baking a fun treat is a must when my four grandchildren come to stay for "Grandma Camp." Sometimes the grandkids help by piping the cake batter.

—Linda Schend, Kenosha, WI

Prep: 45 min. • **Bake:** 10 min./batch + cooling
Makes: about 2 dozen

- 1 **pkg. red velvet cake mix (regular size)**
- 3 **large eggs, room temperature**
- ½ **cup canola oil**
- 2 **tsp. vanilla extract**

FILLING

- 8 **oz. cream cheese, softened**
- ½ **cup butter, softened**
- 2 **cups confectioners' sugar**
- 1 **cup miniature semisweet chocolate chips**

1. Preheat oven to 350°. In a large bowl, combine cake mix, eggs, oil and extract; beat on low speed 30 seconds. Beat on medium 2 minutes.
2. Transfer batter to pastry bag; cut a ½-in. hole in the tip of bag. Pipe 1½x1-in. hearts onto parchment-lined baking sheets, spacing hearts 1 in. apart. Bake until edges are set, 6-8 minutes. Cool on pans 2 minutes. Remove to wire racks to cool completely.
3. For filling, in a large bowl, beat the cream cheese and butter until blended. Gradually beat in confectioners' sugar until smooth. Stir in chocolate chips. Spread filling on bottoms of half the cookies. Top with remaining cookies. Refrigerate leftovers.

1 whoopie pie: 267 cal., 16g fat (6g sat. fat), 44mg chol., 194mg sod., 30g carb. (23g sugars, 1g fiber), 2g pro.

Dazzling Desserts

When it's time to end the meal, sign off in style with one of these sweet recipes. Whether you're creating a rich, indulgent dessert for a harvesttime feast or a light, refreshing treat that puts summer fruits forward, the 27 delectable recipes in this chapter are ready to round out your menu!

LODGE

EASY BOURBON PECAN PIE

This pie has a mellow bourbon flavor that is not too strong and not too sweet. And it's easy, crunchy and chewy—just what you want in a pecan pie.

—Nick Iverson, Denver, CO

Prep: 10 min. + freezing
Bake: 1¼ hours + cooling • **Makes:** 10 servings

- **12 oz. toasted pecan halves, divided**
- **4 large eggs, room temperature**
- **½ cup packed dark brown sugar**
- **¼ cup sugar**
- **1 cup dark corn syrup**
- **8 Tbsp. unsalted butter, melted**
- **¼ cup bourbon**
- **2 tsp. vanilla extract**
- **¼ tsp. salt**
- **1 sheet refrigerated pie crust**
- **Vanilla ice cream, optional**

1. In a food processor, pulse half the pecans until coarsely chopped; reserve remaining pecans. Combine eggs and sugars until well mixed. Add the next 5 ingredients and the chopped pecans.
2. Unroll crust into a 9-in. metal pie plate; flute edge. Pour filling into crust. Arrange reserved pecan halves over filling. Place filled pie in freezer for 30 minutes.
3. Preheat oven to 425°. Bake until crust is set, about 15 minutes. Reduce oven setting to 350°; continue baking until the pie is puffed and set in the middle, about 1 hour (tent loosely with foil if needed to prevent overbrowning). Cool. If desired, serve with vanilla ice cream.

1 slice: 600 cal., 41g fat (11g sat. fat), 103mg chol., 221mg sod., 56g carb. (43g sugars, 3g fiber), 7g pro.

PEANUT BUTTER CHOCOLATE TART

Anyone who loves peanut butter cups will be in heaven when they take a bite of this rich, sensational tart. While it looks spectacular, it is very easy to put together.

—Mary Ann Lee, Clifton Park, NY

Prep: 40 min. + chilling • **Makes:** 16 servings

- **1 pkg. (9 oz.) chocolate wafers**
- **½ cup peanut butter chips**
- **2 Tbsp. sugar**
- **½ cup butter, melted**

FILLING

- **1 cup creamy peanut butter**
- **½ cup butter, softened**
- **4 oz. cream cheese, softened**
- **1 cup confectioners' sugar**
- **¼ cup light corn syrup**
- **1 tsp. vanilla extract**

GANACHE

- **¾ cup semisweet chocolate chips**
- **½ cup heavy whipping cream**
- **1½ tsp. sugar**
- **1½ tsp. light corn syrup**
- **¼ cup chopped salted peanuts**

1. In a food processor, place the wafers, peanut butter chips and sugar; cover and process until finely crushed. Stir in melted butter. Press onto the bottom and up the sides of an ungreased 9-in. fluted tart pan with removable bottom. Refrigerate for 30 minutes.
2. For filling, in a large bowl, beat the peanut butter, butter and cream cheese until fluffy. Add the confectioners' sugar, corn syrup and vanilla; beat until smooth. Pour into crust. Refrigerate while making the ganache.
3. Place the chocolate chips in a small bowl. In a small saucepan, bring the cream, sugar and corn syrup just to a boil. Pour over the chips; whisk until melted and smooth. Pour over the filling. Sprinkle with peanuts. Refrigerate for at least 2 hours.

1 slice: 448 cal., 32g fat (15g sat. fat), 48mg chol., 299mg sod., 37g carb. (23g sugars, 2g fiber), 8g pro.

BLUEBERRY DREAM PIE

This showstopping pie can be decorated to fit any season. I like to make hearts for Valentine's Day, flowers for spring, stars for Independence Day or even leaves for fall!
—Kerry Nakayama, New York, NY

Prep: 40 min. • **Bake:** 35 min. + cooling
Makes: 8 servings

Dough for a double-crust pie

CHEESE FILLING
- **4 oz. reduced-fat cream cheese**
- **½ cup confectioners' sugar**
- **1 Tbsp. lemon juice**
- **1 large egg yolk, room temperature**

BLUEBERRY FILLING
- **½ cup plus 1 Tbsp. sugar, divided**
- **2 Tbsp. all-purpose flour**
- **1 Tbsp. cornstarch**
- **¼ cup cold water**
- **6 cups fresh or frozen blueberries, divided**
- **2 Tbsp. lemon juice**
- **1 Tbsp. minced fresh mint or 1 tsp. dried mint**
- **1 large egg white, beaten**

1. On a floured surface, roll each dough disk to fit a 9-in. deep-dish cast-iron or other cast-iron skillet. Line skillet with bottom crust. Trim crust to ½ in. beyond edge of plate; flute edges. Line unpricked crust with a double thickness of heavy-duty foil. Bake at 450° for 8 minutes. Remove foil; bake 5 minutes longer. Cool on a wire rack. Reduce heat to 375°.
2. In a small bowl, beat the cream cheese, confectioners' sugar and lemon juice until light and fluffy. Beat in the egg yolk until blended. Spread into crust.
3. In a large saucepan, combine ½ cup sugar, the flour and cornstarch; stir in water until smooth. Stir in 2 cups berries. Bring to a boil; cook and stir 1-2 minutes or until thickened. Cool slightly. Gently stir in the lemon juice, mint and remaining berries. Pour over cheese filling.
4. Cut decorative cutouts in remaining crust; arrange over filling, leaving center uncovered. Brush crust with egg white; sprinkle with remaining sugar.
5. Bake at 375° until the crust is golden brown and filling is bubbly, 35-40 minutes. If necessary, cover the edges with foil during the last 15 minutes to prevent overbrowning. Cool on a wire rack. Refrigerate leftovers.

1 piece: 442 cal., 18g fat (8g sat. fat), 46mg chol., 269mg sod., 67g carb. (35g sugars, 3g fiber), 5g pro.

Dough for a double-crust pie: Combine 2½ cups all-purpose flour and ½ tsp. salt; cut in 1 cup cold butter until crumbly. Gradually add ⅓-⅔ cup ice water, tossing with a fork until dough holds together when pressed. Divide dough in half. Shape each into a disk. Cover and refrigerate 1 hour to overnight.

LEMONY LIMONCELLO TIRAMISU

This is a delightful citrus twist on a classic Italian dessert. It's always a favorite at holiday meals and summer family gatherings!
—Deena Resnick, Oregon City, OR

Prep: 25 min. + chilling • **Makes:** 12 servings

- **2 cartons (8 oz. each) mascarpone cheese**
- **6 large egg yolks**
- **¾ cup sugar**
- **⅔ cup 2% milk**
- **1¼ cups heavy whipping cream**
- **½ tsp. vanilla extract**
- **¼ cup lemon juice**
- **½ cup limoncello**
- **1 pkg. (7 oz.) crisp ladyfinger cookies**
- **1 jar (10 oz.) lemon curd**
- **Candied lemon slices**

1. Stir the mascarpone cheese; let stand at room temperature 30 minutes. Whisk the egg yolks, sugar and milk in top of a double boiler until mixture is thickened (ribbon stage) and a thermometer reads 160°. Remove from heat; cool completely. Whisk in mascarpone cheese until almost smooth. Whip heavy cream and vanilla until soft peaks form.
2. Combine lemon juice and limoncello. Briefly dip 24 ladyfingers into the lemon mixture and place in the bottom of an 11x7-in. baking dish. Top with half the mascarpone mixture, half the lemon curd and half the whipped cream. Repeat layers. Refrigerate, covered, 6 hours or overnight. To serve, garnish with candied lemon peel as desired.

1 piece: 509 cal., 31g fat (17g sat. fat), 204mg chol., 80mg sod., 47g carb. (40g sugars, 0 fiber), 7g pro.

CHOCOLATE POUND CAKE

This cake goes well with ice cream, but it's also delicate enough to serve in small pieces with tea.
—Ann Perry, Sierra Vista, AZ

Prep: 20 min. • **Bake:** 1½ hours + cooling
Makes: 12 servings

- **8 milk chocolate bars (1.55 oz. each)**
- **2 Tbsp. water**
- **½ cup butter, softened**
- **2 cups sugar**
- **4 large eggs, room temperature**
- **2 tsp. vanilla extract**
- **2½ cups cake flour, sifted**
- **½ tsp. salt**
- **¼ tsp. baking soda**
- **1 cup buttermilk**
- **½ cup chopped pecans, optional**
- **Confectioners' sugar, optional**

1. Preheat oven to 325°. In a saucepan, melt chocolate with water over low heat. Mixture will begin to harden.
2. In a large bowl, cream butter and sugar until light and fluffy, 5-7 minutes. Add eggs, 1 at a time, beating well after each addition. Beat in vanilla and the chocolate mixture. Combine the flour, salt and soda; add to creamed mixture alternately with buttermilk. Fold in nuts if desired.
3. Pour into a greased and floured 10-in. tube pan or fluted tube pan. Bake for 1½ hours or until a toothpick inserted in the center comes out clean. Let stand for 10 minutes before removing from pan to a wire rack to cool. Sprinkle with confectioners' sugar if desired.

1 slice: 353 cal., 11g fat (6g sat. fat), 93mg chol., 248mg sod., 59g carb. (36g sugars, 1g fiber), 5g pro.

APPLE PIE CUPCAKES WITH CINNAMON BUTTERCREAM

These apple pie cupcakes are always a hit! They are so easy to make and the flavor just screams fall—of course, they're just as delicious any other time of year, too.
—Jennifer Stowell, Deep River, IA

Prep: 20 min. • **Bake:** 20 min. + cooling
Makes: 2 dozen

- **1 pkg. yellow cake mix (regular size)**
- **2 Tbsp. butter**
- **4 medium tart apples, peeled and finely chopped (about 4 cups)**
- **¾ cup packed brown sugar**
- **1 Tbsp. cornstarch**
- **1 Tbsp. water**

FROSTING

- **1 cup butter, softened**
- **3 cups confectioners' sugar**
- **2 Tbsp. heavy whipping cream**
- **1 tsp. vanilla extract**
- **1½ tsp. ground cinnamon**
- **Thinly sliced apples, optional**

1. Prepare and bake cake mix according to package directions for cupcakes.
2. In a large skillet, heat the butter over medium heat. Add the apples and brown sugar; cook and stir until the apples are tender, 10-12 minutes. In a small bowl, mix cornstarch and water until smooth; stir into pan. Bring to a boil; cook and stir until thickened, 1-2 minutes. Remove from heat; cool completely.
3. Using a paring knife, cut a 1-in.-wide cone-shaped piece from the top of each cupcake; discard the removed portion. Fill cavity with apple mixture.
4. In a large bowl, combine the 5 frosting ingredients; beat until smooth. Frost the cupcakes. If desired, top with apple slices to serve.

1 cupcake: 300 cal., 15g fat (7g sat. fat), 48mg chol., 221mg sod., 41g carb. (32g sugars, 1g fiber), 1g pro.

BLACKBERRY WHITE CHOCOLATE CHEESECAKE CUPS

I read that white chocolate intensifies the flavor of blackberries. It's true! The crunch of baking chips, the blackberry puree, and the sweet and salty pretzel crust make this a fabulous mini dessert.

—Arlene Erlbach, Morton Grove, IL

Prep: 25 min. + chilling • **Makes:** 6 servings

- **1½ cups miniature pretzels**
- **2 Tbsp. plus ⅓ cup sugar, divided**
- **3 Tbsp. butter, melted**
- **1 cup heavy whipping cream**
- **1 pkg. (8 oz.) cream cheese, softened**
- **½ cup confectioners' sugar**
- **1 tsp. vanilla extract**
- **½ cup white baking chips**
- **1½ cups fresh blackberries**
- **Additional blackberries**

1. Pulse pretzels in a food processor until fine crumbs form. Add 2 Tbsp. granulated sugar and melted butter; pulse just until combined. Divide the mixture among 6 half-pint canning jars or dessert dishes.
2. For cheesecake layer, beat cream until stiff peaks form. In another bowl, beat cream cheese, confectioners' sugar and vanilla until smooth. Fold in 1½ cups of whipped cream, then the baking chips. Spoon over pretzel mixture. Refrigerate, covered, until cold, about 3 hours.
3. Meanwhile, in a clean food processor, puree 1½ cups blackberries with the remaining sugar; remove to a bowl. Cover and refrigerate berry mixture and the remaining whipped cream until serving.
4. To serve, top with blackberry mixture, reserved whipped cream and additional blackberries.

1 serving: 553 cal., 38g fat (23g sat. fat), 102mg chol., 359mg sod., 49g carb. (38g sugars, 2g fiber), 6g pro.

LIME OPTION

For a blackberry-lime variation, omit the vanilla and add ½ tsp. of grated lime zest along with an extra tablespoon of confectioners' sugar.

AUTUMN APPLE TORTE

During apple season, we always make room for a slice of this heartwarming torte. It has a cream cheese layer and apples galore.
—Margaret Wilson, San Bernardino, CA

Prep: 40 min. • **Bake:** 35 min. + cooling
Makes: 12 servings

- **½ cup butter, softened**
- **½ cup sugar, divided**
- **½ tsp. vanilla extract**
- **1 cup all-purpose flour**
- **1 pkg. (8 oz.) cream cheese, softened**
- **1 large egg, room temperature, lightly beaten**
- **½ tsp. almond extract**
- **2 cups thinly sliced, peeled Granny Smith apples (about 2 medium)**
- **2 cups thinly sliced, peeled Cortland apples (about 2 medium)**
- **¼ cup cinnamon sugar**
- **¼ tsp. ground nutmeg**
- **½ cup confectioners' sugar**
- **2 Tbsp. 2% milk**
- **2 Tbsp. sliced almonds, toasted**

1. Preheat oven to 450°. In a small bowl, cream butter and ¼ cup sugar until light and fluffy, 5-7 minutes. Beat in the vanilla. Gradually beat in flour. Press onto bottom and 1 in. up the sides of a greased 9-in. springform pan.
2. In a small bowl, beat cream cheese and remaining sugar until smooth. Add egg and almond extract; beat on low speed just until blended. Pour into crust.
3. Place the apples in a large bowl. Mix cinnamon sugar and nutmeg; add to apples and toss to coat. Arrange over cream cheese mixture. Bake 5 minutes.
4. Reduce oven setting to 400°. Bake 30-35 minutes longer or until apples are tender. Cool on a wire rack.
5. Remove rim from pan. In a small bowl, mix confectioners' sugar and milk until smooth. Drizzle over torte; sprinkle with almonds. Refrigerate leftovers.

Note: To toast nuts, place in a dry skillet; cook and stir over low heat until lightly browned.

1 slice: 270 cal., 15g fat (9g sat. fat), 57mg chol., 136mg sod., 31g carb. (22g sugars, 1g fiber), 3g pro.

CARAMEL DUMPLINGS

My family loves these tender dumplings in the sweet, rich sauce. They turn out wonderful every time I make them, which is a lot!
—Faye Johnson, Connersville, IN

Prep: 10 min. • **Cook:** 30 min.
Makes: 8 servings

- **2 Tbsp. butter**
- **1½ cups packed brown sugar**
- **1½ cups water**

DUMPLINGS

- **1¼ cups all-purpose flour**
- **½ cup sugar**
- **2 tsp. baking powder**
- **½ tsp. salt**
- **½ cup whole milk**
- **2 Tbsp. butter, softened**
- **2 tsp. vanilla extract**
- **½ cup coarsely chopped peeled apple, optional**
- **Vanilla ice cream, optional**

1. In a large skillet, heat the butter, brown sugar and water to boiling. Reduce heat to simmer.
2. Meanwhile, combine the dumpling ingredients; add apple if desired. Drop by tablespoonfuls into the simmering sauce. Cover tightly and simmer for 20 minutes. Do not lift lid. If desired, serve warm with vanilla ice cream.

½ cup: 336 cal., 6g fat (4g sat. fat), 17mg chol., 329mg sod., 68g carb. (53g sugars, 1g fiber), 3g pro.

LEMON BERRY DUMP CAKE

This sweet-tart cake recipe is so much fun to make with my grandkids. They love just dumping it all in and watching it magically become a pretty, yummy dessert.
—Nancy Heishman, Las Vegas, NV

Prep: 10 min. • **Bake:** 45 min. + cooling
Makes: 15 servings (3 cups lemon topping)

- **6 cups fresh or frozen blueberries**
- **1 tsp. ground cinnamon**
- **¾ cup butter, melted**
- **1 pkg. lemon cake mix (regular size)**

TOPPING

- **2 containers (6 oz. each) lemon yogurt**
- **1 container (8 oz.) frozen whipped topping, thawed**
- **½ cup marshmallow creme**
- **⅓ cup lemon curd**
- **Additional blueberries, optional**

1. Preheat oven to 350°. Toss blueberries with cinnamon; spread into a greased 13x9-in. baking dish. Drizzle with half the melted butter. Sprinkle with cake mix; drizzle with the remaining butter. Bake until golden brown and fruit is bubbly, 45-55 minutes. Cool on a wire rack.
2. Beat together the yogurt, whipped topping, marshmallow creme and lemon curd. Serve cake with yogurt mixture and, if desired, additional blueberries.

1 serving: 340 cal., 15g fat (9g sat. fat), 31mg chol., 297mg sod., 48g carb. (33g sugars, 1g fiber), 3g pro.

DIRTY BANANA TRIFLE

What could be better than bananas, cookies and Kahlua? You can adjust this to suit your taste, depending on whether you like a stronger or weaker Kahlua flavor.
—Laurie Handlin, Ocean View, DE

Prep: 40 min. + chilling • **Makes:** 24 servings

- **2 pkg. (8 oz. each) cream cheese, softened, divided**
- **2 cans (14 oz. each) sweetened condensed milk, divided**
- **1½ cups Kahlua (coffee liqueur), chilled**
- **2½ cups cold 2% milk, divided**
- **2 pkg. (3.9 oz. each) instant chocolate pudding mix**
- **3 cartons (8 oz. each) frozen whipped topping, thawed, divided**
- **9 whole chocolate graham crackers, coarsely crushed**
- **2 pkg. (3.4 oz. each) instant banana cream pudding mix**
- **1½ cups coarsely crushed vanilla wafers (about 45 wafers)**
- **5 medium bananas, sliced**
- **Additional wafers, crushed chocolate graham crackers and sliced bananas**

1. In a large bowl, beat 1 package cream cheese and 1 can condensed milk until blended. Beat in Kahlua, ½ cup milk and chocolate pudding mixes until thickened, about 2 minutes. Fold in 1 carton of whipped topping, then the chocolate graham crackers. Set aside.
2. In another large bowl, beat remaining cream cheese and condensed milk until blended. Beat in the remaining 2 cups milk and the banana pudding mixes until thickened, about 2 minutes. Fold in 1 carton whipped topping, vanilla wafers and bananas.
3. Spread the chocolate pudding mixture in the bottom of a 6- or 7-qt. trifle bowl or glass bowl. Layer with 1½ cups whipped topping and banana pudding mixture; top with remaining 1½ cups whipped topping. Cover and refrigerate overnight.
4. Before serving, garnish with the additional wafers, crushed chocolate graham crackers and sliced bananas.

1 cup: 381 cal., 16g fat (11g sat. fat), 33mg chol., 326mg sod., 46g carb. (33g sugars, 1g fiber), 5g pro.

CREAMY LAYERED BLUEBERRY ICE POPS

These delicious ice pops can also be made with raspberries or blackberries. The rosemary sprig and lemon zest bring another layer of flavor. The pops are quick, easy, kid-friendly and freezable.
—*Gloria Bradley, Naperville, IL*

Prep: 25 min. + freezing
Cook: 10 min. + cooling
Makes: 10 servings

- ⅓ **cup agave nectar**
- ¼ **cup water**
- 1 **fresh rosemary sprig**
- 1 **lemon zest strip (2 in.)**
- 1 **Tbsp. lemon juice**
- 2 **cups fresh or frozen blueberries**
- 2 **Tbsp. sugar**
- 2¼ **cups frozen whipped topping, thawed**
- 10 **freezer pop molds or 10 paper cups (3 oz. each) and wooden pop sticks**

1. For the lemon syrup, place the first 4 ingredients in a small saucepan; bring to a boil, stirring occasionally. Remove from heat; let stand, covered, 10 minutes. Remove rosemary and lemon zest. Stir in lemon juice; cool completely.
2. Place the blueberries and sugar in another saucepan; cook and stir over medium heat until the berries pop, 5-7 minutes. Cool completely.
3. Add whipped topping to the lemon syrup, whisking to blend. Transfer half the mixture to a pastry bag. Pipe into molds. Layer with blueberries. Pipe the remaining whipped topping mixture over top. Close molds with holders. If using paper cups, top with foil and insert sticks through foil.
4. Freeze until firm, about 4 hours. To serve, dip the pop molds briefly in warm water before removing.

1 pop: 104 cal., 3g fat (3g sat. fat), 0 chol., 0 sod., 19g carb. (18g sugars, 1g fiber), 0 pro.
Diabetic exchanges: 1 starch, ½ fat.

AGAVE INSIGHTS

Agave nectar, made from the same plant used to make tequila, is a sweetener that can be used like sugar or honey.

EASY STRAWBERRY LEMONADE FREEZER PIE

Three simple ingredients mixed together and spread into a graham crust make magic while your freezer does the all the work. Prep this pie ahead and freeze it overnight or even longer. Feel free to vary the fruit if you'd like!
—Debbie Glasscock, Conway, AR

Prep: 15 min. + freezing • **Makes:** 8 servings

- **1 container (23.2 oz.) frozen sweetened sliced strawberries, thawed (2½ cups thawed)**
- **1 pkg. (3.4 oz.) instant lemon pudding mix**
- **1 carton (8 oz.) frozen whipped topping, thawed**
- **1 graham cracker crust (9 in.)**
  Optional: Additional whipped topping and fresh strawberries

1. In a large bowl, combine strawberries (with juices) and pudding mix; let stand until slightly thickened, about 5 minutes. Fold in whipped topping. Spread into graham cracker crust.
2. Freeze at least 8 hours or overnight. Let stand 5-10 minutes before serving. If desired, serve with additional whipped topping and strawberries.

1 piece: 306 cal., 10g fat (6g sat. fat), 0 chol., 273mg sod., 51g carb. (45g sugars, 2g fiber), 1g pro.

CHOCOLATE MALT CHEESECAKE

For a change of pace, substitute pretzel crumbs for the graham cracker crumbs—they make a surprisingly good crust!
—Anita Moffett, Rewey, WI

Prep: 25 min. • **Bake:** 1 hour + chilling
Makes: 14 servings

- **1 cup graham cracker crumbs (about 16 squares)**
- **¼ cup sugar**
- **⅓ cup butter, melted**

FILLING

- **3 pkg. (8 oz. each) cream cheese, softened**
- **1 can (14 oz.) sweetened condensed milk**
- **¾ cup chocolate malt powder**
- **4 large eggs, room temperature, lightly beaten**
- **1 cup semisweet chocolate chips, melted and cooled**
- **1 tsp. vanilla extract**
  Optional: Confectioners' sugar and chocolate curls

1. Preheat oven to 325°. Combine the cracker crumbs, sugar and butter. Press onto the bottom of a greased 9-in. springform pan; set aside.
2. In a large bowl, beat cream cheese and milk until smooth. Add malt powder; beat well. Add the eggs; beat on low speed just until combined. Stir in melted chocolate and vanilla just until blended. Pour over crust. Place pan on a baking sheet.
3. Bake until the center is almost set, 60-65 minutes. Cool on a wire rack for 10 minutes. Carefully run a knife around edge of pan to loosen; cool 1 hour longer. Refrigerate overnight, covering when completely cooled.
4. Remove sides of pan. Garnish with confectioners' sugar and chocolate curls if desired. Refrigerate leftovers.

1 piece: 369 cal., 19g fat (11g sat. fat), 101mg chol., 291mg sod., 47g carb. (35g sugars, 1g fiber), 7g pro.

MAMA'S BLACKBERRY COBBLER

Alabama has some tasty fresh blackberries. Many years ago my mama was planning on picking blackberries to make a cobbler—but she went to the hospital to have me instead! This is her mama's recipe.
—Lisa Allen, Joppa, AL

Prep: 15 min. • **Bake:** 45 min.
Makes: 6 servings

- **½ cup plus 2 Tbsp. melted butter, divided**
- **1 cup self-rising flour**
- **1½ cups sugar, divided**
- **1 cup 2% milk**
- **½ tsp. vanilla extract**
- **3 cups fresh blackberries or frozen unsweetened blackberries**

1. Preheat oven to 350°. Pour ½ cup melted butter into an 8-in. square baking dish. In a small bowl, combine flour, 1 cup sugar, the milk and vanilla until blended; pour into the prepared dish. In another bowl, combine the blackberries and the remaining ½ cup sugar and remaining 2 Tbsp. melted butter; toss until combined. Spoon over batter.
2. Bake until topping is golden brown and the fruit is tender, 45-50 minutes. Serve warm.

¾ cup: 491 cal., 21g fat (13g sat. fat), 54mg chol., 421mg sod., 75g carb. (56g sugars, 4g fiber), 5g pro.

WHOLE WHEAT STRAWBERRY SHORTCAKES

Nothing says spring better than a fresh strawberry shortcake. It is heavenly! My mother and I usually make this with strawberries we picked ourselves.
—Sarah Hatter, Brodhead, WI

Prep: 45 min. + chilling
Bake: 15 min. + cooling
Makes: 6 servings

- **2½ cups fresh strawberries, hulled, divided**
- **1 to 2 Tbsp. maple syrup**

SHORTCAKES

- **2 cups whole wheat flour**
- **2½ tsp. baking powder**
- **½ tsp. salt**
- **¼ tsp. baking soda**
- **½ cup cold butter, cubed**
- **1 large egg, room temperature**
- **½ cup 2% milk**
- **¼ cup honey**
- **Whipped cream**

1. In a bowl, thoroughly mash ¾ cup strawberries; stir in syrup. Cut remaining strawberries into ¼-in. slices; add to the crushed strawberries and toss to coat. Refrigerate, covered, 1 hour.
2. Meanwhile, preheat oven to 400°. In a large bowl, whisk flour, baking powder, salt and baking soda. Cut in butter until mixture resembles coarse crumbs. In a small bowl, whisk egg, milk and honey until blended; stir into the flour mixture just until moistened.
3. Turn onto a lightly floured surface; knead gently 8-10 times. Pat or roll the dough to ¾-in. thickness; cut with a floured 2½-in. biscuit cutter. Place 2 in. apart on parchment-lined baking sheets. Bake 12-15 minutes or until light brown. Remove to wire racks to cool slightly.
4. To serve, split shortcakes in half. Fill with the strawberry mixture and whipped cream. Top with additional whipped cream.

1 shortcake: 362 cal., 17g fat (10g sat. fat), 77mg chol., 549mg sod., 49g carb. (18g sugars, 6g fiber), 8g pro.

APPLE BUTTER CAKE ROLL

This spicy gingerbread cake is a new take on a classic pumpkin roll. It might make you think back fondly to your grandma's Christmas cookies.

—Debbie White, Williamson, WV

Prep: 35 min. • **Bake:** 15 min. + chilling
Makes: 15 servings

- **3 large eggs, separated**
- **1 cup all-purpose flour, divided**
- **2 Tbsp. plus ½ cup sugar, divided**
- **2 tsp. ground cinnamon**
- **1 tsp. baking powder**
- **1 tsp. ground ginger**
- **1 tsp. ground cloves**
- **¼ tsp. baking soda**
- **¼ cup butter, melted**
- **¼ cup molasses**
- **2 Tbsp. water**
- **1 Tbsp. confectioners' sugar**
- **2 cups apple butter**

1. Preheat the oven to 375°. Place the egg whites in a small bowl; let stand at room temperature for 30 minutes. Line a greased 15x10x1-in. baking pan with waxed paper and grease the paper. Sprinkle with 1 Tbsp. flour and 2 Tbsp. sugar; set aside.
2. In a large bowl, combine remaining flour and sugar; add cinnamon, baking powder, ginger, cloves and baking soda. In another bowl, whisk the egg yolks, butter, molasses and water. Add to the dry ingredients and beat until blended. Beat egg whites on medium speed until soft peaks form; fold into batter. Pour into prepared pan.
3. Bake for 12-14 minutes or until cake springs back when lightly touched. Cool for 5 minutes. Turn cake onto a kitchen towel dusted with confectioners' sugar. Gently peel off waxed paper. Roll up the cake in the towel jelly-roll style, starting with a short side. Cool completely on a wire rack.
4. Unroll cake; spread the apple butter to within ½ in. of edges. Roll up again. Cover and chill for 1 hour before serving. Refrigerate leftovers.

1 slice: 186 cal., 4g fat (2g sat. fat), 45mg chol., 100mg sod., 35g carb. (26g sugars, 1g fiber), 2g pro. **Diabetic exchanges:** 2 starch, 1 fat.

MAMA'S COCONUT PIE

My mama showed me how to make this pie about 40 years ago, just as her mama showed her how to make it. I was 6 when Mawmaw passed away, but I can still remember her cooking in the kitchen in her beautiful cotton dresses dusted with flour. I am honored to teach my daughter how to make this dessert.

—Lisa Allen, Joppa, AL

Prep: 20 min. • **Bake:** 50 min.
Makes: 8 servings

Dough for single-crust pie
1 cup sugar
3 large eggs
½ cup buttermilk
½ cup unsalted butter, melted and cooled
2 Tbsp. all-purpose flour
1½ tsp. vanilla extract
Dash salt
1½ cups sweetened shredded coconut

1. Preheat oven to 325°. On a lightly floured surface, roll dough to a ⅛-in.-thick circle; transfer to a 9-in. pie plate. Trim to ½ in. beyond rim of plate; flute edge. Place the pie plate on a rimmed baking sheet.
2. In a large bowl, beat the sugar, eggs, buttermilk, melted butter, flour, vanilla and salt until blended. Stir in coconut. Pour into crust. Bake until light golden brown and the center is almost set, 50-60 minutes. Cool on a wire rack; serve or refrigerate within 2 hours.

Note: It is important not to overbake this pie or the surface will crack as it cools. The center of the pie will still be slightly wobbly after baking but will set up as it cools.

1 piece: 550 cal., 35g fat (23g sat. fat), 142mg chol., 318mg sod., 54g carb. (34g sugars, 1g fiber), 6g pro.

Dough for single-crust pie: Combine 1½ cups all-purpose flour and ¼ tsp. salt; cut in ⅔ cup cold butter until crumbly. Gradually add 3-6 Tbsp. ice water, tossing with a fork until dough holds together when pressed. Cover and refrigerate 1 hour.

ROASTED STRAWBERRY SHEET CAKE

My Grandma Gigi loved summer berry cakes. Almost any time I'd call her during the warmer months, she'd invite me over to taste her latest masterpiece. This cake is a tribute to her.

—Kristin Bowers, Rancho Palos Verdes, CA

Prep: 1 hour • **Bake:** 30 min. + cooling
Makes: 24 servings

4 lbs. halved fresh strawberries
½ cup sugar

CAKE

1 cup butter, softened
1½ cups sugar
2 large eggs, room temperature
2 tsp. almond extract
3 cups all-purpose flour
3 tsp. baking powder
2 tsp. salt
1 cup 2% milk
¼ cup turbinado (washed raw) sugar

1. Preheat oven to 350°. Place the strawberries on a parchment-lined rimmed baking sheet. Sprinkle with sugar and toss to coat. Bake until just tender, 35-40 minutes. Cool slightly.
2. Meanwhile, grease a 15x10x1-in. baking pan. In a large bowl, cream butter and sugar until light and fluffy, 5-7 minutes. Add eggs, 1 at a time, beating well after each addition. Beat in extract. In another bowl, whisk flour, baking powder and salt; add to creamed mixture alternately with milk, beating well after each addition (batter may appear curdled).
3. Transfer to prepared pan. Top with 3 cups roasted strawberries; sprinkle with turbinado sugar. Reserve remaining strawberries for serving. Bake until a toothpick inserted in center comes out clean, 30-35 minutes. Cool completely in pan on a wire rack. Serve with reserved roasted strawberries.

1 piece: 235 cal., 9g fat (5g sat. fat), 37mg chol., 329mg sod., 37g carb. (23g sugars, 2g fiber), 3g pro.

RHUBARB ICEBOX DESSERT

A light and fluffy marshmallow layer tops the tart rhubarb filling in this delicious make-ahead recipe.

—Renee Schwebach, Dumont, MN

Prep: 15 min. • **Bake:** 10 min. + chilling
Makes: 15 servings

1¾ cups graham cracker crumbs, divided
3 Tbsp. butter, melted
1 cup sugar
2 Tbsp. cornstarch
4 cups diced fresh or frozen rhubarb
1 pkg. (3 oz.) raspberry or strawberry gelatin
1 carton (8 oz.) frozen whipped topping, thawed
1½ cups miniature marshmallows
2 cups cold whole milk
1 pkg. (3.4 oz.) instant vanilla pudding mix

1. Preheat oven to 350°. In a small bowl, combine 1½ cups cracker crumbs and butter. Press mixture into a greased 13x9-in. baking dish. Bake until lightly browned, about 10 minutes. Cool on a wire rack.
2. In a large saucepan, combine the sugar, cornstarch and rhubarb. Bring to a boil; cook and stir until thickened and rhubarb is tender, 2-3 minutes. Remove from the heat; stir in gelatin until dissolved. Cover and refrigerate until partially set, about 1 hour.
3. Spoon rhubarb mixture over the crust. Combine the whipped topping and marshmallows; spread over the rhubarb mixture.
4. In a large bowl, whisk milk and pudding mix for 2 minutes. Let stand until soft set, about 2 minutes. Carefully spread over marshmallow topping (the dish will be full). Sprinkle with remaining cracker crumbs. Refrigerate for at least 2 hours before serving.

1 piece: 247 cal., 7g fat (5g sat. fat), 11mg chol., 206mg sod., 43g carb. (31g sugars, 1g fiber), 3g pro.

MIXED BERRY TIRAMISU

Because I love tiramisu, I came up with this deliciously refreshing twist on the traditional coffee-flavored Italian dessert. Fresh softened berries star with crisp ladyfinger cookies and mascarpone cheese. Serve it from a glass bowl or in clear dishes to show off the luscious layers.
—Najmussahar Ahmed, Ypsilanti, MI

Prep: 35 min. + chilling • **Makes:** 12 servings

3 cups fresh raspberries
3 cups fresh blackberries
2 cups fresh blueberries
2 cups fresh strawberries, sliced
1⅓ cups sugar, divided
4 tsp. grated orange zest
1 cup orange juice
1 cup heavy whipping cream
2 cartons (8 oz. each) mascarpone cheese
1 tsp. vanilla extract
2 pkg. (7 oz. each) crisp ladyfinger cookies
Additional fresh berries, optional

1. Place berries in a large bowl. Mix ⅓ cup sugar, the orange zest and orange juice; toss gently with berries. Refrigerate, covered, 45 minutes.
2. Beat cream until soft peaks form. In another bowl, mix mascarpone cheese, vanilla and the remaining sugar. Fold in whipped cream, a third at a time.
3. Drain berries over a shallow bowl, reserving juices. Dip the ladyfingers in reserved juices, allowing excess to drip off; arrange in a single layer on bottom of a 13x9-in. dish. Layer with half the berries and half the mascarpone mixture; repeat layers, starting with ladyfingers.
4. Refrigerate, covered, overnight. If desired, top with additional berries before serving.

Note: This recipe was prepared with Alessi brand ladyfinger cookies.

1 piece: 501 cal., 26g fat (14g sat. fat), 105mg chol., 77mg sod., 63g carb. (45g sugars, 5g fiber), 8g pro.

PLUM & HAZELNUT PIE

My mom taught me about Italian prune plums and pie. Sprinkling the crust with ground hazelnuts gives it a luscious flavor and also keeps it from getting soggy.
—Trisha Kruse, Eagle, ID

Prep: 15 min. + chilling
Bake: 45 min. + cooling
Makes: 8 servings

- **Dough for single-crust pie**
- **4 cups sliced fresh plums (about 8)**
- **2 Tbsp. hazelnut liqueur, optional**
- **½ cup sugar**
- **¼ cup all-purpose flour**
- **¼ tsp. salt**

TOPPING

- **½ cup packed brown sugar**
- **⅓ cup all-purpose flour**
- **¼ cup finely chopped hazelnuts, toasted**
- **3 Tbsp. cold butter, cubed**

1. On a lightly floured surface, roll dough to a ⅛-in.-thick circle; transfer to a 9-in. deep-dish pie plate. Trim the crust to ½ in. beyond rim of plate; flute the edge. Refrigerate 30 minutes.
2. Preheat oven to 375°. Toss the plums with liqueur if desired. Mix sugar, flour and salt; add to plums and toss to coat. Transfer to crust.
3. For topping, combine brown sugar, flour and hazelnuts; cut in butter until crumbly. Sprinkle over plum mixture.
4. Bake until crust is golden brown and filling is bubbly, about 45-55 minutes. Cool on a wire rack.

1 piece: 454 cal., 22g fat (13g sat. fat), 52mg chol., 308mg sod., 61g carb. (34g sugars, 2g fiber), 5g pro.

Dough for single-crust pie: Combine 1½ cups all-purpose flour and ¼ tsp. salt; cut in ⅔ cup cold butter until crumbly. Gradually add 3-6 Tbsp. ice water, tossing with a fork until dough holds together when pressed. Cover and refrigerate for 1 hour.

Contest Winner

BLACKBERRY DAIQUIRI SHERBET

This summer I decided to try making sherbet, which is one of my favorites. Blackberries were in season in my mom's garden, and I love the flavor of daiquiris. The two blend together beautifully!
—Shelly Bevington, Hermiston, OR

Prep: 15 min. • **Process:** 30 min. + freezing
Makes: 1¼ qt.

- **3 cups fresh or frozen blackberries, thawed**
- **1 cup sugar**
- **¼ tsp. salt**
- **1 can (12 oz.) evaporated milk**
- **2 Tbsp. lime juice**
- **1 tsp. rum extract**
- **½ tsp. citric acid**

1. Place blackberries, sugar and salt in a food processor; process until smooth. Press through a fine-mesh strainer into a bowl; discard seeds and pulp. Stir the remaining ingredients into the puree.
2. Fill the cylinder of ice cream maker no more than two-thirds full; freeze according to manufacturer's directions. Transfer sherbet to freezer containers, allowing headspace for expansion. Freeze until firm, 8 hours or overnight.

½ cup: 147 cal., 3g fat (2g sat. fat), 12mg chol., 96mg sod., 28g carb. (26g sugars, 2g fiber), 3g pro.

LEAVE OUT THE BOOZE!

Substituting rum for the extract might seem like a fun idea, but the alcohol will keep your dessert from freezing solid.

Upside-Down Delights

Topsy-turvy desserts are truly delightful, and these recipes prove it. Baking a dessert upside down lets the bottom layer (actually the top!) soak up flavor without the cake soaking in too much juice.

UPSIDE-DOWN PEAR GINGERBREAD CAKE

The aroma of baking gingerbread stirs up such warm memories. This cake looks festive and is even on the lighter side.
—Nancy Beckman, Helena, MT

Prep: 25 min. • **Bake:** 25 min. + cooling
Makes: 8 servings

- 3 **Tbsp. butter**
- ⅓ **cup packed dark brown sugar**
- 2 **medium Bosc pears, peeled and thinly sliced**

CAKE

- ½ **cup 2% milk**
- 1 **Tbsp. cider vinegar**
- 1 **large egg, room temperature**
- ½ **cup packed dark brown sugar**
- ⅓ **cup molasses**
- ¼ **cup butter, melted**
- 1¼ **cups all-purpose flour**
- 2 **tsp. ground cinnamon**
- 1 **tsp. baking soda**
- 1 **tsp. ground ginger**
- ¼ **tsp. salt**
- ¼ **tsp. ground cloves**
- **Whipped cream, optional**

1. Preheat the oven to 350°. In a small saucepan, melt butter over medium heat; stir in brown sugar. Spread over bottom of greased 9-in. round baking pan. Arrange pears over top.

2. For cake, mix the milk and vinegar; let stand 5 minutes. In a large bowl, beat egg, brown sugar, molasses, melted butter and milk mixture until well blended. In another bowl, whisk flour, cinnamon, baking soda, ginger, salt and cloves; gradually beat into the molasses mixture. Spoon carefully over pears.

3. Bake for 25-30 minutes or until a toothpick inserted in center comes out clean. Cool 10 minutes before inverting onto a serving plate. Serve warm or at room temperature with whipped cream, if desired.

1 slice: 331 cal., 11g fat (7g sat. fat), 51mg chol., 348mg sod., 56g carb. (37g sugars, 2g fiber), 4g pro.

HOMEMADE RHUBARB UPSIDE-DOWN CAKE

This light and airy yellow cake is moist but not too sweet, and the caramelized rhubarb topping adds tangy flavor and visual appeal. We like it served with strawberry ice cream.
—Joyce Rowe, Stratham, NH

Prep: 30 min. • **Bake:** 40 min. + cooling
Makes: 12 servings

- ⅔ **cup packed brown sugar**
- 3 **Tbsp. butter, melted**
- 2¼ **cups diced fresh or frozen rhubarb**
- 4½ **tsp. sugar**

BATTER

- 6 **Tbsp. butter, softened**
- ¾ **cup sugar**
- 2 **large eggs, separated, room temperature**
- 1 **tsp. vanilla extract**
- 1 **cup plus 2 Tbsp. all-purpose flour**
- 1½ **tsp. baking powder**
- ½ **tsp. salt**
- ¼ **cup milk**
- ¼ **tsp. cream of tartar**
- **Optional: Whipped cream or vanilla ice cream**

1. Preheat oven to 325°. In a small bowl, combine brown sugar and butter. Spread into a greased 10-in cast-iron or other ovenproof skillet. Layer with rhubarb; sprinkle with sugar. Set aside.

2. In a large bowl, cream butter and sugar until light and fluffy, 5-7 minutes. Beat in egg yolks and vanilla. Combine the flour, baking powder and salt; add to creamed mixture alternately with milk, beating well after each addition.

3. In a small bowl, beat egg whites and cream of tartar on medium speed until stiff peaks form. Gradually fold into the creamed mixture, about ½ cup at a time. Gently spoon over rhubarb.

4. Bake until the cake springs back when lightly touched, 40-50 minutes. Cool for 10 minutes before inverting onto a serving plate. Serve warm with whipped cream or ice cream as desired.

1 piece: 240 cal., 10g fat (6g sat. fat), 59mg chol., 254mg sod., 36g carb. (27g sugars, 1g fiber), 3g pro.

Contest Winner

APPLE-PUMPKIN UPSIDE-DOWN CAKE

We love the combination of classic fall fruits in this terrific cake. I bake the apples on the bottom to keep them plump and moist, then flip the cake so we can dig in at any time of day. It's best served warm with vanilla ice cream.

—Christina Yahraes, San Francisco, CA

Prep: 15 min. • **Bake:** 30 min. + cooling
Makes: 8 servings

- **2 large eggs**
- **2 Tbsp. plus ¼ cup softened butter, divided**
- **2 Tbsp. plus ¾ cup sugar, divided**
- **1 tsp. ground cinnamon, divided**
- **2 medium apples (about 10 oz.), peeled and thinly sliced**
- **½ cup canned pumpkin**
- **1¼ cups all-purpose flour**
- **1 tsp. baking soda**
- **½ tsp. salt**
- **½ cup buttermilk**
- **Vanilla ice cream, optional**

1. Preheat oven to 350°. Let eggs stand at room temperature 30 minutes. In a microwave, melt 2 Tbsp. butter. Stir in 2 Tbsp. sugar and ½ tsp. cinnamon; spread the mixture into a 9-in. pie plate. Arrange apples in a single layer over the butter mixture.
2. Cream the remaining butter and remaining sugar until light and fluffy, 5-7 minutes. Beat in the pumpkin. Add eggs, 1 at a time, beating well after each addition. In another bowl, whisk together the flour, baking soda, salt and remaining cinnamon; add to the creamed mixture alternately with buttermilk, beating well after each addition.
3. Spread batter evenly over apples. Bake until a toothpick inserted in center comes out clean, 30-35 minutes. Loosen sides of the cake from pie plate with a knife. Cool 10 minutes before inverting onto a serving plate. Serve warm and, if desired, with vanilla ice cream.

1 slice: 278 cal., 10g fat (6g sat. fat), 70mg chol., 422mg sod., 43g carb. (27g sugars, 2g fiber), 4g pro.

UPSIDE-DOWN PUMPKIN PECAN TARTS

These are a superb twist on pumpkin pie and can be prepared ahead. You'll love the flaky phyllo combined with the rich pumpkin filling.

—Darlene Buerger, Peoria, AZ

Prep: 45 min. • **Bake:** 45 min. + cooling
Makes: 12 servings

- **1¼ cups melted butter, divided**
- **⅓ cup packed brown sugar**
- **¼ cup maple syrup**
- **½ cup chopped pecans**
- **12 oz. cream cheese, softened**
- **½ cup sugar**
- **1 tsp. vanilla extract**
- **2 large eggs, room temperature**
- **¾ cup canned pumpkin**
- **2 Tbsp. all-purpose flour**
- **2 tsp. pumpkin pie spice**
- **36 sheets phyllo dough (14x9-in. size)**
- **Optional: Whipped cream and additional pumpkin pie spice**

1. Preheat oven to 325°. In small bowl, combine ¼ cup melted butter, brown sugar and maple syrup. Divide between 12 greased jumbo muffin cups. Sprinkle with pecans; set aside.
2. In a large bowl, beat the cream cheese, sugar and vanilla until smooth. Add eggs, 1 at a time, until blended. Remove 1 cup for filling. Stir in pumpkin, flour and pie spice to remaining cream cheese mixture; set aside.
3. Place 1 sheet of phyllo dough on a work surface; brush with butter. Layer with 5 additional phyllo sheets, brushing each layer. (Keep the remaining phyllo covered with a damp towel to prevent it from drying out.) Cut sheets into a 9x7-in. rectangle. Carefully press each stack into prepared muffin cups. Repeat with the remaining phyllo.
4. Spoon 1 heaping Tbsp. plain cream cheese mixture into each phyllo cup. Top with 3 Tbsp. pumpkin mixture. Pinch the corners of phyllo together and twist to seal; brush with remaining butter. Bake until golden brown, 45-50 minutes. Cool 5 minutes before inverting onto wire racks to cool completely. If desired, serve with whipped cream and sprinkle with additional pumpkin pie spice.

1 tart: 487 cal., 34g fat (18g sat. fat), 111mg chol., 392mg sod., 42g carb. (22g sugars, 2g fiber), 7g pro.

Substitutions & Equivalents

EQUIVALENT MEASURES

3 teaspoons = 1 tablespoon	**16 tablespoons** = 1 cup
4 tablespoons = ¼ cup	**2 cups** = 1 pint
5⅓ tablespoons = ⅓ cup	**4 cups** = 1 quart
8 tablespoons = ½ cup	**4 quarts** = 1 gallon

FOOD EQUIVALENTS

Macaroni	1 cup (3½ ounces) uncooked = 2½ cups cooked
Noodles, Medium	3 cups (4 ounces) uncooked = 4 cups cooked
Popcorn	⅓-½ cup unpopped = 8 cups popped
Rice, Long Grain	1 cup uncooked = 3 cups cooked
Rice, Quick-Cooking	1 cup uncooked = 2 cups cooked
Spaghetti	8 ounces uncooked = 4 cups cooked

Bread	1 slice = ¾ cup soft crumbs or ¼ cup fine dry crumbs
Graham Crackers	7 squares = ½ cup finely crushed
Buttery Round Crackers	12 crackers = ½ cup finely crushed
Saltine Crackers	14 crackers = ½ cup finely crushed

Bananas	1 medium = ⅓ cup mashed
Lemons	1 medium = 3 tablespoons juice + 2 teaspoons grated zest
Limes	1 medium = 2 tablespoons juice + 1½ teaspoons grated zest
Oranges	1 medium = ¼-⅓ cup juice + 4 teaspoons grated zest

Cabbage	1 head = 5 cups shredded	**Green Pepper**	1 large = 1 cup chopped
Carrots	1 pound = 3 cups shredded	**Mushrooms**	½ pound = 3 cups sliced
Celery	1 rib = ½ cup chopped	**Onions**	1 medium = ½ cup chopped
Corn	1 ear fresh = ⅔ cup kernels	**Potatoes**	3 medium = 2 cups cubed

Almonds	1 pound = 3 cups chopped	**Pecan Halves**	1 pound = 4½ cups chopped
Ground Nuts	3¾ ounces = 1 cup	**Walnuts**	1 pound = 3¾ cups chopped

EASY SUBSTITUTIONS

WHEN YOU NEED...		USE...
Baking Powder	1 teaspoon	½ teaspoon cream of tartar + ¼ teaspoon baking soda
Buttermilk	1 cup	1 tablespoon lemon juice or vinegar + enough milk to measure 1 cup (let stand 5 minutes before using)
Cornstarch	1 tablespoon	2 tablespoons all-purpose flour
Honey	1 cup	1¼ cups sugar + ¼ cup water
Half-and-Half Cream	1 cup	1 tablespoon melted butter + enough whole milk to measure 1 cup
Onion	1 small, chopped (⅓ cup)	1 teaspoon onion powder or 1 tablespoon dried minced onion
Tomato Juice	1 cup	½ cup tomato sauce + ½ cup water
Tomato Sauce	2 cups	¾ cup tomato paste + 1 cup water
Unsweetened Chocolate	1 square (1 ounce)	3 tablespoons baking cocoa + 1 tablespoon shortening or oil
Whole Milk	1 cup	½ cup evaporated milk + ½ cup water

HONEY: BW FOLSOM/SHUTTERSTOCK

Cooking Terms

Here's a quick reference for some of the most common cooking terms used in recipes:

BASTE To moisten food with melted butter, pan drippings, marinades or other liquid to add more flavor and juiciness.

BEAT A rapid movement to combine ingredients using a fork, spoon, wire whisk or electric mixer.

BLEND To combine ingredients until just mixed.

BOIL To heat liquids until bubbles form that cannot be stirred down. In the case of water, the temperature will reach 212°.

BONE To remove all meat from the bone before cooking.

CREAM To beat ingredients together to a smooth consistency, usually in the case of butter and sugar for baking.

DASH A small amount of seasoning, less than ⅛ teaspoon. If using a shaker, a dash would be a quick flick of the container.

DREDGE To coat foods with flour or other dry ingredients. Most often done with pot roasts and stew meat before browning.

FOLD To incorporate several ingredients by careful and gentle turning with a spatula. Often used with beaten egg whites or whipped cream when mixing into the rest of the ingredients to keep the batter light.

JULIENNE To cut foods into long thin strips much like matchsticks. Used most often for salads and stir-fry dishes.

MINCE To cut into very fine pieces. Used often for garlic or fresh herbs.

PARBOIL To cook partially. Usually used in the case of chicken, sausages and vegetables.

PARTIALLY SET Describes the consistency of gelatin after it has been chilled for a short amount of time. Mixture should resemble the consistency of egg whites.

PUREE To process foods to a smooth mixture. Can be prepared in an electric blender, food processor, food mill or sieve.

SAUTE To fry quickly in a small amount of fat, stirring almost constantly. Most often done with onions, mushrooms and other chopped vegetables.

SCORE To cut slits partway through the outer surface of foods. Often used with ham or flank steak.

STIR-FRY To cook meats and/or vegetables with a constant stirring motion in a small amount of oil in a wok or skillet over high heat.

Alphabetical Index

A

Aberdeen Beef Pie, 79
Air-Fryer Apple Fritters with Brown Butter Glaze, 151
Air-Fryer Chicken Tenders, 151
Air-Fryer Pretzel-Crusted Catfish, 150
Air-Fryer Sweet Potato Fries, 150
Amish Sugar Cookies, 161
Angel Food Christmas Candy, 160
Appetizer Tomato Cheese Bread, 13
Apple Butter Cake Roll, 181
Apple-Glazed Chicken Thighs, 106
Apple Pie Cupcakes with Cinnamon Buttercream, 174
Apple-Pumpkin Upside-Down Cake, 187
Asian Slaw with Steak, 111
Autumn Apple Torte, 176

B

Bacon & Date Goat Cheese Burgers, 53
Bacon Lima Beans, 136
Bacon-Sausage Quiche Tarts, 12
Bacon-Wrapped Corn, 39
Baked Chicken with Bacon-Tomato Relish, 115
Baked Chili-Lime Corn, 39
Baked Simple Meatball Stroganoff, 80
Baked Vidalia Onions, 131
Balsamic Braised Pot Roast, 99
Barley Corn Salad, 55
Basil & Heirloom Tomato Toss, 49
BBQ Chicken & Apple Bread Pudding, 96
BBQ Country-Style Ribs, 85
Beef & Mushrooms with Smashed Potatoes, 110
Beef & Tater Bake, 97
Best Curried Pumpkin Soup, 49
Best Ever Sweet Pickles, 32
Black & Blue Cobbler, 147
Blackberry Daiquiri Sherbet, 185
Blackberry White Chocolate Cheesecake Cups, 175
Blackened Halibut, 110
Blueberry Dream Pie, 173
Blueberry-Orange Muffins, 69
Bourbon Peach Jam, 28
Bourbon-Spiced Glazed Ham, 80
Breaded Pork Tenderloin, 102
Bruschetta Chicken Wraps, 44
Brussels Sprouts & Kale Saute, 33
Buffalo Chicken Pockets, 20
Butternut Squash & Pear Soup, 43

C

Caramel Dumplings, 176
Cassoulet for Today, 95
Cast-Iron Favorite Pizza, 84
Ceylon Chicken Curry & Rice Noodle Soup, 57
Chai-Spiced Star Bread, 75
Cheesy Caramelized Onion Skillet Bread, 11
Cheesy Ham & Egg Sandwiches, 48
Chewy Honey Granola Bars, 16
Chewy Salted Peanut Bars, 156
Chicken & Cheddar Biscuit Casserole, 85
Chicken & Swiss Casserole, 86
Chicken Biscuit Skillet, 102
Chicken Cucumber Pitas, 47
Chicken Paella, 123
Chicken Potpie Galette with Cheddar-Thyme Crust, 83
Chipotle Mexican Street Corn Dip with Goat Cheese, 16
Chipotle-Orange Chicken, 122
Chipotle Pulled Chicken, 55
Chocolate Chip Red Velvet Whoopie Pies, 169
Chocolate Chip Zucchini Cookies, 163
Chocolate Lace Cookies, 157
Chocolate Malt Cheesecake, 179
Chocolate Pear & Cherry Salad, 131
Chocolate Pecan Pie Snack Mix, 11
Chocolate Pound Cake, 174
Chocolate-Raspberry Whoopie Pies, 168
Cinnamon Blueberry Jam, 27
Citrus-Herb Roast Chicken, 95
Classic Chicken & Waffles, 109
Coffee-Glazed Molasses Cookies, 158
Coffee Shop Fudge, 156
Cold-Brew Coffee, 9
Contest-Winning Eggplant Parmesan, 87
Country Crust Sourdough Bread, 67
Crab Crescent Triangles, 21
Cranberry Eggnog Muffins, 74
Crawfish Etouffee, 82
Creamy Butterscotch Pudding for 2, 122
Creamy Layered Blueberry Ice Pops, 178
Creamy Lemon Almond Pastries, 62
Creamy Roasted Garlic & Spinach Orzo, 26
Creamy Sweet Potatoes, 28
Creamy Twice-Baked Potatoes, 124
Crispy Asian Chicken Salad, 133
Crispy Baked Zucchini Fries, 27
Curry Coconut Chicken, 124

D

Dad's Creamed Peas & Pearl Onions, 30
Dark Chocolate Pecan Cake, 127
Date-Nut Honey Bars, 165
Dirty Banana Trifle, 177
Dutch-Oven Bread, 63

E

Easy Bourbon Pecan Pie, 172
Easy Cheese-Stuffed Jalapenos, 9

Easy Chicken Tamale Pie, 137
Easy Strawberry Lemonade
Freezer Pie, 179
Easy Stuffed Poblanos, 107
Eggnog Bread, 75
"Everything" Stuffing, 137

F

Four-Cheese Stuffed Shells, 120
Fried Mushrooms Marinara, 19

G

Garden Chickpea Salad, 132
Garden-Fresh Seafood Cocktail, 17
Garlic Chicken with
Maple-Chipotle Glaze, 91
Garlic-Rosemary Brussels Sprouts, 29
Gentleman's Whiskey Bacon Jam, 30
German Bratwurst with
Sauerkraut & Apples, 89
Gingerbread Cinnamon Rolls, 73
Gingerbread Meringue Bars, 167
Gingerbread Oatmeal Cookies, 155
Go Bananas Whoopie Pies, 169
Goat Cheese & Spinach
Stuffed Chicken, 129
Gooey Chocolate Caramel Bars, 161
Grampa's German-Style Pot Roast, 99
Grandma's Baked Ham
Sandwiches, 46
Grandma's Pressure-Cooker
Chicken Noodle Soup, 57
Greek Tortellini Skillet, 115
Green Chile Corn Fritters, 71
Grilled Corn in Husks, 38
Grilled Veggies with Mustard
Vinaigrette, 37
Ground Beef Wellington, 121

H

Ham & Green Onion Biscuits, 67
Ham, Potato & Pepper Chowder, 54
Hearty Beef & Vegetable Soup, 48
Hearty Split Pea Soup, 44
Heavenly Drinking Chocolate, 6
Homemade Apple Cider Beef Stew, 86
Homemade Honey Grahams, 165
Homemade Rhubarb
Upside-Down Cake, 186
Honey Garlic Green Beans, 35
Honey-Orange Broccoli Slaw, 51
Hot Shrimp Dip, 10

I

Iced Raspberry Tea, 17
Italian Chicken Skillet Supper, 131

J

Jalapeno Cornbread Filled with
Blueberry Quick Jam, 69
Jalapeno Mac & Cheese, 140

K

Kale Caesar Salad, 45
Korean Beef & Rice, 103

L

Lamb Pitas with Yogurt Sauce, 45
Lavender Lemon Bars, 154
Lemon Berry Dump Cake, 177
Lemon Chicken Skewers, 113
Lemon Pudding Cake, 120
Lemon Thyme Icebox Cookies, 165
Lemony Bacon-Artichoke Dip, 7
Lemony Coconut Bars, 162
Lemony Limoncello Tiramisu, 173
Linguine with Broccoli Rabe
& Peppers, 112
Lisa's All-Day Sugar & Salt
Pork Roast, 43
Loaded Twice-Baked Potato
Casserole, 36
Lone Star Pot Roast, 98
Louisiana Jambalaya, 97

M

Mama's Blackberry Cobbler, 180
Mama's Coconut Pie, 183
Marinated Broccoli, 131
Mini Chicken & Biscuit Sandwiches, 51
Mini Party Burgers, 21
Mini Pizza Cups, 14
Mixed Berry Tiramisu, 184
Mixed Nut Clusters, 162
Movie Theater Pretzel Rods, 15

N

Nanny's Fruitcake Cookies, 167

O

Oatmeal Rolls, 66
Oktoberfest Casserole, 90
Old-Fashioned Whoopie Pies, 168
Open-Faced Turkey Sandwich, 53
Orange Pistachio Cookies, 157

P

Pan-Seared Cod, 126
Peach-Basil Lemonade Slush, 15
Peach Cobbler Cookies, 160
Peanut Butter Chocolate Tart, 172
Pear Pandowdy, 125
Pecan-Coconut Crusted Tilapia, 112
Pecan Pie Thumbprints, 166
Pepper Jack Hash Brown
Casserole, 35
Peppered Pork with
Mushroom Sauce, 113
Pepperoni Cheese Bread, 61
Pizza Rolls, 13
Plum & Hazelnut Pie, 185
Po'Boy Tacos, 117
Porcini Mac & Cheese, 81
Pork & Cheesy Macaroni Sliders, 42
Pork Chops with Apples & Stuffing, 78
Pressure-Cooker Beef
& Veggie Sloppy Joes, 142
Pressure-Cooker Cheesy Egg
Casserole, 138
Pressure-Cooker Cinnamon
Applesauce, 138
Pressure-Cooker Cola BBQ
Chicken, 136
Pressure-Cooker Country
Captain Chicken, 147

Pressure-Cooker Eggs in Purgatory, 141
Pressure-Cooker Herbed Turkey Breasts, 139
Pressure-Cooker Lentil & Sausage Soup, 143
Pressure-Cooker Light Deviled Eggs, 140
Pressure-Cooker Raisin Nut Oatmeal, 141
Pressure-Cooker Smoked Sausage & White Beans, 144
Pressure-Cooker Spaghetti Squash with Tomatoes, 149
Pressure-Cooker Summer Squash, 143
Pumpkin Cookies with Browned Butter Frosting, 159
Pumpkin Egg Braid, 71
Pumpkin Pie Bars, 166

Q

Quick Tacos al Pastor, 116

R

Raspberry Sorbet for Two, 128
Red, White & Blue Summer Salad, 47
Rhubarb-Apricot Barbecued Chicken, 89
Rhubarb Bread, 61
Rhubarb Icebox Dessert, 183
Rich Seafood Chowder, 46
Roadside Diner Cheeseburger Quiche, 89
Roasted Strawberry Sheet Cake, 183
Roasted Carrots & Fennel, 25
Roasted Cauliflower with Tahini Yogurt Sauce, 31
Roasted Pumpkin Nachos, 19
Rosemary-Thyme Lamb Chops, 114

S

Saturday Afternoon Oven Pot Roast, 98
Sausage & Cornbread Dressing, 24
Sausage-Stuffed Butternut Squash, 104
Savory Blueberry-Onion Jam, 24
Savory Skillet Popover, 65
Scalloped Sweet Corn Casserole, 25
Seared Salmon with Strawberry Basil Relish, 104
Seasoned Tilapia Fillets, 128
Sesame, Sunflower & Carrot Salad, 53
Sharp Cheddar Scalloped Potatoes, 36
Shrimp & Scallops Tropical Salad, 133
Shrimp Cobb Salad, 132
Shrimp with Warm German-Style Coleslaw, 105
Simple Herbed Scallops, 127
Skillet Apple Muffin Bread, 62
Skillet Plum Chicken Tenders, 96
Skillet-Roasted Lemon Chicken with Potatoes, 81
Skillet Stout Brownies, 158
Slow-Cooked Corn on the Cob, 38
Slow-Cooked Short Ribs with Salt-Skin Potatoes, 93
Slow-Cooker Breakfast Burritos, 147
Slow-Cooker Cheddar Bacon Beer Dip, 145
Slow-Cooker Chipotle Pork Chops, 144
Slow-Cooker Meatball Stew, 82
Slow-Cooker Memphis-Style Ribs, 148
Slow-Cooker Pumpkin Yeast Bread, 71
Smoked Sausage & Veggie Sheet-Pan Supper, 109
Smoky Spanish Chicken, 108
Sour Cream Cut-Out Biscuits, 60
Sour Cream Rolls with Walnut Filling, 65
Southern Barbecue Spaghetti Sauce, 149
Southern Brunch Pastry Puff, 60
Southwestern Bean Chowder, 51
Southwestern Egg Rolls, 7
Spiced Sweet Potato Doughnuts, 68
Spicy Corn Kabobs, 39
Spicy Shepherd's Pie, 106
Spinach & Shrimp Fra Diavolo, 92
Spinach Turnovers, 20
Spring Green Risotto, 33
Sticky Sesame Cauliflower, 6
Stollen Butter Rolls, 74
Strawberry Pretzel Dessert, 123
Stuffed Baked Tomatoes, 37
Sunday Best Stuffed Pork Chops, 91
Swedish Rye Bread, 61
Sweet Potato & Turkey Couscous, 114
Sweet Potato Dutch Baby with Praline Syrup, 72
Sweet Zucchini Relish, 31

T

Tacos on a Stick, 117
Texas-Style Brisket, 78
Tomato-Onion Phyllo Pizza, 8
Tuna Noodle Casserole, 92
Turkey Focaccia Club, 51

U

The Ultimate Chicken Noodle Soup, 56
Upside-Down Pear Gingerbread Cake, 186
Upside-Down Pumpkin Pecan Tarts, 187

V

Veggie-Stuffed Tomatoes, 125

W

Waffle-Fry Reuben Bites, 19
Watermelon-Lime Cooler, 14
Whole Wheat Butterhorns, 72
Whole Wheat Strawberry Shortcakes, 180
Wholesome Wheat Bread, 64

Y

Yummy Corn Chip Salad, 42

Z

Zesty Chicken Soft Tacos, 116
Zucchini & Sausage Stovetop Casserole, 105
Zucchini Brownies, 154